S0-ACA-032

Culturally Affirming Literacy Practices for Urban Elementary Students

Culturally Affirming Literacy Practices for Urban Elementary Students

Edited by Lakia M. Scott and Barbara Purdum-Cassidy

A sincere "thank you" for all of your support!

Lakia M Scott & Barbara Purdum-Cassidy

ROWMAN & LITTLEFIELD
Lanham • Boulder • New York • London

Published by Rowman & Littlefield
A wholly owned subsidiary of The Rowman & Littlefield Publishing Group, Inc.
4501 Forbes Boulevard, Suite 200, Lanham, Maryland 20706
www.rowman.com

Unit A, Whitacre Mews, 26-34 Stannary Street, London SE11 4AB

Copyright © 2016 by Lakia M. Scott and Barbara Purdum-Cassidy

All rights reserved. No part of this book may be reproduced in any form or by any
electronic or mechanical means, including information storage and retrieval systems,
without written permission from the publisher, except by a reviewer who may quote
passages in a review.

British Library Cataloguing in Publication Information Available

Library of Congress Cataloging-in-Publication Data

Names: Scott, Lakia, editor. | Purdum-Cassidy, Barbara, editor.
Title: Culturally affirming literacy practices for urban elementary students / edited by Lakia M. Scott
    and Barbara Purdum-Cassidy.
Description: Lanham, Maryland : Rowman & Littlefield, 2016. | Includes bibliographical references
    and index.
Identifiers: LCCN 2016019194 (print) | LCCN 2016031507 (ebook) | ISBN 9781475826418 (cloth :
    alk. paper) | ISBN 9781475826425 (pbk. : alk. paper) | ISBN 9781475826449 (Electronic)
Subjects: LCSH: Language arts (Elementary)--United States. | City children--Education (Elemen-
    tary)--United States. | Culturally relevant pedagogy--United States.
Classification: LCC LB1576 .C852 2016 (print) | LCC LB1576 (ebook) | DDC 372.6--dc23
LC record available at https://lccn.loc.gov/2016019194

♾ ™ The paper used in this publication meets the minimum requirements of American
National Standard for Information Sciences Permanence of Paper for Printed Library
Materials, ANSI/NISO Z39.48-1992.

Printed in the United States of America

Contents

Foreword

[W]e are the sum of all the moments of our lives—all that is ours is in them; we cannot escape or conceal it. If the writer has used the clay of life to make [*her or*] his book, [*she or*] he has only used what all [*humans*] men must, what none can keep from using. Fiction is not fact, but fiction is fact selected and understood, fiction is fact arranged and charged with purpose.
—Thomas Wolfe (1929)

Historically, the peoples of the United States have framed its dominating culture as white, male, upper middle class, educated, and Christian; this culture has been promoted primarily by itself through its power and control of mass marketing visible in our government, education, commerce, and so forth. The country's narrative has been communicated through both factual and fictional accounts via spoken, written, and viewed representations offered formally and informally, directly and indirectly.

Far too often these accounts perpetuate events that may or may not have occurred and have morphed into myths based on little or no authenticity and have become the accepted stories passed on to generations of young learners in our schools and classrooms. Accounts and myths are then passed through these young learners to their children and grandchildren, which perpetuates inaccurate narratives and magnified beliefs.

The population of the United States is composed of many different people whose ancestors immigrated to the United States both voluntarily and involuntarily. Immigrants continue to relocate within the United States, impacting the country's composition and character. The dominating culture attempts to maintain its power; control emanates across the nation through legislative acts and social norms, both of which influence decisions guiding educational issues and relevant recourses needed and wanted to prepare today's youth for tomorrow's experiences in college, career, community, and civic life.

However, the population of the United States has continued to change since the day it was founded. Although the dominant culture has expected nondominate individuals to assimilate into their desired preconceived "melting pot," the country's population has been experiencing dramatic changes that cannot be swirled into one (nor ever should have been considered a single entity). Individuals identifying with the dominant culture are no longer the dominating culture mathematically or socially. Concomitantly, the concept of marketing the nation as a single dominating culture is not meaningful or productive other than a nation that "values liberty and justice for all" (Bellamy, 1892).

Schools and teachers have always been cognizant of and challenged by the continuous changes in the country's population. Although individuals from nondominate cultures may try to evade the center of society, especially families who are not comfortable, cannot speak English, those who have experienced legal conflicts, are not citizens, or do not appear to belong, they want their children to attend schools, become educated, and have a better life.

Throughout our country's history, some schools and teachers have welcomed all learners and their families, finding avenues to accommodate needs and interests to engage all learners, promote achievement, and communicate with families. Yet other schools and teachers have been unaccepting, insensitive, discouraging, resistant, oppositional, and even hostile when expected to teach all learners. It would appear that resistant schools and teachers disregarded their roles and responsibilities for teaching *all* learners by marginalizing these children and their families.

Sadly, marginalization also occurs for many learners who may appear to belong but who have adopted coping skills to avoid bringing attention to themselves. Just as children consciously and unconsciously internalize their parents' behaviors, even at early ages most children recognize the patterns and preferences exhibited by schools and teachers. Throughout their education (and later into their careers), learners mindfully negotiate their learning (and employment) environments, balancing the complexities associated with chance and choice.

It is presumed that schools and teachers are trusted to prepare *all* learners—from all cultures—for college, career, community, and civic life. The most effective and efficient educational approaches capitalize on providing learners at all ages with information, access, and opportunities resulting in confidence for making powerful connections with and about oneself, others, and society in ways that honor and respect all cultures and cultural characteristics.

Too often teacher candidates may have been initially prepared for valuing cultural diversity and for teaching all learners. However, during their induction to and continuing throughout their professional careers, teacher candidates and then classroom teachers must be guided and supported by their schools in their abilities to reflect on their practices and enhance their self-efficacy for accommodating every learner and be aware of every learner's individual needs and wants based on the learner's background, experiences, and perceptions.

Schools and teachers must take meaningful steps to modify restricted curricula, limited instruction, biased assessments, and prejudicial classroom management and school expectations with expanded concepts and practices that invite all learners into the conversation; excite all learners to discover more knowledge that tells their stories; and ignite all learners as they are taught and learn in ways that promote engagement and achievement through expression and exchange of learners' ideas reflective of their backgrounds and interests.

Many educational researchers recommend that school administrators and classroom teachers try to experience life in the same ways that their learners and their families exist . . . sometimes survive. When educators become part of their learners' lived experiences, the outcomes can be quite eye-opening and life changing. Educators are encouraged to walk in the neighborhoods, visit the shops, and attend the events.

Learners' lived experiences include individuals' backgrounds, experiences, and perspectives . . . all of which are encompassed in rhetoric and interpretation. Each of us has developed individual competence and confidence with language and expression that communicate our thoughts and feelings. In return, other people analyze our expressed language through individual understanding and importance. Therefore, educators should offer an array of literacies that comprises the lives of their learners, families, and cultures.

Substantiating their lived experiences, validating their personal narratives, and authenticating their cultural identities and individual existence with texts, via reading, writing, speaking, listening, and viewing, allows individuals to seek information, access, and opportunities that enrich our lives with confidence and competence. Individuals often talk about their fictional and nonfictional texts (books, magazines, newspapers, websites, movies, television programs, and so forth) to develop a shared literacy that becomes the basis of their cultural characteristics and understanding. Throughout our lives, each of us wants to learn more about our pasts, comprehend the present, and prepare for the future.

Ultimately, to fulfill individuals' purposes and to develop our individual and shared lived experiences, young learners must be guided and supported in their cultural literacy so each learner is equipped and empowered to discover an array of accounts (both factual and fictional) that align with their cultural identities and individual existence.

As a nation that values "liberty and justice for all," the roles and responsibilities of all educators (i.e., school administrators, professional developers, classroom teachers, teacher educators, and teacher candidates) are to ensure that every learner is fully prepared for college, career, community, and civic life. Teaching, learning, and schooling must contribute purposely to the sum of all the moments of our lives.

This text provides educators—in K–12 schools and classrooms as well as in higher education, particularly teacher preparation—information and insights to stimulate their awareness and increase their understanding of the broad range of cultural literacies that inform and support learners' lived experiences.

Equipped and empowered with the research and practices found in these meaningful and pragmatic chapters, educators expand both their content knowledge and their pedagogical content knowledge to enhance their self-efficacy benefitting all learners. Learning and living as holistic experiences, this text challenges educators' beliefs and presents both frames and fluencies for advancing the literacies needed for preparing today's learners as tomorrow's adults.

The editors of this text, Lakia Scott and Barbara Purdum-Cassidy, both come from varied experiences that have provided them the platform needed to understand how to meet the literacy needs of culturally and linguistically diverse elementary students. In particular, Scott has worked in and studied urban education with special focus on the role of language and dialect in school settings for more than a decade. She provides a valid and authentic perspective on why most of today's classrooms have restricted students' cultural and linguistic identities through curricula, pedagogical practices, and education policies, which stands to detriment the student, as well as his or her peers, the teacher, and the aims of a true education.

Purdum-Cassidy also shares nearly three decades of educational experiences that span from the classroom to teacher educator and scholar. In addition, she has been a resource clearinghouse for helping pre-service and in-service educators understand how to teach using the processes of inquiry and project-based instruction. Having known them both as educators, scholars, and teachers of teachers, Scott and Purdum-Cassidy are a literacy force to be reckoned with, and the culmination of *Culturally Affirming Literacy Practices for Urban Elementary Students* is a manifestation of conceptual and instructional approaches that will make a valuable contribution to the field of education and educational practice.

Nancy P. Gallavan, PhD
    Professor of Teacher Education, University of Central Arkansas
    2013–2014 Association of Teacher Educators President

Dr. Nancy P. Gallavan is professor of teacher education at University of Central Arkansas specializing in classroom assessments, cultural competence, and social studies education. She earned her undergraduate degree from Missouri State University; her master's degree from the University of Colorado–Boulder; and her doctorate from the University of Denver. Before entering higher education at the University of Nevada–Las Vegas, Gallavan taught elementary and middle school for twenty years, primarily in the Cherry Creek School District of Colorado. Author of more than 160 publications, she is a 2013 KDP Eleanor Roosevelt Legacy Chapter member and was the 2013–2014 Association of Teacher Educators president.

REFERENCES

Bellamy, F. (1892). United States Pledge of Allegiance. Retrieved from http://www.ushistory.org/documents/pledge.htm.
Wolfe, T. (1929). *Look homeward, angel.* Project Gutenberg Australia. Retrieved from http://gutenberg.net.au/ebooks03/0300721.txt.

Acknowledgments

First, I would like to thank my creator for pouring unto my spirit the ability and capacity to see this project to the end. Often, we go throughout the day criticizing how much time we don't have, but seldom are the opportunities that we reflect in thanks for the things we get done within the time in which we are afforded. I know without your will, none of this would be done, so I say thank you, Lord.

Second, I would like to recognize my family for their continued support by allowing me the space and time to work on this book. I want to acknowledge my son, Chadley, who continues to remind me that being Dr. Mommy is a never-ending adventure, but always a memorable journey. It is he who also reminds me that there is much work to be done for the future of public school education. To my husband, Chadwick, I thank you for your patience and understanding. And to my parents, Paul and Collette Jones, I honor the sacrifices you have made to propel me forward in my education and career; I will forever cherish you and the lessons you have taught me.

Next, I would like to thank my Baylor University faculty colleagues for all of their support and collegiality. In particular, I thank Dr. Barbara Purdum-Cassidy, the co-editor of this project. You are and continue to be a beacon of light and a source of academic strength for me. I'm grateful for having the opportunity to collaborate and look forward to future endeavors.

Finally, a special and heart-felt thanks to our acquisitions editor, Sarah Jubar, for her kindness, professionalism, and considerate feedback throughout the process. Your guidance and wisdom has been invaluable, and for that I am forever grateful.

—**Lakia M. Scott**

First, I must thank our publisher, Rowman & Littlefield. Our editor, Sarah Jubar, gave us thoughtful feedback and provided the right information at the right time to move the book forward. Thank you, Sarah, for your support and belief in our work. Thanks also to the authors that contributed chapters. The ideas you have shared challenge me to reflect upon my teaching practices.

I am indebted to the marvelous undergraduate students at Baylor University I have taught over the years. A special thanks goes to the pre-service teachers who agreed to be part of the Connecting Content project. Your work and accomplishments deserve to be heard.

Thank you to my family. To my children, Shannon, Courtney, and Tanner, thanks for the inspiration you never knew you gave. To my husband, Dan, thanks for your love, friendship, and encouragement. And last, but not least, thank you to my grandchildren, Declan, Payton, Taylor, Carter, Layne, and Thomas, you are the reasons I remain passionate about the teaching of reading and writing.

Finally, a big thank you to Lakia. Without your vision, the book would have never been. Our collaboration has been one of the best things that has happened to me professionally. I have learned so much.

—**Barbara Purdum-Cassidy**

Chapter One

Introduction: A Continued Era of Language Discrimination

Implications for Culturally Affirming Literacy Practices in Urban Elementary Schools

Lakia M. Scott

"The educational foundations of our society are presently being eroded by a rising tide of mediocrity that threatens our very future as a Nation and a people." Even though more than thirty years have passed, this statement still rings true (National Commission on Excellence in Education, 1983). The highly publicized national report *A Nation at Risk* was released in 1983 in an effort to gain public and political support to improve the inadequate quality of U.S. education. The report provides recommendations in educational content, standards and expectations, instructional time, teaching, administrative leadership, and fiscal support.

However, when comparing the chief recommendations to what has been done to increase educational quality for all students since its publication, our nation is still considered at risk (Graham, 2013). Some might refer to U.S. academic disparities and racial disproportionalities in consideration of literacy levels, graduation rates, and college enrollment. In particular, urban districts and schools have reportedly higher academic disproportionalities than suburban and rural areas (Dillon, 2010; Goodman & Hilton, 2010; Ladson-Billings, 2006; Milner, 2012).

Other literature has accredited the difference between urban and suburban/rural to a lack of funding resources (Anyon, 2005; Biddle & Berliner, 2002; Hudley, 2013; Lynch, 2014), teacher and administrator turnover (Darling-Hammond & Green, 1990; Guin, 2004; Jacob, 2007), perceptions about urban youth (Murray & Zvoch, 2011), and the overall educational treatment

1

of traditionally marginalized students (Allen, Scott, & Lewis, 2013; Cook, 2015; Kucsera, Seigel-Hawley, & Orfield, 2015; Ladson-Billings, 2006; Milner, 2012).

Some also look to international achievement trends that demonstrate through the Progress in International Ready Literacy Study (PIRLS) that despite moderate gains within the last fifteen years, the United States is still not recognized as "top performing" country (Mullis, Martin, Foy, & Drucker, 2011). These sobering statistics further support the fact that the United States is failing today's students and leaving much to question about tomorrow and the future of our country.

In particular, *A Nation at Risk* suggests that high school graduates "know our literacy heritage and how it enhances imagination and ethical understanding, and how it relates to the customs, ideas, and values of today's life and culture" (National Commission on Excellence in Education, 1983). The report also affirms it is important to create engaged and critically informed citizens. However, understanding how one acquires and develops literacy and its relation to life, culture, and society starts much earlier than the high school years; it begins with the formation of language itself. Therefore, literacy foundations become a vital component in the primary years of learning.

A Nation at Risk also highlights how students should become proficient in languages other than English (as early as the elementary grades) because it "introduces students to non-English speaking cultures, heightens awareness and comprehension of one's native tongue, and serves the Nation's needs in commerce, diplomacy, defense, and education" (National Commission on Excellence in Education, 1983). Despite the acclaim for language diversity to serve as an influential factor in how our nation is positioned with the global world, linguistic hegemony continues to exist.

Both historical and contemporary federal- and state-level laws and policies continue to reinforce language discrimination by upholding the notion that English is the standard form for which all Americans can and will excel to be a leading global competitor. This chapter will briefly review historical language policies and statutes that have influenced the current landscape of language discrimination.

Next, a discussion on contemporary reform movements will demonstrate how language minority students are continually marginalized through culturally deficit curricula and biased assessment practices. In particular, the ways in which the *rising tide of mediocrity* is reinforced through a continued era of language discrimination in U.S. public elementary schools will be detailed. Finally, this chapter will provide a concise summary of the following chapters that will highlight implications for policy and classroom practice in efforts to advance literacy and academic outcomes for traditionally marginalized elementary students.

HISTORICAL LANGUAGE DEBATES

Little has been done to celebrate linguistic diversity in U.S. public schools since the formation of schooling. As early as the 1920s, English immersion (also known as "sink-or-swim" policies) threatened educational opportunity for language minority students. In the 1960s, Title VI of the Civil Rights Act of 1964 prohibited discrimination on the basis of race, color, or national origin in federally assisted programs.

And in 1968, Title VII of the Elementary and Secondary Education Act (also referred to as the Bilingual Education Act) established federal funding for bilingual education programs to support students who were economically disadvantaged and non-English speaking. Despite these federal policies, language debates continued. As illustrated in table 1.1, legislation before *A Nation at Risk* served the primary purpose of identifying discriminatory practices for linguistically diverse students but not actually eradicating them.

Still, court rulings provided grounds for schools to better support bilingual education programming. Amendments to Title VII allowed for expanded eligibility for students with limited English proficiency, family English literacy programs, and teacher training (Texas Education Agency [TEA], 2010b).

Five years after the release of *A Nation at Risk*, amendments to the Bilingual Education Act were made to increase state-level funding for professional training on language variety, foreign language instruction, and immigrant education (TEA, 2010a). The No Child Left Behind Act of 2001 (NCLB) reauthorized the appropriation of funds to states to improve achievement for students with limited English proficiency (LEP).

The act permits parents to enroll their children in a bilingual education program, but the student may only stay in the program for a maximum of three years. After that time, the student must then receive English-only instruction, regardless of their English-speaking ability. NCLB also mandates that bilingual teachers be fluent in English and any other language used in the classroom.

The problem with students having a three-year time limit in bilingual education is that they may still need the support services to meet academic standards. After all, students' home and cultural experiences directly conflict with classroom language practices, so the amount of time for them to learn how to speak another language proficiently may take longer than three years. As such, educational programming for language minority students should reflect individualized curriculum structures to facilitate growth at a pace that will also ensure the student's academic success.

NCLB is recognized for making schools and districts more accountable by addressing students' academic needs and developing instructional and curriculum interventions. However, in the process of doing this, the policy

Table 1.1.   U.S. Supreme Court and Federal Court Cases Impacting Language Minority Students before *A Nation at Risk* Report

1971	*United States v. State of Texas, et al.*	The state cannot discriminate on grounds of race, color, or national origin in Texas public and charter schools.
1974	*Lau v. Nichols*	Schools must work diligently to overcome barriers faced by non-English speakers.
1974	*Serna v. Portales*	Schools must implement a bilingual curriculum, provide instructional resources, revise assessment procedures to accommodate language difference, and hire bilingual personnel.
1978	*Cintron v. Brentwood*	Courts ruled against unnecessarily segregating Spanish-speaking students from English-speaking peers in bilingual programs.
1978	*Rios v. Reed*	Court ruling that students must continue to receive equal educational opportunities by providing more extensive Spanish instruction in bilingual programs.
1981	*Castañeda v. Pickard*	To maintain compliance with the Equal Educational Opportunities Act (EEOA), schools examine and use research-based programs that will yield results. This is also known as the Castañeda test.
1982	*Plyler v. Doe*	The state cannot deny free public education to undocumented children, as sanctioned by the Fourteenth Amendment of the U.S. Constitution.

also furthered discriminatory practices, particularly for language minority students, as a result of inappropriate (and invalid) assessment measures, academic tracking, and a shift toward English-only instruction to meet adequate yearly progress (AYP) and annual measurable achievement objectives (AMAOs).

CONTEMPORARY LANGUAGE REFORM MOVEMENTS

Although immigrant languages were treated with more tolerance in the early years of nation building, the symbolism of the 1900s' Americanization movement that was able to link speaking English and assimilation with being an American (and fulfilling the American Dream) continues to shape policies toward immigrant languages (Olneck, 1989).

More recently, state-level policies have continued to reinforce discriminatory language practices on Hispanic/Latino(a) and African American students through English-only legislation and culturally diminishing classroom practices. These policies and practices reinforce systems of social and racial stratification through language in the traditional classroom (Orozco, 2011).

English-Only Legislation

Educational policies in Arizona public schools have vehemently continued language discrimination for Spanish-speaking students. According to the U.S. Census Bureau (2011), the state of Arizona's Hispanic and Latino populations represent 30.2 percent, third to only Texas and California. With a high concentration of Spanish-speaking families, language education policies directly influence educational access, opportunity, and outcomes for minority language students. In 2000, Proposition 203 (commonly referred to as *English for the Children*) mandated sheltered English instruction (SEI) to improve English language acquisition and academic achievement (Crawford, 2001).

And in 2008, the Arizona English Language Learners Task Force mandated a four-hour English Language Development (ELD) block that provided additional instruction on Standard English structure, syntax, and semantics. It is also important to consider the context of Arizona: Arizona SB 1070 was passed in 2010 and it allows law officials to question a person's immigration on the sole basis of race.

A study conducted by Lillie and colleagues (2010) criticizes SEI programs for hindering students' academic abilities in core academic courses because of the intensive instructional block. In particular, Lillie and colleagues (2010) note that students are physically and academically separated from their English-proficient peers and that contributes to further academic and social isolation as well as negative attitudes about education and personal identity.

The implications of English-only policies have been detrimental for English language learners (ELLs). National Assessment of Educational Progress (U.S. Department of Education, 2009) data revealed that within states that have adopted English-only educational policies, academic achievement gaps continue to widen between ELLs and native English speakers. In addition, the number of ELLs who receive special education services has significantly increased (Rumberger & Tran, 2010). Similarly, in Massachusetts (another state that has enacted English-only policies since 2002), the dropout rate for ELLs has risen (Rumberger & Tran, 2010).

These policies force monolinguistic instruction, which explicitly *and* implicitly diminishes the cultural value of native languages. Additionally, the concentrated SEI blocks further reinforce systems of cultural and social stratification by reducing the amount of time students have in core academic courses and other specified content fields. In this way, language becomes a gatekeeper to academic opportunity (King & Scott, 2014).

The Urban Dialect: African American Vernacular English

Though not within the same ethnic group, some African American students have also been victimized by language discrimination. Consider the Ebonics controversy. Wolfram and Torbert (2005) report that African American Vernacular English (AAVE) is an ancestral connection stemming from the African slave trade. They assert: "Africans speaking a rich assortment of West African languages such as Mandinka, Mende, and Gola—among many others—learned English subsequent to their shackled emigration from Africa to North America" (Wolfram & Torbert, 2005). Robert Williams first introduced the term *Ebonics* in 1973 at the Cognitive and Language Development Conference (Baugh, 2005). *Black English* is another popular phrasing used to identify how students communicated.

In 1979, California's State Board of Education adopted a policy to address the need for Ebonics or Black English speakers to develop English language proficiency (Baugh, 2005). In 1996, the Oakland School Board passed a resolution defining Ebonics as the native language of more than twenty-eight thousand African American students within the district, allowing access to Title VII bilingual funds. However, former Secretary of Education Richard Riley immediately rejected the board's notion because of fear that the action would target other districts to do the same for African American students (Tamura, 2002).

This particular case highlights the power of language in educational policy and curricular practice. Even though sociolinguists have validated the equality of various English dialects and recognize AAVE or Ebonics as logical and rule-governed with unique grammatical, phonological, and stylistic features (Escher & Godley, 2012), the Oakland Ebonics controversy sheds light on the mainstream perspective about languages and dialects that vary from Standard American English (SAE).

This potentially damaging perspective continues today, as Wolfram and Torbert (2005) assert: "Observations about African American speech have never been far removed from the politics of race in American society, so that it is hardly surprising that the status of African American Vernacular English (AAVE) has been—and continues to be—highly contentious and politically sensitive" (p. 1).

The Ban on Ethnic Studies

Language discrimination also persists when examining the elimination of ethnic studies programs. Consider the case of the Mexican American/Raza Studies (MARS) Program in Tucson Unified School District. In 2007, Arizona Superintendent of Public Instruction Tom Horne authored a public letter calling for the end of ethnic studies in the Tucson Unified School District.

The implications of Horne's letter would end the MARS program. Consequently, in 2010 Arizona passed the Prohibited Courses Law (PCL). According to the Arizona State Board of Education, the law seeks to prohibit courses that are determined to promote resentment toward a race or class of people, is designed for a particular ethnic group, or advocates for ethnic solidarity. A school or district found to violate the PCL has sixty days to comply or will be denied 10 percent of its apportioned state aid.

The PCL in Arizona promotes language discrimination because it lawfully allows the authentication of a status quo by promoting institutional and structural racism. PCL veils itself in neutrality by seeking to eliminate the promotion of any one race or ethnicity; however, the law protects the White experience in K–12 curriculum through the exclusion of minority perspectives.

Language discrimination arises through the elimination of ethnic studies programs by blatantly prohibiting culturally relevant and diverse curriculum and instruction. Terminating ethnic studies programs also normalizes the White experience in the United States as "American" while discounting the experiences of the minoritized which thereby further marginalizes non-White students.

From the sum of this research, herein lies the purpose of this book: to highlight ways in which curriculum and practice can become culturally affirming for urban elementary students. In doing so, the following chapters will provide practical insights guided by conceptual and contextual knowledge in understanding how to teach urban African American and Hispanic/Latino(a) students by discussing issues associated with critical pedagogies, literacy, and culturally appropriate instructional strategies that have demonstrated success for traditionally marginalized students.

ORGANIZATION OF THE TEXT

Many researchers support the notion of a culturally affirming pedagogy: students of color in urban educational settings demonstrate marked academic growth in literacy when the content, materials, and instructional practices used to facilitate their learning are culturally aligned (Allen, Scott, & Lewis, 2013; Paciga, Hoffman, & Teale, 2011). This book extends the conversation for culturally affirming pedagogy by showcasing successful models for teaching reading and writing to urban students through a discussion of topics that foster culturally inclusive instruction through critical pedagogy and in-quiry-based learning.

In chapter 2, Dana Stachowiak elaborates on the benefits of teaching through a social justice lens: critical literacy pedagogy enhances students' levels of metacognitive awareness, critical analyses, social reasoning, and activism. In chapter 3, Melanie Acosta discusses the importance of recon-structing a framework for effective literacy instruction by examining the role of pedagogical excellence and the influence of sociocultural complexities that are deeply embedded in teaching and learning.

Next, in chapter 4, Marcia Watson highlights the CDF Freedom School model for its continued success in providing culturally relevant learning opportunities for low-income students through supplementary and summer literacy programs. In chapter 5, Barbara Purdum-Cassidy and Karon Le-Compte provide a framework for project-based instruction that involves civic literacy and inquiry-based learning.

In chapter 6, Catherine Reischl and Debi Khasnabis elaborate on peda-gogical principles for teaching early adolescent English learners by sharing key findings from a culturally responsive project-based unit of instruction for upper elementary students. In chapter 7, Cherese Childers-McKee, Libra Boyd, and Corliss Brown Thompson explore ways in which the tenets of critical pedagogies can be integrated in core reading and writing instruction for ELLs.

In chapter 8, Elena King and Michelle Plaisance use experiential educa-tion concepts to discuss the use of learning gardens to enhance ELLs' vocab-ulary acquisition and writing development. And in chapter 9, Jessica Meehan discusses how teachers can affirm students' cultural identities and academic self-concept by examining the influence of culturally appropriate texts. Elena Venegas encourages urban elementary educators to use critical media litera-cy tools to counter hegemonic media messages and empower youth to be creators of their own media identities and perspectives in chapter 10.

In chapter 11, Lakia Scott and Marcia Watson highlight the importance of empowering Black students through the reteaching of Black history, using relevant Black curriculum as a core tenet to learning, and increasing the academic expectations of Black students through the affirmation of positive self-concept. Next, in chapter 12, Jason Trumble and Michael Mills discuss digital literacy concepts, software, applications, and social media platforms that can enhance instructional uses for technology in the urban elementary classroom.

The concluding chapters provide implications for teacher education pro-grams and models. Leanne Howell and Brent Merritt discuss how technology can be used to support and scaffold instruction in urban elementary class-rooms in chapter 13. And finally, in chapter 14, Sherry McElhannon and

Jessica Rogers provide instructional resources and materials for fostering a culturally affirming literacy program.

FINAL THOUGHTS

In conclusion, by choosing to ignore the role and power of language, we as teachers, educators, and scholars are prescribing failure for future generations of leaders. Federal and state laws and policies have and continue to restrict educational opportunities for language minority students through reiterating that English mastery is the *only* conduit to understanding language and the world around us. As a result, today's public schools face incredible challenges in educating students from linguistically different backgrounds even though the classroom is more diverse now than it has ever been.

However, there are ways in which policy can positively shape educational practices, mainly by allowing the school grounds to become conduits of culture between students, their families, and the neighboring community. This collection of works serves as a resource for pre-service and in-service literacy educators who currently or will work with urban elementary students. This book has the potential to impact and influence the way in which language and literacy is taught, valued, and respected. And most importantly, it provides a framework for how culturally affirming literacy practices will positively impact academic achievement for traditionally marginalized student populations.

REFERENCES

Allen, A., Scott, L. M., & Lewis, C. W. (2013). Racial micro-aggressions and African American and Hispanic students in urban schools: A call for culturally affirming education. *Interdisciplinary Journal of Teaching and Learning, 3*(2), 117–29.

Anyon, J. (2005). *Radical possibilities: Public policy, urban education, and a new social movement.* New York: Routledge.

Baugh, J. (2005). *Ebonics timeline.* Retrieved from http://www.pbs.org/speak/seatosea/americanvarieties/AAVE/timeline/.

Biddle, B. J., & Berliner, D. C. (2002). A research synthesis: Unequal school funding in the United States. *Beyond Instructional Leadership, 59*(8), 48–59.

California Department of Education. (2014). *Q and A for Test Variations.* Retrieved from http://www.cde.ca.gov/ta/tg/hs/qandatestvar.asp.

Cook, L. (2015). US education: Still separate and unequal. Retrieved from http://www.usnews.com/news/blogs/data-mine/2015/01/28/us-education-still-separate-and-unequal.

Crawford, J. (2001). Bilingual education: Strike two. *Rethinking schools.* Retrieved from http://www.rethinkingschools.org/special_reports/bilingual/Az152.shtml.

Darling-Hammond, L., & Green, J. (1990). Teacher quality and equality. In J. Goodlad & P. Keatings (Eds.), *Access to knowledge: An agenda for our nation's schools* (pp. 237–59). New York: College Entrance Examination Board.

Dillon, S. (2010). Racial disparity in school suspensions. *New York Times.* Retrieved from http://www.nytimes.com/2010/09/14/education/14suspend.html?emc=eta1.

Escher, A., & Godley, A. (2012). Bidialectal African American adolescents' beliefs about spoken language expectations in English classrooms. *Journal of Adolescent & Adult Literacy, 55*(8), 704–13. http://dx.doi.org/10.1002/JAAL.00085.

Goodman, G. S., & Hilton, A. A. (2010). *Urban dropouts: Why persist?* In Steinburg, S. R. (Ed.), *19 Urban Questions* (pp. 55–67). New York: Peter Lang.

Graham, E. (2013, April 25). 'A Nation at Risk' Turns 30: Where did it take us? *NEA Today.* Retrieved from http://neatoday.org/2013/04/25/a-nation-at-risk-turns-30-where-did-it-take-us-2/.

Guin, K. (2004). Chronic teacher turnover in urban elementary schools. *Education Policy Analysis Archives, 12*(42), 1–30.

Hudley, C. (2013, May). Education and urban schools. *American Psychological Association.* Retrieved from http://www.apa.org/pi/ses/resources/indicator/2013/05/urban-schools.aspx.

Jacob, B. A. (2007). The challenge of staffing urban schools with effective teachers. *The Future of Children, 17*(1), 129–53.

King, E. T., & Scott, L. M. (2014). English as a gatekeeper: A conversation of linguistic capital and American schools. *Journal for Multicultural Education, 8*(4), 226–36.

Kucsera, J., Siegel-Hawley, G., & Orfield, G. (2015, July). Are we segregated and satisfied? Segregation and inequality in southern California schools. *Urban Education, 50*(5), 535–71.

Ladson-Billings, G. (2006). From the achievement gap to the education debt: Understanding achievement in US schools. *Educational Researcher, 35*(7), 3–12.

Lillie, K. E., Markos, A., Estrella, A. Nguyen, T., Trifiro, A., Arias, M. B., & Perez, K. (2010). Policy in practice: The implementation of structured English immersion in Arizona. Retrieved from http://civilrightsproject.ucla.edu/research/k-12-education/language-minority-students/policy-in-practice-the-implementation-of-structured-english-immersion-in-arizona/lillie-policy-practice-sei-2010.pdf.

Lynch, M. (2014, October 15). Poverty and school funding: Why low-income students often suffer. *Huff Post Education.* Retrieved from http://www.huffingtonpost.com/matthew-lynch-edd/poverty-and-school-fundin_b_5989490.html.

Milner, H. R. (2012). Beyond a test score: Explaining opportunity gaps in educational practice. *Journal of Black Studies, 43*(6), 693–718.

Mullis, I. V., Martin, M. O., Foy, P., & Drucker, K. T. (2011). *PIRLS 2011 International Results in Reading.* Chestnut Hill, MA: TIMSS & PIRLS International Study Center.

Murray, C., & Zvoch, K. (2011). Teacher–student relationships among behaviorally at-risk African American youth from low-income backgrounds: Student perceptions, teacher perceptions, and socioemotional adjustment correlates. *Journal of Emotional and Behavioral Disorders, 19*(1), 41–54.

National Commission on Excellence in Education. (1983). *A nation at risk: The imperative for educational reform. A report to the Nation and the Secretary of Education, United States Department of Education.* Washington, DC: The Commission.

Olneck, M. R. (1989). Americanization and the education of immigrants, 1900–1925: An analysis of symbolic action. *American Journal of Education, 97*(4), 398–423.

Orozco, R. A. (2011). 'It is certainly strange . . .': Attacks on ethnic studies and whiteness as property. *Journal of Education Policy, 26*(6), 819–838. http://dx.doi.org/10.1080/02680939.2011.587540.

Paciga, K. A., Hoffman, J. L., & Teale, W. H. (2011). The national early literacy panel report and classroom instruction: Green lights, caution lights, and red lights. *Young Children, 66*(6), 50–57.

Rumberger, R., & Tran, L. (2010). State language policies, school language practices, and the English learner achievement gap. In P. Gandara & M. Hopkins (Eds.), *Forbidden language: English Learners and restrictive language policies* (pp. 86–101). New York: Teachers College Press

Tamura, E. H. (2002). African American Vernacular English and Hawaii Creole English: A comparison of two school board controversies. *The Journal of Negro Education, 71*(1/2), 17–30.

Texas Education Agency (TEA). (2009). Historical overview of assessment in Texas. *Technical Digest 2008–2009.* Retrieved from http://tea.texas.gov/student.assessment/techdigest/yr0809/.

Texas Education Agency (TEA). (2010a). English Language Learners (ELLs) and the State of Texas Assessments of Academic Readiness (STAAR) program. *House Bill 3 Transition Plan,* pp. I-67–I-74.

Texas Education Agency (TEA). (2010b). *Language Proficiency Assessment Committee Framework Manual.* Retrieved from http://portal.esc20.net/portal/page/portal/esc20public/bilesl/LPACFramework/Files/LPAC_Framework_Manual_Accessible_2011-12_2.pdf.

U.S. Census Bureau. (2011, March 10). U.S. Census Bureau delivers Arizona's 2010 census population totals, including first look at race and Hispanic origin data for legislative redistricting. Retrieved from http://www.census.gov/2010census/news/releases/operations/cb11-cn76.html.

U.S. Department of Education. (2009). National Center for Education Statistics, National Assessment of Educational Progress (NAEP), NAEP 1999 Trends in Academic Progress; and 2004 and 2008 Long-Term Trend Reading Assessments. Retrieved from the Long-Term Trend NAEP Data Explorer. Retrieved from http://nces.ed.gov/nationsreportcard/naepdata/.

Wolfram, W., & Torbert, B. (2005). *American varieties: African American English—When worlds collide.* Public Broadcasting Station (PBS). Retrieved from http://www.pbs.org/speak/seatosea/americanvarieties/AAVE/worldscollide/.

Chapter Two

A Framework for Critical Social Justice Literacy in Urban Elementary Schools

Dana Stachowiak

From pre-kindergarten through graduate school, classrooms are grounded in standards-based, and oftentimes stagnant, curricula that force students to conform to educational, cultural, and societal norms. This modern-day form of colonization leaves little room for students to value individual cultures, viewpoints, and lived experiences as a part of their own schooling experiences.

Students are rarely invited to bring their own self to the classroom; they are left unheard, silenced, and invisible. This is especially true for minoritized (Sensoy & DiAngelo, 2012) students (i.e., gay or lesbian students, gender nonconforming students, students of color, students of lower socioeconomic statuses, non-Christian students, etc.).

As Au (2009) writes, "when classes are not grounded in the lives of students, do not include the voices and knowledge of communities being studied, and are not based in dialogue, they create environments where not only are white students miseducated, but students of color feel as if their very identities are under attack" (p. 249). There is an important need for educators of urban elementary students to create classrooms that encourage engagement, critical consciousness, and community. Therefore, it is vital to decolonize the classroom, seek social justice, and teach with it in mind.

WHY TEACH WITH SOCIAL JUSTICE IN MIND?

It is common that when thinking about teaching culturally affirming literacy to urban elementary students, educators look to the tenets of multicultural education (e.g., see the work of James Banks) and culturally relevant pedagogy (e.g., see the work of Geneva Gay and Gloria Ladson-Billings), and this is with good reason.

Both multicultural education and culturally relevant pedagogy demand that teachers see and value the cultures of the students they teach and adjust their teaching practices accordingly. This means using "the cultural characteristics, experiences, and perspectives of . . . diverse students as conduits for teaching" culturally affirming literacy to urban elementary students (Gay, 2002, p. 106).

Even further, culturally relevant pedagogy also requires that teachers recognize that there is often incompatibility between the school culture and culture of minoritized students (Gay, 2002; Ladson-Billings, 1992, 1995). This incompatibility is especially important to recognize in urban elementary school settings because there tends to be a disproportionate ratio of white teachers to students of color, and therefore students of color are taught through a white cultural lens.

No matter how good the teaching is, if teachers are unconscious about this cultural mismatch, optimal learning does not and cannot occur. To this end, culturally relevant pedagogy increases student learning and success.

Banks and McGee Banks (2012) describe five central tenets of multicultural education that have much the same aim as culturally relevant pedagogy. The first, Integration, is where teachers begin to put different cultures into the curriculum, such as providing more books with African American or Muslim characters. Knowledge Construction and Prejudice Reduction are the next two tenets, and with these, teachers are responsible for noticing and teaching students to notice implicit bias, and for "helping students develop positive attitudes towards different racial, ethnic, and cultural groups" (p. 22), respectively.

The fourth tenet, Equity Pedagogy, asks that teachers take it one step further and change the way they teach to be more culturally responsive. And finally, multicultural education requires that students and teachers work to Empower School Culture and Social Structure to be more culturally affirming.

This idea of multicultural education is largely embraced in schools, generally as a means to follow district initiatives or state mandates to support diversity. In literacy classrooms, this often translates to purchasing and using more multicultural texts, which is a part of Integration (Banks & McGee Banks, 2012). All too often, however, this is as far as teachers go. Although a district's initiative to support diversity is noble, understanding how to support that initiative falls short. This forces teachers to focus mostly on celebrating diversity rather than asking students to think critically about social issues.

Culturally relevant pedagogy also falls short in practice because there is often a problematic conflation that culture *only* equals teaching about race and ethnicity. This makes room for a superficial application of culturally relevant pedagogy in the classroom, where teachers tend to "home in on more simplistic notions of culture" (Gorski & Stallwell, 2015, p. 36), therefore leaving out considerations of class, gender, and sexual orientation, to name a few.

Although culturally relevant pedagogy requires teachers to be aware of who, what, and how they are teaching, this understanding does not require teachers to think critically about who, what, and how they are teaching.

Thinking critically about teaching "means to continuously seek out the information that lies beyond our common sense ideas about the world," and to think about "who benefits from [a] knowledge claim and whose lives are limited by it" (Sensoy & DiAngelo, 2012, p. 2). Culturally relevant pedagogy without critical thinking compromises its central tenets of equity and empowerment and completely misses the mark.

A literacy teacher who practices culturally relevant pedagogy and critical thinking in tandem recognizes that (1) there are more (and oftentimes subtle) cultural messages in the text that shape our knowledge about the social construction of identity (e.g., race, class, gender, sexual orientation, religion, etc.), and (2) school and the literature content used in classrooms are incompatible with students' cultures.

As such, when literacy teachers apply culturally relevant pedagogy and critical thinking into their literary practices and classrooms, it is also important that they demand critical literacy. The practice of critical literacy "invites [students] to move beyond passively accepting the text's message to question, examine, or dispute" the author and the status quo (McLaughlin & DeVoogd, 2004, p. 14). Students use their cultural experiences and perspectives to question the messages in the text related to the social construction of knowledge and issues of equity, power, and justice.

Practicing critical literacy is akin to Gorski's and Stallwell's (2015) Equity Literacy and Banks and McGee Banks's (2012) fourth tenet of multicultural education, Equity Pedagogy, where equity, not culture, is at the center. Together, culturally relevant pedagogy and critical literacy require both teacher and student be actively involved in rethinking the culture of school, as well as rethinking the literature and how it is used to convey messages about certain cultures and cultural values.

Culturally relevant pedagogy and critical literacy practices most certainly build an important foundation for work in classrooms where teaching culturally affirming literacy is the objective; however, these two alone or in tandem still leave room for a disconnect between work inside the classroom and the work outside the classroom.

A critical social justice framework is a means by which this disconnect can be lessened. Culturally affirming literacy practices need a foundation built on multicultural education, culturally relevant pedagogy, and critical literacy to enhance the framework of critical social justice literacy.

According to Bell (2007), "social justice is both a process and a goal," in which people from all groups are "active and equal participants" (p. 3) in breaking down inequities and injustices and forging transformation of thinking and learning. Thus, where culturally relevant pedagogy and critical literacy call for thought and awareness, social justice calls for action. Culturally relevant pedagogy and critical literacy, then, do not operate separately from a critical social justice framework, but rather the two are a part of the process (see figure 2.1).

A critical social justice framework for literacy is an evolving process in which teachers and students always consider cultural relevancy, employ critical literacy, and work for social justice as they relate to the word and the world (Freire & Macedo, 1987). With this, they actively address issues of privilege, power, and oppression. This "means guiding students in critical self-reflection of their socialization" in ways that critically question and challenge the status quo, but also in ways that guide students to become activists to promote equity and justice (Cochran-Smith, 2004, p. x).

Within a critical social justice framework for literacy, students might ask, "What do we do about it?" when they recognize stereotypes are present in a text. Consider, for example, Patricia Polacco's (2009) text, *In Our Mothers' House*, that presents the story of a lesbian couple who faces confrontation and challenges from their neighborhood community for being different.

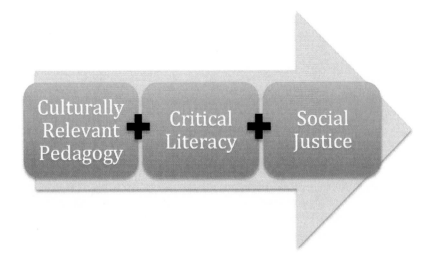

Figure 2.1.   Critical Social Justice Framework for Literacy

Students can think about how to use the text in ways that promote equitable and transformational learning and engagement. In this way, students move from passive to active participants in and out of the classroom within the critical social justice literacy framework.

HOW TO TEACH WITH A CRITICAL SOCIAL JUSTICE FRAMEWORK FOR LITERACY

Teaching within a critical social justice framework for literacy requires teachers to consider cultural relevancy, employ critical literacy, work for social justice, and be continuously self-reflective. This means that teachers need to continuously "recognize," "respond to," and "redress" their own and others' assumptions and biases related to issues of equity (Gorski & Stallwell, 2015, p. 37), as well as be well-versed in multicultural and diversity content and concepts.

A critical social justice framework for literacy also requires teachers to set up their classrooms in ways that focus on social justice. Paulo Freire (2000) first encouraged educators to move from a traditional banking method of teaching, where teachers are the knowledge-givers and students are the knowledge-receivers, to teaching with a social justice focus, where both teachers and students are both active participants in teaching and learning.

Nieto and Bode (2011) build on this and lay out four components for social justice in education that can be applied to all classrooms that operate within a critical social justice framework for literacy.

A literacy classroom must operate in ways that: (1) challenge, confront, and disrupt misconceptions, untruths, and stereotypes that lead to structural inequality and discrimination based on race, social class, gender, and other social and human differences; (2) provide all students with the resources necessary to learn to their full potential; (3) draw on the talents and strengths that students bring to their education; (4) and create a learning environment that promotes critical thinking and supports agency for social change (Nieto & Bode, 2011, p. 6–7).

Additionally, it is essential that teachers have a deep knowledge of literacy content and related pedagogical strategies so that the work for social justice operates with, rather than in addition to, these literacy strategies.

An important pedagogical strategy that is especially supportive of a critical social justice framework for literacy is the practice of close reading. Lehman and Roberts (2013), in their book *Falling in Love with Close Reading: Lessons for Analyzing Texts—and Life*, pull together several important and overlapping definitions to share their vision for effective close reading. They assert that students engage in multiple close reads by critically analyzing texts, "while also valuing their lives and experiences" (p. 4). Clearly, what drives close reading is directly in line with a critical social justice framework in literacy because of the necessity of critical engagement with the word and the world.

Lehman and Roberts (2013) outline three essential steps for close reading, and the following is meant to explain what close reading looks like within a critical social justice framework. The first step is to read through lenses, which they name as text evidence, word choice, structure, and point-of-view and argument. When teaching with a critical social justice literacy framework, however, teachers need to coach students on how to read through an anti-oppressive lens (Kumashiro, 2000).

An anti-oppressive lens is one by which students read with a critical consciousness of social justice. Some questions students could ask during this part of the close reading include: (1) what is the knowledge claim that the author is trying to make in this text? and (2) who benefits from or is limited by that knowledge claim?

When students are analyzing word choice, for example, they need to specifically hone in on this analysis through a social justice lens. In the fictional book *Nappy Hair*, Carolivia Herron (1997) writes that a community calls out to God, "Why you gotta be so ornery, thinking about giving that nappy, nappy hair to that innocent little child" (p. 12). Here, the knowledge claim appears to be that nappy hair is the result of someone being ornery, and a critical analysis of the word *ornery*, used in conjunction with "nappy hair," sends a message that nappy hair is not a good thing to possess.

An analysis of this knowledge claim through a social justice lens exposes that the claim limits student understanding that one type of hair is not more acceptable than another. As such, African American students who see themselves in the main character with nappy hair may walk away thinking their hair is not as good as smooth, soft hair. White students with smooth, soft hair, on the other hand, benefit from this knowledge claim because it asserts that their hair is better than that of their African American peers.

The next step in close reading as outlined by Lehman and Roberts (2013) is to use the lenses to find patterns. The patterns that students need to look for as they read through an anti-oppression lens need to be centered on issues of racism, sexism, classism, heterosexism, ableism, anti-semitism/religious oppression, and colonialism, as well as the intersections of these *–isms*. Considering intersections of these *–isms* simply means to not look at these issues in isolation.

For example, when reading the nonfiction text, *Malala Yousafzai: Warrior of Words*, by Karen Legett Abouraya (2014), it is important to read and analyze the ways in which the young girl is portrayed related to issues of gender, as well as how the Muslim faith is portrayed related to issues of religion. It is also important to read and analyze the ways the Muslim girl is portrayed; thus, reading and analyzing the portrayal of gender and religion as they intersect. The questions students should ask as they read for patterns will largely depend on issues in the text but should build on the two questions students ask as they read through an anti-oppression lens. Some basic questions that readers can begin to ask as they read for patterns could include: (1) who or what does the author's knowledge claim give power to? and (2) what stereotypes, biases, and myths are challenged or upheld?

The third step in close reading is to use patterns to develop a new understanding of the text (Lehman & Roberts, 2013). As students begin to find these patterns, they can ask critically conscious questions to develop a new understanding of not only the text, but also the larger system of oppressions that are at play in the text and the world.

Bomer and Bomer (2001) present readers with a substantial list of questions for critical reading that are helpful with close reading in a social justice framework, but there are three that are particularly useful when developing a new understanding: "(1) At what points do you notice yourself resisting the book, the characters, or the author? (2) What does your resistance say about the book, and what does it say about you? and (3) How does this book help you think about social issues you care about or causes you are committed to?" (p. 52). Together, these questions encourage critical thinking about both the word and the world, which is a central component of a social justice framework for literacy.

A CRITICAL SOCIAL JUSTICE FRAMEWORK FOR LITERACY IN ACTION

Teaching within a critical social justice framework for literacy requires certain teacher dispositions, pedagogical methods, and student expectations. What is taught within a social justice framework, however, is a creative and dynamic process that is largely dependent on school and classroom demographics, resources, state and local standards, and teacher preferences.

It is recommended that the workshop approach be used to teach literacy within a critical social justice framework (e.g., see the work of Lucy Calkins, Irene Fountas, and Gay Su Pinnell). That is, explicit teacher modeling, read-alouds, mini-lessons, independent reading and writing time, student notebooks, and individual and group conferences should be used to maximize instructional time and student success.

The purpose of this section is to share and discuss one example of how a social justice framework was implemented into a literacy classroom. It is important to note that, although the unit discussed is specifically related to a fourth-grade reading and writing research unit on issues of inequity in a community, a critical social justice framework should not be isolated to one unit. Culturally relevant pedagogy, critical literacy, social justice, and close reads need to remain at the foundation of all class work.

The unit discussed in this chapter is broken up into four main components that can easily be incorporated into all units throughout the year. These components include: (1) immersion, (2) generating ideas, (3) researching/reading, and (4) promoting social justice. A brief description of each component, as well as sample lessons/activities and student work, are shared.

Immersion

The immersion component for this unit on reading and writing about inequity in a community serves as an introduction to social justice and general definitions of power, equity, and activism. This is when teachers need to begin discussions of anti-oppression topics described previously. During this time, students immerse themselves in reading and writing about social justice–related poetry, music, speeches, and stories, and consequently begin to gauge the world around them through a social justice lens.

When using critical social justice framework for literacy, it is important that students early on spend some time considering who they are as individuals, as well as part of a collective group, and it is especially important to revisit their interconnectedness with the others at the start of this unit on issues of equity. Linda Christensen's (2000), "Where I Am From: Inviting Students' Lives Into the Classroom," (p. 18) is a useful activity here. In this activity, students begin to think about *who* they are as individuals, as well as *who* they are in the context of their family, school, communities, and larger society.

The use of mentor authors is essential as students immerse themselves in a social justice framework (Bomer & Bomer, 2001). This prepares the students to consider the different ways that people choose to publish their work, as well as react to and reflect on different approaches to the same topic. Mentor authors not only help students understand the topics at hand, but also help them to think about ways in which they can be activists themselves. The fourth-grade teachers highlighted in this chapter provided several examples of mentor authors for close reading, but also encouraged their students to seek out their own mentor authors during this unit.

During a lesson on using mentor authors to understand racism, one teacher, Jeff, provided students with several excerpts of speeches, song lyrics, and poems. Along with close reads of each, he had the students respond to questions to get them thinking about the impact the words had on supporting their understanding of the social issues at hand, and how the words did or did not inspire action. Among the excerpts for this particular assignment were Martin Luther King Jr.'s (1963) "I Have a Dream" speech; song lyrics to Lori

McKenna's "Ruby's Shoes (1998)"; and the poem "I, Too" by Langston Hughes (2006).

Of the three excerpts, one student, Cristina, found King's "I Have a Dream" speech to be particularly inspiring. Although the overarching issue being studied in this lesson was racism, she journaled about how acceptance of individuals needed to move beyond race alone and also encompass sexuality and religion—issues she saw as reflective of her school and larger community.

In response, Cristina crafted her own "I Have a Dream" speech about how she wanted to "globalize acceptance." In writing her speech, Cristina considered the intersections of *-isms* as she did close reads through an anti-oppression lens and was able to use a mentor author to help in her analysis of the text.

Generating Ideas

In this next component, students began to generate ideas about what to research related to issues of equity that they saw playing out in their classroom, school, and the larger world. The work done during Immersion most certainly overlapped with the work in this component. Students generated ideas and narrowed topics to conduct specific research.

Chapman, Hobbel, and Alvarado (2011) suggest that students think about what issues concern them personally and then narrow those issues down to the ones that concern their families, communities, and finally society on a global level. Asking students to generate ideas and reflect on and analyze their feelings and knowledge claims about issues of equity gives them an opportunity to also think about the ways in which they might address these issues.

Another teacher, Shonda, had students "notice issues of justice, power, and association inside the school and out in the community." Antonio, a student in Shonda's classroom, spent a few days observing and taking meticulous notes about issues that plagued the school and the community news. His notebook became filled with personal observations, reactions, and thoughts about pressing social justice issues that were labeled as: violence, robberies, poverty, illnesses, groups, class, and fairness/justice.

While generating ideas, students wrote entries about their thoughts and reactions to mentor authors, personal observations, and classroom discussions related to equity issues. After Antonio spent a few days observing and taking notes, he wrote:

> I see in this school the issue of voice & silence, like when someone calls [another person] names and you don't say anything about it because you're afraid to say it. When I see this issue going [on], I feel like speaking up for the person because I know what they have been told is wrong but then I feel afraid

to show it, to speak up, the fear wins and in the end I'm not doing anything that is supportive. This get's [*sic*] me frustrated, frustrated, FRUSTRATED, about when someone judge you about how you look or your race color and don't even know you, don't even know what is inside of that person. When I see this issue, I feel I should get out of these walls of this box I am in and speak out, but then the fear overcomes me and I'm still in the box.

This journal entry was titled "Issue: Voice & Silence" and is a good example of the process of generating ideas. The entry stemmed from Antonio's reading of mentor authors who wrote about bullying in connection with a follow-up activity assigned by the teacher. He eventually chose to do his research on bullying.

Another student in Shonda's class, Shay, made a graphic organizer that was broken down into three columns, titled "Bugging Me/Worrying Me," "Questions," and "What I Can Do." Among the issues "bugging her" were typical elementary school issues, such as backstabbers, hunger, Miley Cyrus, as well as a not-so-typical topic of gay students. In her notebook, the student wrote, "I think gay kids should be able to be open about their sexuality. This means we'd need to stop making fun of gay kids [and] give them support."

The student bridged her findings from her close reads of different mentor texts along with her own perspective of her school community and saw a need to address the equitable treatment of lesbian, gay, bisexual, transgender, and queer (LGBTQ) students. She ultimately chose this as her topic because she felt that bullying of students who were perceived to be LGTBQ was getting out of hand at the school.

When generating ideas within a critical social justice framework for literacy, it is important to engage students in peer discussions that address differing viewpoints, counter-stories, and varying perspectives. The student who generated ideas on voice and silence watched and compared information from several news channels, talked to other students about bullying, and asked teachers about their insight on how bullying was handled in the school. Likewise, the student who generated ideas on equitable treatment of LGBTQ students perused several authors and spoke with students to get a pulse on the issue within the school and in society.

Reading/Researching

After choosing a topic, students then moved to reading about and researching the equity issue(s) of their choosing. Close reading comes into full swing in this part of the unit, and it is a continuous cycle of reading through an anti-oppression lens, finding patterns, and developing new understandings of the texts. Students located their own mentor authors and engaged in close reads of multiple texts. As is with any research, reading each text for information is also important as students read and research on their topic.

As students read their texts for information, another teacher, Sofia, had them pull out direct quotes that helped strengthen their understanding of the equity issues they chose. The students then had to give an explanation as to why each quote was important or useful for others to know. This helped students delineate the culturally responsive and anti-oppressive textual information from the inequitable and oppressive information, a task that is at the foundation of using a critical social adjust framework for literacy.

Shay, who chose to research the equitable treatment of LGBTQ students, did several close reads of related kid-friendly books and websites. During her close reads, she noted the lack of inclusion the LGBTQ topics, the lack of support for LGTBQ students, and especially the negative language used to describe LGBTQ individuals. In her research, she also found one site that she was able to use as a mentor for how to speak out against injustices.

This prompted Shay to conduct a close read of the school's discrimination policy to see what type of support was offered, as well as juxtapose it with the information she had gathered from the close reads of other texts. This close read revealed that the policy was similar to the other texts, specifically in that mention of LGBTQ students was lacking and word choice regarding safety was vague, leaving out any protection of LGBTQ students. It was at this point that Shay was ready to move to the action phase of the critical social justice framework for literacy.

Promoting Social Justice

Even if a unit is taught about researching equity issues, unless it is framed around critical social justice literacy, the culminating student projects are often traditional, in the form of written papers. Student work is graded, then handed back, or filed away. Sometimes, students are allowed be creative and create informative posters or brochures that educate others on their topics, and displays of their work might be used in the hallway to spread their message to anyone who chooses to stop and read them. Social action, however, is often weak, or missing altogether.

A critical social justice framework demands social action beyond classroom walls and is especially important because students are asked to read and research the word and the world both in and out of the classroom (Bomer & Bomer, 2001). Shay wrote and delivered a letter to the superintendent about changing the discrimination policy to have inclusive language for LGBTQ students. Antonio gathered student stories and school data on bullying, then created and handed out a booklet with the information, as well information on how to prevent bullying and where to go for resources.

Sofia's class used their understanding of equity and justice to collectively challenge the school administration on the removal of the equity unit on the grounds that the topics being researched were "too controversial." They created a wall display titled "Stirring Up Justice," where they each made posters to advocate for equity in the community and formed a human barrier around the display in protest. A pair of students in Jeff's classroom wrote a letter to the librarian requesting that more culturally relevant and inclusive books be ordered on topics that matched the demographics of the school.

No matter the size of the culminating project, the reach must be beyond the classroom when working within a critical social justice framework for literacy.

FINAL THOUGHTS

The level of student achievement and engagement is telling of transformative power in literacy classrooms that embody a critical social justice framework. The students in this chapter changed mind-sets, challenged inequities, struck up mini-revolutions, and deepened their love for and success in reading and writing. This type of literacy learning allows our urban youth more equitable opportunities to be successful in college, have higher paying jobs, display social and civic efficacy, and effect social change (Morrell, 2008).

Built on the concepts of culturally relevant pedagogy, critical literacy, and social justice, a critical social justice framework for literacy pushes both students and teachers to actively address issues of privilege, power, and oppression in the word and the world.

When applied to literacy, a critical social justice framework has the power to decolonize current classroom practices that silence and restrict the voices of minoritized students in urban elementary schools. Student perspectives, experiences, and lives are invited into the classroom in ways that transform mainstream culture and thinking and increase student success. Students need and deserve this type of education—always.

REFERENCES

Abouraya, K. L. (2014). *Malala Yousafzai: Warrior with words*. Great Neck, NY: StarWalk Kids Media.

Au, W. (2009). *Rethinking multicultural education: Teaching for racial and cultural justice*. Milwaukee, WI: Rethinking Schools, Ltd.

Banks, J. A., & McGee Banks, C. (2012). *Multicultural education: Issues and perspectives* (8th ed.). Hoboken, NJ: Wiley Publishing.

Bell, L. A. (2007). Theoretical foundations for social justice education. In M. Adams, L. A. Bell, & P. Griffin (Eds.), *Teaching for diversity and social justice* (pp. 1–14). New York: Routledge.

Bomer, R., & Bomer, K. (2001). *For a better world: Reading and writing for social action*. Portsmouth, NH: Heinemann.

Chapman, T. K., Hobbel, N., & Alvarado, N. V. (2011). A social justice approach as a base for teaching writing. *Journal of Adolescent & Adult Literacy, 54*(7), 539–41.

Christensen, L. (2000). *Reading, writing, and rising up: Teaching about social justice and the power of the written word*. Milwaukee, WI: Rethinking Schools.

Cochran-Smith, M. (2004). *Walking the road: Race, diversity, and social justice in teacher education*. New York: Teachers College Press.

Freire, P. (2000). *Pedagogy of the oppressed* (30th Anniversary Ed.). New York: Bloomsbury Academic.

Freire, P., & Macedo, D. (1987). *Literacy: Reading the word and the world*. Westport, CT: Praeger Publishers.

Gay, G. (2002). Preparing for culturally responsive teaching. *Journal of Teacher Education, 53*(2), 106–16.

Gorski, P., & Stallwell, K. (2015). Equity literacy for all. *Educational Leadership, 72*(6), 34–40.

Herron, C. (1997). *Nappy hair*. New York, NY: Dragon Fly Books.

Hughes, L. (2006). I, too. In D. Roessel & A. Rampersad (Eds.), *Poetry for young people: Langston Hughes* (p. 22). New York: Scholastic.

King, M. L., Jr. (1963). I have a dream. Retrieved from http://www.archives.gov/press/exhibits/dream-speech.pdf.

Kumashiro, K. K. (2000). Toward a theory of anti-oppressive education. *Review of Educational Research, 70*(1), 25–53.

Ladson-Billings, G. (1992). Liberatory consequences of literacy: A case of culturally relevant instruction for African-American students. *Journal of Negro Education, 61*, 378–91.

Ladson-Billings, G. (1995). But that's just good teaching! The case for culturally relevant pedagogy. *Theory Into Practice, 34*(3), 159–65.

Lehman, C., & Roberts, K. (2013). *Falling in love with close reading: Lessons for analyzing texts—and life*. New York: Heinemann.

McKenna, L. (1999). Ruby's Shoes. On *Paper wings and halo* [Audio CD]. Portland, OR: CD Baby.

McLaughlin, M., & DeVoogd, G. (2004). *Critical literacy: Enhancing students' comprehension of text*. New York: Scholastic.

Morrell, E. (2008). *Critical literacy and urban youth: Pedagogies of access, dissent, and liberation*. New York: Routledge.

Nieto, S., & Bode, P. (2011). *Affirming diversity: The sociopolitical context of multicultural education* (6th ed.). Upper Saddle River, NJ: Pearson.

Polacco, P. (2009). *In our mothers' house*. New York: Philomel Books.

Sensoy, O., & DiAngelo, R. (2012). *Is everyone really equal? An introduction to key concepts in social justice education*. New York: Teachers College Press.

Chapter Three

Reauthorizing Excellence in Literacy Teaching for African American Learners

Melanie Acosta

Over the last three decades, scores of reading researchers have studied teacher effectiveness in the literacy classroom and the residual effects of this work exists in many schools today (Afflerbach, 2007; Morrow, Tracy, Woo, & Pressley, 1999; Pressley, Mohan, Fingeret, Reffit, & Raphael-Bogaret, 2007; Snow, Burns, & Griffin, 1998; Wharton-McDonald, Pressley, & Hampston, 1998).

Yet, many of the studies documenting effective literacy teaching have been driven by a color-blind approach that fails to recognize the centrality of race and ethnicity in teaching and learning experiences, despite an emphasis on meeting the needs of all students (Lazar, Edwards, & Thompson-McMillion, 2012; Powell & Rightmeyer, 2011).

When this research has attempted to address the sociological complexities embedded in American literacy teaching and learning contexts, discussion has been encapsulated in a deficit discourse in which code language such as *at-risk, disadvantaged,* and *struggling* have been used to describe African American children (Edwards, Thompson-McMillion, & Turner, 2010; Lazar, et al., 2012; Powell & Rightmeyer, 2011).

As a result, there has been little improvement in reading achievement for African American young readers. According to the National Assessment of Educational Progress standardized reading assessment data, less than 20 percent of African American fourth graders read at or above proficiency levels (U.S. Department of Education, 2014). Furthermore, these patterns persist over time and characterize a trajectory of literacy underachievement.

As Tatum (n.d.) contends the looming questions that bear critical consideration regarding the reading achievement of African American children are "Who is authorizing these practices and policies inside and outside of schools that can adversely impact the reading, writing, and intellectual development of African Americans. And, what will it take to reauthorize practices that will serve their best interest?" (p. 1). These questions point to the urgency to rethink existing conceptualizations of effective literacy instruction in ways relevant to African American learners.

This chapter begins to reauthorize the scope of effective literacy instruction by situating effective literacy teaching in a framework that emphasizes the underlying sociocultural aspects of exemplary teaching as well as instructional strategies. This is important because it creates an important link between teacher effectiveness in literacy teaching and African American student success.

RACE, CULTURE, AND EFFECTIVE ELEMENTARY LITERACY INSTRUCTION: WHERE HAVE WE BEEN?

Literacy has been inherently linked to race, citizenship, and universal human freedom for centuries, particularly for African Americans (Anderson, 1995; Ladson-Billings, 2012; Lee & Slaughter-Defoe, 2002; Perry, 2003). As European colonization seized the new world under a racial caste system that positioned people of darker-skinned hues at the bottom of the social hierarchy, literacy became appropriated as an indicator of Whiteness (Ladson-Billings, 2012). As a result, African Americans were institutionally denied the right to learn to read and write. However, as Anderson (1995) writes, African Americans maintained ideas and values about literacy that fueled their determination to master the alphabetic principle. These ideals reflected "a consciousness of literacy as a means of resistance as well as an understanding of anti-literacy movements as mechanisms of oppression" (p. 3). This consciousness spurred intentional efforts by African Americans to demand free public schooling as a way to promote the teaching of literacy as a matter of justice. This justice-oriented insight about the utility of literacy teaching contributed to massive efforts among African American adults to ensure that their children were able to learn to read, which led to rapid increases in literacy among young, southern African Americans by the early 1900s (Anderson, 1995).

Despite this inherent connection, the influence of race on literacy teaching and learning exists primarily as a justification of the moral failures of people of color rather than as a proxy for effective literacy instruction. Moreover, many researchers have student elementary literacy achievement from a de-racialized perspective.

For example, researchers (Pressley, Rankin, & Yokoi, 1996; Wharton-McDonald, et al., 1998; Pressley et al., 2001) used qualitative methods to delineate the characteristics of effective elementary literacy instruction. Findings revealed characteristics that distinguish exemplary teachers. Researchers also concluded that student engagement, motivation, and actual reading and writing were critical factors in literacy acquisition.

Although high teacher expectations were mentioned as a key factor of exemplary elementary reading teachers, there was no interrogation of teachers' racialized and cultural perspectives and how these beliefs influenced their teaching practice. Moreover, while the researchers mentioned the importance of positive classroom environment and student engagement in effective literacy teaching, they did not address the central role cultural relevance and responsiveness plays in creating positive classroom communities and in engaging students in learning (Gay, 2000; Hollins, 1982; Ladson-Billings, 1994).

Morrow and colleagues (1999) and Allington (2002) sought to describe the nature of effective literacy teaching at the elementary level. Both studies found that reading achievement was the result of exemplary teachers responding to the individual needs of students. These studies also demonstrated that expert teachers knew not only how to provide explicit instruction, but also how to "foster transfer of the strategies from the structured practice activities to students' independent use of them while engaged in reading" (Allington, 2002, p. 744).

In both studies, researchers used predominantly European American teachers and findings were generalized across all cultural groups. Thus, Eurocentric ideals were elevated as the standard of quality, which marginalized the wisdoms of practice of teachers of color.

Block, Oakar, and Hurt (2002) conducted a qualitative study to develop a descriptive database of teaching expertise in literacy from preschool to grade five. The study found eighty-eight indicators of expertise with forty-four of these indicators specific to grade levels.

This study was important because it began to legitimize the social context of effective literacy teaching and learning by highlighting teacher-student relationships, motivation, and teacher values. However, researchers gave no analytical attention to the influence of cultural synchronization in relating to students, motivating students to read, and reading behaviors valued by the teacher.

Finally, the report of the National Reading Panel (NRP) (2000) compiled the results of a study examining effective reading instruction. The study looked at effective instructional practices in the early elementary grades and brought to focus specific instructional practices related to five pillars of literacy instruction (NRP, 2000). Phonics, phonemic awareness, fluency, vocabulary, and comprehension were the five core areas identified by the panel.

Here again, researchers privileged content expertise over sociocultural knowledge in designating the areas of reading instruction where teachers should direct the majority of their effort.

This research has provided descriptions of literacy teaching practices that promote achievement in young readers. However, each of these studies is limited in its ability to meet the needs of African American learners. These studies seem to position the teacher as an objective technician. That is, each study does not capture teacher perspectives that undoubtedly influence instructional practices such as beliefs about student abilities, perspectives on the purpose of literacy and education, the ideological construction of blackness (Acosta, 2015).

What a teacher values, believes, and assumes about students, their capabilities, and the kind of instruction they need to be successful readers is critical to promoting excellence in reading education for African American children (Compton-Lilly, 2004; Lazar et al., 2012; Tatum, n.d.). Popkewitz (2006) posits that standardized curriculums, discussions about best practices, and evidenced-based or scientifically based instruction are not neutral but are "inscriptions of cultural theses about who the child is and should be" (p. 129). Any discussion of effective literacy teaching should necessarily address the ideological characteristics of effective reading teachers because it is these factors that drive the instructional approaches documented as effective practice (Acosta, 2015).

Despite these significant limitations, many of these studies are used as the backdrop to frame the way teachers and researchers talk about, think about, and learn about effective elementary literacy instruction (Compton-Lilly, 2004; Lazar et al., 2012; Powell & Rightmeyer, 2011; Tatum, n.d.). The exclusive reliance on ethnocentric ways of thinking and knowing about effective instruction is what Acosta (2013) conceptualizes as pedagogical hegemony.

Pedagogical hegemony takes direction from research on dysconsciousness (King, 1991) among teachers because it thrives off of an uncritical habit of mind in thinking about teaching, learning, and appropriate practices for educating children. Without critical study of social inequity and its impact on teaching and learning, many teachers see no reason to change their instructional practices.

In other words, pedagogical hegemony keeps teachers bound to instructional practices that actually constrain the achievement of African Americans readers (Tatum, n.d.). For example, teachers are less likely to create challenging instructional activities or provide students with scaffolding (Ladson-Billings, 2002; Lazar et al., 2012; Tatum, 2012).

Previously, Woodson (1933) explained the scope of pedagogical hegemony. The author wrote that when racism is unchallenged and hegemony remains the foundation of societal institutions, the instructional practices touted as most effective could be the most damaging to the development of African American children.

There are at least two debilitating consequences of pedagogical hegemony in relation to effective elementary literacy instruction. First, pedagogical hegemony silences the voices and wisdoms of practice of teachers of color who maintain an expansive pedagogical vision dually focused on educational and pedagogical equity (Acosta, 2015; Siddle-Walker, 2012). Second, pedagogical hegemony reifies a color-blind mentality because it treats race and ethnicity as irrelevant variables that have little to do with the ability of teachers to enact effective literacy practices.

CONCEPTUAL FRAMEWORK: PEDAGOGICAL EXCELLENCE

"Pedagogical excellence represents an intentional attempt to crystallize, or bind together the research that outlines the features of effective teaching for African American children by making connections between the ideological premises that often undergirds these teaching approaches" (Acosta, 2015, p. 62). This is important because it provides a way to think about the symbiotic nature of the cultural, political, and historical factors that influence the quality of instruction of African American learners. However, this is a key indicator missing from many discussions about teacher quality (Acosta, 2015).

For example, the U.S. Department of Education (2013) defined a highly qualified teacher as one who has a bachelor's degree, has full state certification or licensure, and can prove that he or she knows each subject he or she teaches by passing a subject area exam.

This set of criteria encourages K–12 schools, policymakers, and some teacher education programs to privilege content expertise and color-blindness over pedagogy and social context in educator preparation, despite the importance of each on teaching and learning. This results in the cultivation of a generation of teachers who have graduated from preparation programs, achieved national teaching certification, yet are unprepared to meet the educational needs of today's public school students who are the most culturally diverse in history.

Hollins (2011) and Sleeter (2008) reported that many prospective teachers are young, White, English-speaking females who have led culturally encapsulated lives and have been socialized into the culture of power. This culture of power reifies a deficit-based, pathologizing set of assumptions about *who* African American children are, what their reading ability and potential is, and how they should be taught in the elementary reading classroom. Many teachers carry these assumptions into their classrooms and use them to guide the design and delivery of instruction, which results in lower expectations and lower achievement for African American students (Lazar et al., 2012; Powell & Rightmeyer, 2011).

Pedagogical excellence emphasizes the sociological influences on teacher quality, which includes cultural, historical, and political considerations (Acosta, 2013, 2015). In other words, it is a way of thinking about effective teaching as intricately connected to the world we live in. It rejects the assumption that teaching is neutral work and that teachers have little impact on or responsibility for improving society. Instead, pedagogical excellence encapsulates the nature of teacher quality within a justice-oriented mission that positions teachers as essential agents of change, and it is this sociological connectedness that provides the foundation for effective teachers' enactment of instructional practices that promote student educational success (Acosta, 2015).

Pedagogical excellence builds on three theoretical frameworks that describe effective pedagogy for African American children (see figure 3.1). These frameworks include culturally relevant pedagogy, effective Black educators, and African American schooling before the end of legalized public school segregation on the basis of skin color. These frameworks have been used to illuminate key facets of pedagogical excellence, which include race consciousness, cultural solidarity, resistance, and humanity (Acosta, 2015).

Though these frameworks have been conceptualized separately, there is a high degree of overlap and fluidity between each and it is difficult to distinguish between them. Rather than separate them, however, it may be more promising to analyze their connections to each toward a larger vision of teacher quality. It must be noted that pedagogical excellence does not seek to replace the existing interpretive frameworks documenting the instructional practices and beliefs associated with good teaching of African American children. These works have been pivotal in shifting the thinking about improving African American education from a deficit perspective to an effective teaching paradigm.

Deficit-based ideologies locate the source of student academic failure within the child, family, and community, whereas effective teaching perspectives posit that improving the quality of instruction can mitigate systemic

IDEOLOGY	BELIEFS	INSTRUCTIONAL PRACTICES
Political clarity	Intellectual capacity of African American children	Insistence
Racial uplift	Positive views of African American families and communities	Connectedness
Affirmative views of African	All children can learn	Interdependent learning community
American culture	Accountability for student learning	Collective success
Culturally relevant critical teacher care		Curriculum connected to student experiences
Opposition		Curriculum relevant to students' lives

Figure 3.1.   Pedagogical Excellence for African American Learners: Conceptual Connections

challenges that impose on student academic achievement. In building on the effective teaching paradigm pedagogical excellence binds these frameworks together by emphasizing the liberatory philosophy that undergirds each.

REAUTHORIZING EFFECTIVE ELEMENTARY LITERACY INSTRUCTION FROM THE "INSIDE OUT"

To date, many literacy education reform efforts have had not made a significant impact on the reading achievement of a growing population of young readers, particularly African American children.

Reconceptualizing effective elementary literacy instruction within the framework of pedagogical excellence is a promising start to challenging pedagogical hegemony in literacy instruction and improving African American student outcomes in reading achievement. This is because pedagogical excellence demands teachers build an effective elementary literacy practice from the "inside out." That is, it encourages teachers to conceptualize effective literacy instruction as the alignment of teacher self-knowledge, perspectives, dispositions, and practices with a focus on student learning and development.

For teachers to fully understand what it means to teach literacy effectively, they must interrogate their own positionality, perspectives, and privilege from a critical purview as it relates to literacy teaching and learning experiences and literacy achievement.

Using pedagogical excellence as a framework for encapsulating effective elementary literacy instruction can be effective because it does not treat teachers politically neutral and teaching as disconnected from our social world. Instead, it situates the practice of effective literacy teaching within the social milieu in ways that help teachers make connections between their role, responsibility, and teaching actions in the classroom with larger equity-oriented agendas.

Finally, pedagogical excellence is promising because it can move educators from the passive position of awareness to a position of action through the cultivation of agency and moral responsibility to change the outcomes for African American readers through good teaching. Mere awareness of social inequities, without intentional deconstruction of the deficit ideologies that are used to rationalize inequities, is not powerful enough to dislodge the grip of pedagogical hegemony on teacher literacy practice.

Pedagogical excellence, on the other hand, is a revolutionary conceptual framework that is poised to directly confront the irrationality of pedagogical hegemony, challenge teacher dysconsciousness, and usher in a way of understanding literacy teaching success as the explicit and synergistic symbiotic alignment of ideology, dispositions, and practices that promote literacy learning and development for African American young readers.

Teachers can begin to reauthorize pedagogical excellence as their framework for quality literacy instruction by developing theories of effective teaching ground in the perspectives and everyday practices of African American community members. African American communities have led efforts to help their children acquire literacy for centuries and have done so with ideas about democracy, morality, and justice in mind (Anderson, 1988; Perry, 2003).

Classroom teachers must develop similar perspectives and skills as this can facilitate their enactment of teaching in ways that promote student intellectual and social development without diminishing their cultural identity and heritage. To move toward this more expansive, morally engaged literacy teaching practice, teachers must develop collaborative partnerships with community members (King, 2008). These partnerships should be predicated on promoting community well-being by encouraging teachers to work with community members to investigate, study, and develop theories of effective literacy teaching.

Within these partnerships, teachers, parents, children, and other community members can engage in collaborative study and theory-building around effective literacy teaching, which teachers can then foreground in their instructional approaches.

African American theorizing on effective teaching is often rooted in the daily, lived experiences within a complex sociocultural structure (Acosta, 2015; Gordon, 1990). That is, African American theorizing uses a sociocultural lens to articulate a vision of effective teaching and develop instruction that aligns with this vision. It expresses how African Americans formulate theories and approaches to teaching and liberation within a society structured in domination by race, class, and gender (Anderson, 1988; Gordon, 1990; Perry, 2003; Siddle-Walker, 2000).

Drawing on the knowledge, values, and experiences embedded in African American communities, literacy teaching recognizes that this cultural knowledge does not exist solely as the antithesis of an ethnocentric ideology. Rather it recognizes that knowledge generated from and within people's culture and experience can be liberating because it legitimizes African American community knowledge as expressed by African American people outside of ethnocentric interpretation.

Through the formulation of collaborative partnerships with African American community groups, teachers can systematically build a pedagogy of excellence in literacy teaching that can be transformative and promote student achievement because it aligns with the experiences, cultural frameworks, and values embedded within the community.

Hyland and Meacham (2004), Murrell (2001), Noffke (1999) have made similar arguments and conclude that educators have largely failed to draw on the localized knowledge, perspectives, and cultural frameworks of culturally diverse communities and this failure is a significant contributor to alienating schooling experiences for African American children. Anderson (1995) found that all successful reform efforts for African American children have built on the strengths inherent in communities, families, students, and teachers. He argued that this aspect of improving education "should be developed and relied on, not ignored or dismissed as pathological" (p. 15).

The partnerships suggested in this chapter positions community and teachers as partners in collaborative theory-building and problem solving. This helps to redistribute power and decision-making ability among the group, and it works to dismantle power inequities that situate the teacher as the sole authority and parents and caregivers as void of know-how related to literacy, teaching, and learning (Miller, 2010).

Preparing teachers to demonstrate pedagogical excellence is a promising approach to rewriting the narrative on what it means to be an effective literacy teacher. Pedagogical excellence represents a bold step toward re-envisioning effective teaching in ways that align with the cultural frameworks and perspectives of African American communities. Though not a panacea for ending all issues involved in promoting reading achievement for African American young readers, it moves teachers in the direction necessary for reconnecting young African American children to academic and cultural excellence in literacy.

REFERENCES

Acosta, M. (2013). A culture-focused study with accomplished black educators on pedagogical excellence for African American children (PhD diss.). University of Florida, Gainesville.

Acosta, M. (2015). Quality of implementation as the "IT" factor in preparing teachers of African American children. *African American Learners Journal, 4*(1).

Afflerbach, P. (2007). Best practices in literacy assessment. In L. B. Gambrell, L. M. Morrow, & M. Pressley (Eds.), *Best practices in literacy instruction* (3rd ed., pp. 264–83). New York: Guilford Press.

Allington, R. L. (2002). What I've learned about effective reading instruction from a decade of studying exemplary elementary classroom teachers. *Phi Delta Kappan, 83*(10), 740–47.

Anderson, J. D. (1988). *The education of Blacks in the South 1860–1935*. Chapel Hill, NC: University of North Carolina Press.

Anderson, J. D. (1995). *A historical context for understanding the test score gap*. Unpublished manuscript.

Block, C. C., Oakar, M., & Hurt, N. (2002). The expertise of literacy teachers: A continuum from preschool to grade 5. *Reading Research Quarterly, 37*, 178–206.

Compton-Lilly. C. (2004). *Confronting racism, poverty, and power: Classroom strategies to change the world*. Portsmouth, NH: Heinemann.

Edwards, P., Thompson-McMillion, G., & Turner, J. (2010). *Change is gonna come: Transforming literacy edcuation for African American students*. New York: Teachers College Press.

Gay, G. (2000). *Culturally responsive teaching: Theory, research and practice.* New York: Teachers College Press.

Gordon, B. (1990). The necessity of African-American epistemology in educational theory and practice. *Journal of Education, 172*(3), 88–106.

Hollins, E. R. (1982). The Marva Collins story revisited: Implications for regular classroom instruction. *Journal of Teacher Education, 33*(2), 37–40.

Hollins, E. R. (2011). The meaning of culture in learning to teach: The power of socialization and identity formation. In A. Ball & C. A. Tyson (Eds.). *Studying diversity in teacher education* (pp. 385–98). Lanham, MD: Rowman & Littlefield Publishers, Inc.

Hyland, N. E., & Meacham, S. (2004). Community-centered teacher education: A paradigm for socially just education transformation. In J. L. Kincheloe, A. Bursztyn, & S. Steinberg (Eds.), *Teaching teachers: Building a quality school of urban education* (pp. 113–34). New York: Peter Lang.

King, J. E. (1991). Dysconscious racism: Ideology, identity, and the miseducation of teachers. *Journal of Negro Education, 60*(2), 133–46

King, J. E. (2008). Critical and qualitative research in teacher education: A blues epistemology, a reason for knowing for cultural well-being. In M. Cochran-Smith, S., Feiman-Nemser, & J. McIntyre (Eds.), *Handbook of research on teacher education: Enduring issues in changing contexts* (3rd ed., pp. 1094–135). Mahwah, NJ: Lawrence Erlbaum, Publishers.

Ladson-Billings, G. (1994). *The dreamkeepers: Successful teachers of African American children.* San Francisco, CA: Jossey-Bass

Ladson-Billings, G. (2012). Through a glass darkly: The persistence of race in education research and scholarship. *Educational Researcher, 41*(4), 115–20.

Ladson-Billings, G. L. (2002). I ain't writin' nuttin': Permissions to fail and demands to succeed in urban classrooms. In L. Delpit & J. K. Dowdy (Eds.). *The skin that we speak: Thoughts on language and culture in the classroom* (pp. 107–20). New York: New Press.

Lazar, A. M., Edwards, P. A., & Thompson-McMillion, G. (2012). *Bridging and equity: The essential guide to social equity teaching.* New York: Teachers College Press.

Lee, C., & Slaughter-Defoe, D. (2002). Historical and sociological influences on African American education. In J. Banks & C. A. Banks (Eds.), *Handbook of multicultural education* (2nd ed., pp. 340–62). San Francisco, CA: Jossey Bass.

Miller, E. T. (2010). An integration of the "if only" mentality: One teacher's deficit perspective put on trial. *Early Childhood Journal, 38*(4), 243–49.

Morrow, L., Tracy, D., Woo, D., & Pressley, M. (1999). Characteristics of exemplary first-grade literacy instruction. *The Reading Teacher, 52*, 462–76.

Murrell, P. C. Jr. (2001). *The community teacher: A new framework for effective urban teaching.* New York: Teachers College Press.

National Reading Panel. (2000). *Report of the National Reading Panel: Teaching children to read: An evidence-based assessment of the scientific research literature on reading and its implications for reading instruction.* Washington, DC: National Institute of Child Health and Human Development.

Noffke, S. E. (1999). What's a nice theory like yours doing in a practice like this? And other impertinent questions about practitioner research. *Change: Transformations in Education, 2*(1), 25–35.

Perry, T. (2003). Up from the parched earth: Toward a theory of African-American achievement. In T. Perry, C. Steele, & A. G. Hilliard III (Eds.), *Young, gifted and Black: Promoting high achievement among African-American students* (pp. 1–108). Boston, MA: Beacon.

Popkewitz, T. S. (2006). Hope of progress and fears of the dangerous: Research, cultural theses and planning different human kinds. In G. Ladson-Billings, & W. F. Tate (Eds.), *Education research in the public interest: Social justice, action, and policy* (pp. 119–41). New York: Teachers College Press.

Powell, R., & Rightmeyer, E. (2011). *Literacy for all students: An instructional framework for closing the gap.* New York: Routledge.

Pressley, M., Rankin, J., & Yokoi, L. (1996). A survey of instructional practices of primary teachers nominated as effective in promoting literacy. *Elementary School Journal, 96*(4), 363–84.

Pressley, M., Mohan, L., Fingeret, L., Reffit, K., & Raphael-Bogaret, L. (2007). Writing instruction in engaging and effective elementary settings. In S. Graham, C. A. MacArthur, & J. Fitzgerald (Eds.), *Best practices in writing instruction* (pp. 13–27). New York: Guildford Press.

Pressley, M., Wharton-McDonald, R., Allington, R., Block, C. C., Morrow, L., Tracey, D., . . . Woo, D. (2001). A study of effective first-grade literacy instruction. *Scientific Studies of Reading, 5*(1), 35–58.

Siddle-Walker, V. (2000). Valued segregated schools for African American children in the South, 1935–1969: A review of common themes and characteristics. *Review of Educational Research, 70*(3), 253–85.

Siddle-Walker, V. (2012, October). Original intent: Black educators in an elusive quest for justice. Presented at the AERA Annual Brown Lecture. Washington, DC.

Sleeter, C. E. (2008). Preparing white teachers for diverse students. In M. Cochran-Smith, S. Feiman-Nemser, J. D. McIntyre, & K. E. Demers (Eds.), *Handbook of research on teacher education: Enduring questions in changing contexts* (3rd ed., pp. 559–82). New York: Routledge.

Snow, C., Burns, S., & Griffin, P. (Eds.). (1998). *Preventing reading difficulties in young children*. Washington, DC: National Academy Press.

Tatum, A. (2012). *Literacy practices for African American male adolescents*. Report of the Jobs for the Future Project, Students at the center series. Retrieved from http://www. studentsatthecenter.org/.../literacy-practices-african-american-male.

Tatum, A. (n.d.). *Reauthorizing literacy practices for African American boys*. Coalition of schools educating boys of color blog. Retrieved from http://www.coseboc.org/news-article/alfred-tatum-literacy.

U.S. Department of Education. (2013). *No child left behind flexibility: Highly qualified teachers fact sheet*. Retrieved from http://www.2.ed.gov/nclb/methods/teachers/hqtflexibility. html.

U.S. Department of Education. (2014). *National Assessment of Educational Progress, 2013–2014 Reading assessment*. Washington, DC. Retrieved from http://nces.ed.gov.

Wharton-McDonald, R., Pressley, M., & Hampston, J. (1998). Literacy instruction in nine first-grade classrooms: Teacher characteristics and student achievement. *The Elementary School Journal, 99*, 101–28.

Woodson, C. (1933). *The miseducation of the negro*. Washington, DC: Associated Publishers.

Chapter Four

Harambee!

Successful, Culturally Centered Literacy Instruction for African American Readers through the Children Defense Fund's Freedom School Model

Marcia Watson

The 1964 Freedom Summer was haunted by racial turmoil and educational inequity. Jim Crow laws and Black Codes pervasively manipulated citizenry into two distinct categories: Whites and coloreds. Racial stratification in the 1960s limited all areas of public life, especially occupation and voting access. One area that remained overtly segregated and disenfranchised was education. Ten years after the *Brown v. Board of Education* decision, public schools in 1964 were equally, if not more, segregated than in years prior (Anderson, 1988; Bell, 2004; Span, 2009).

Frontrunners in social justice, such as Ella Baker, Charles Cobb, and Septima Clark, recognized that supplemental literacy education was necessary in Black communities. They, along with the Student Nonviolent Coordinating Committee (SNCC), provided summer and Saturday programs known as "Freedom Schools." The success of Freedom Schools in 1964 was attributed to critical literacy, democratic education, and Black (Negro) history.

Much like education in 1964, today's schools are almost equally segregated and inequitable. To address this systemic issue, Marian Wright Edelman regenerated the Freedom School program nationwide in 1991 to provide low-income students with supplementary education. Today, Freedom Schools advocate for the same educational opportunities as decades prior and are measurably successful for literacy attainment. It is important to further explore Freedom Schools, both as an organization and educational platform, to glean into various successful literacy approaches for students.

HISTORICAL FORMATIONS OF FREEDOM SCHOOLS

Education is the primary tool for social mobility (Freire, 2000). Yet, for African Americans during the Civil Rights era, equitable education was a lofty reverie (Anderson, 1988). The South operated as a microcosm of large-scale injustice. The widest disservice manifested in the limited educational opportunities for Blacks. After emancipation, education for Blacks required much more than reading, writing, and arithmetic (Anderson, 1988; Watson, 2014).

Effective education required knowledgeable navigation of social codes and constitutional laws. African Americans especially needed to become literate for political and voting rights. Yet, Mississippi schools failed to provide adequate equal access. In the 1960s, the Mississippi state government spent almost four times on White students as it did on Black students (Ransby, 2003). Access to schooling meant much more than simply being uneducated; in Mississippi, it meant being denied citizenship.

In 1964, Ella Baker, Charles Cobb, Bob Moses, Septima Clark, and other local advocates designed Freedom Schools, which were incepted to "train and educate people to be active agents in bringing about social change" (Hale, 2011, p. 330). Cobb and Baker, in particular, believed that Mississippi schools restricted and oppressed African American students. Mississippi's pervasive racial policies crippled the Black voice, which was desperately needed at voting polls to overturn ineffective legislature. Thus, because changes in macro policies seemed impossible, grassroots organizers sought ideological change through reformed schooling. The focus for the zealous organizers was critical literacy and citizenship skills.

Cobb, one of the frontrunners of the Civil Rights Movement, solicited the help from the SNCC and wrote a memo describing Mississippi schools as "impoverished" and "burdened" (Ransby, 2003, p. 329). Cobb further explicated that Mississippi schools possessed "a complete absence of academic freedom, and students [were] forced to live in an environment that [was] geared to squash intellectual curiosity and different thinking" (2003, p. 329).

Thus, Cobb, Baker, and SNCC formed Freedom Schools as "third space"—informal locale separate from formal school and home—to teach key skills needed for voting rights and full citizenship attainment. These informal learning spaces met in barbershops, basements of churches, front porches, and even in school buildings after hours (Sturkey, 2010). From their inception, Freedom Schools were designed to motivate students to have a political voice, venturing beyond what schools offered in tradition settings (Chilcoat & Ligon, 1998, 2001).

Freedom Schools taught literacy skills and other academic subjects. However, unlike traditional schools, filled with educational inequity, Freedom Schools aimed to equalize stratification and teach students the skills needed to navigate Mississippi's tumultuous political environment. The primary aim was helping students better navigate political barriers that impeded on Black social mobility (Ransby, 2003; Sturkey, 2010). This was no simple task.

To begin the movement, Baker, a frontrunner in Freedom Schools, sought suspended or at-risk students in the McComb, Mississippi, area. Baker taught "about the underlying economic structures of white supremacy" (Ransby, 2003, p. 299), and in turn, exposed students to supplemental Black history and education. Baker found this curricular approach to be especially advantageous for Black students.

The difference in Freedom School classrooms was witnessed through the implementation of nontraditional educational paradigms, not typically seen in schools. "Rigid hierarchy was abandoned, and the curriculum was designed to reflect the world and heritage of the schools' students. These were different kinds of classrooms that the Mississippi students had previously encountered" (Ransby, 2003, p. 326).

Although Freedom Schools provided overt literacy training to equip students on the constitutional test required by voting laws, Freedom Schools were made special by offering students spaces for critical inquiry (Ransby, 2003; Sturkey, 2010). In short, Freedom Schools went beyond the traditional paradigm. Within the Freedom School curriculum, critical thinking and self-knowledge were encouraged among students and teachers (Ransby, 2003). By the end of Freedom Summer in 1964, more than fifty Freedom Schools were established, impacting over 2,100 students and adults in Mississippi (Ransby, 2003; Sturkey, 2010; Watson, 2014).

INSIDE TWENTY-FIRST-CENTURY SCHOOLS

Sadly, many of the educational conditions during the 1964 Freedom Summer still resonate today. It is important to better understand the educational conditions of today's twenty-first-century schools. Briefly, this section will outline some of the educational inequalities that preoccupy students from learning. First, it is important to acknowledge that students currently learn in high-stakes testing environments (Darling-Hammond, 2010). High-stakes standardized assessments are often used for grade promotion, graduation, and formative testing. As a result, some educators fear that schools have become spaces for rote memorization and drills, not critical spaces of discovery and inquiry (Darling-Hammond, 2010; Watson, 2014).

States are now mandated, through No Child Left Behind (NCLB), Common Core State Standards (CCSS), and Race to the Top (RTTT) initiatives, to monitor student mastery in critical subjects like language arts and mathematics. For an incentive, schools and districts with high-performing scores often get supplemental bonuses or grants (Kim, Losen, & Hewitt, 2010;

Rodriguez, 2013). This intensifies the "high-stakes" environment even further.

Another key component of today's schools is student discipline. This is a widely researched topic in educational discourse. Unfortunately, African American male students, in particular, are three and sixteen times as likely to be suspended and/or expelled from schools than White males and females, respectively (Schott Foundation, 2012; U.S. Department of Education, 2014).

These are troubling statistics when considering that education is still supposedly the primary tool for social mobility. How can students learn if they are removed from school through suspension or expulsion? Not surprisingly, this critical area has been linked to the aforementioned high-stakes nature of today's schools. The overuse of school discipline is a common strategy to remove unwanted, or low performing, students out of classroom environments (Kim et al., 2010).

Yet, the disproportionate numbers of African American and Latino(a) students that are extracted from schools through unwarranted discipline policies lead to a much larger issue: race. Similar to 1964, race still overwhelmingly surrounds classroom pedagogy. Although the *Brown v. Board of Education* decision was supportive of classroom integration more than sixty years ago, schools are equally segregated today (Mickelson, 2001).

Subversive classroom policies, such as school tracking, zip code zoning, and unequal course offerings between schools positions the overarching educational system just as segregated. Within schools, Milner and Hoy (2003) found that classroom dissonance can be directly linked to teacher and student differences. Considering 82 percent of the current teaching force is White, African American and Latino(a) students often learn from teachers of different cultural backgrounds. Although race is in no way an indication of effective teaching, it is nevertheless important to acknowledge this dissonance in today's school.

CONTEMPORARY ANALYSIS OF TODAY'S FREEDOM SCHOOL PROGRAM

These descriptions are undoubtedly daunting. Educational conditions of today are surrounded by inequality, which stunts widespread social mobility. Yet, educational inequity has plagued the United States since its inception (Anderson, 1988; Span, 2009). It is no surprise that the necessity of Freedom School programs in 1964 is still witnessed today.

After the Civil Rights Movement of the 1960s, Freedom Schools were not as prevalent throughout the South. In 1991, Marian Wright Edelman resurfaced Freedom Schools for nationwide implementation (Smith, 2010). There are several commonalities between the original Freedom Schools and more contemporary models, such as culturally relevant textbooks, democratic education, informal learning, and critical literacy, yet twenty-first-century Freedom Schools are much more programmatic. Today's Freedom Schools are sponsored by the Children's Defense Fund (CDF) in Washington, DC, and are spread out nationwide. There are local "sites," which are housed in nearly every state. Today's Freedom School programs operate during the summer to help provide supplementary education to low-income students (Jackson, 2009a, 2009b; Watson, 2014).

THE IMPORTANCE OF NATIONAL TRAINING

Today's Freedom Schools hinge their educational notoriety on their rigorous training process. This training is infused in multiculturalism, research, liberation pedagogy, and African traditions. This training takes place in Clinton, Tennessee, every year on Alex Haley's farm. Haley, a prominent African American writer during the Civil Rights Movement, famously authored *The Autobiography of Malcolm X* and *Roots*. The location of this training embeds attendees in the rich heritage of the 1964 Freedom Summer.

What might seem menial is extremely important when considering Freedom Schools as not only an educational program, but also a social movement. In Tennessee, college students and adults spend time learning with former Civil Rights activists on ways to ignite student learning by tackling real-life issues. This is a community connection not commonly seen in traditional school settings.

After national training in Tennessee, Freedom School programs meet for six to eight weeks over the summer at various "sites" nationwide. Similar to the summer of 1964, Freedom Schools meet informally at local recreation facilities, churches, schools, and community centers in local neighborhoods. College students are typically the teachers, known as *servant leader interns*; meanwhile, local K–12 children are the students, known as *scholars*.

The term *servant leader intern* reinforces the principles of democratic and critical education, as suggested by Freire and Baker. These educational frameworks promote the importance of *all* citizens, not just those with dominant power, to help students reach educational success. The term *scholar* is used to culturally affirm students from low-income communities, where long-term educational attainment is often not a reality.

HARAMBEE! THE START OF THE FREEDOM SCHOOL DAY

The "Freedom School Day" is standardized nationwide. Scholars meet from 8:00 AM to 3:00 PM over the summer and start every morning with *Harambee*, which is a Kiswahili word that means "Let's pull together!" (Children's Defense Fund [CDF], 2005). According to CDF, Harambee reaffirms positivity within children and prepares their bodies and minds for the upcoming day of learning (CDF, 2011).

Harambee is a multi-stimulus pep rally that aims to positively venerate each child for thirty minutes. Harambee follows a schedule that includes community reading, cheers, moment of silence, and meditation. The first part of Harambee is "Read Aloud," which invites community members to read a short story to the students each day (Smith, 2010). The stories must be positive, edifying, and multicultural.

Following the story, students are allowed to "ask the guest reader questions about the book, personal academic experiences, or thematic issues that were relevant to the story. This allows scholars to engage with the Read Aloud guest, leveling and promoting equality among adults and students" (Watson, 2014, p. 180).

Next, students participate in singing a motivational song, then followed by "Cheers and Chants." This section is the most energetic portion of the morning, which encourages participants to incorporate rhythm, dance, song, positive affirmations, call and responses, and sequencing to provide scholars with a chance to release energy.

After "Cheers and Chants" is a portion called "Recognitions." This allows any scholar or intern to highlight something positive in someone else. Recognitions often spotlight positive student behavior, birthdays, or community accomplishments. The next and final stage is the "Moment of Silence," where scholars are encouraged to meditate quietly with a guided reflection conducted by an intern. This allows scholars to recenter their energy for the upcoming Freedom School Day.

INTEGRATED READING CURRICULUM

After Harambee, scholars spend the rest of their day completing the Integrated Reading Curriculum (IRC). This curriculum centers on the mantra: *I can make a difference in myself, family, community, nation, and world* (Smith, 2010). Aside from Harambee, the IRC is what makes Freedom Schools unique. IRC promotes multicultural readings that embrace all forms of diversity, including race, gender, sexuality, class, and ability. These are all used for greater social awareness and advocacy.

Scholars focus on the theme: *I can make a difference in myself, family, community, nation, and world* using critical literacy (Bethea, 2012). IRC books and resources encourage scholars to critically think about the world around them and ponder how they can become change agents within their local communities. For sake of reference, during the 2015 Freedom School summer, some of the sixty IRC books included: *Tomás and the Library Lady* (Mora, 1997), *Uncle Jed's Barbershop* (Mitchell, 1998), *Nasreen's Secret School: A True Story from Afghanistan* (Winter, 2009), *Copper Sun* (Draper, 2006), and *Families Are Different* (Pellegrini, 1991). Each of these books highlights diverse heroes, both past and present, who responded to community issues and fostered social change. In short, these books go beyond rote memorization and test preparation; rather, the IRC books provide students with contextual examples of *true* social mobility.

It is important to note that after IRC, scholars spend the afternoons in their communities invoking neighborhood change and positive social action. Past efforts have included: voter registration, anti-gun violence rallies, early childhood advocacy, and poverty awareness. Similar to the 1964 Freedom School Summer, whose mission was to prepare students for voting tests, today's Freedom Schools also prepare scholars for informed adult citizenry. Considering that most Freedom Schools service low-income African American and Latino(a) children, this is especially important with the lack of educational access in traditional schools.

THE NECESSITY OF CULTURAL RELEVANCE IN LEARNING

One of the most notable differences that Freedom Schools offer, both historically and contemporarily, is increased access to culturally relevant curriculum and critical literacy. Researchers often use these terms today; but even fifty years ago, the founders of Freedom Schools recognized the role *relevancy* plays in learning. A common connection among many U.S. schools is that critical education is not typically offered to students. Moreover, critical literacy, one that challenges the status quo and places students at the center of analysis and inquiry, is also often unavailable. In years past, critical education was overshadowed by unattainable social mobility; today, critical education is supplanted with testing.

Ladson-Billings (1994) and Gay (2000) advocate for culturally relevant teaching in light of today's subpar educational conditions. In the midst of standardized assessments, high-stakes testing, and streamlined curriculum standards, it is important to modify pedagogy to adapt to students. In literacy, this role is especially important (Gay, 2000; Ladson-Billings, 1994).

For students to be successful learners, the connection between textbooks, stories, and curricula must be multicultural, reflexive, and critical (Freire, 2000; Gay, 2000; Ladson-Billings, 1994; Nieto, 1992). By exposing students to critical information, students can make vital connections between education and social problems. In the most organic sense, education becomes a tool for critical inquiry and questioning. Through literacy, students must examine issues of equality—political, economic, racial, social, etc.—as they did in the 1964 Freedom School Summer (Hale, 2007, 2011; Kumaravadive-lu, 2012).

According to Gay (2000), culturally relevant teaching has six distinct characteristics: (a) validating, (b) comprehensive, (c) multidimensional, (d) empowering, (e) transformative, and (f) emancipatory. An examination of the historical significance of Freedom Schools explains how supplemental information, through cultural exploration, was imperative for student learning in 1964:

> Freedom School students studied African American history and literature, which were not part of the regular public school curriculum. . . . The Freedom School teachers taught and assigned authors who articulated what it meant to be African American in the United States. Culturally relevant sources assisted teachers in challenging notions of citizenship in a racialized society. (Hale, 2011, p. 332)

Teachers of the original Freedom Schools acknowledged that education played a direct role in citizenship (Hale, 2011; Ransby, 2003). Thus, lessons and discussions centered on equipping students to be more knowledgeable on these critical issues.

In short, Freedom Schools embraced culturally relevant teaching. Yet, culturally relevant teaching is also found in Freedom Schools today. In fact, the implementation of culturally relevant children's books for students is a visible distinction of the Freedom Schools program. Freedom School book selections culturally and racially reflect student demographics. This form of hegemonic resistance also fosters critical literacy in the classroom.

NATIONAL AND URBAN CITY DATA TRENDS

Longitudinal data on the impact of Freedom Schools are limited. Yet, secondary national and regional data documents Freedom School's impact as an organization today. The Children's Defense Fund's © national office found that Freedom Schools participation increased elementary student achievement (CDF, 2015). More specifically, students who participated in Freedom Schools for at least three years saw reading skills increased by 2.2 grade equivalents (CDF, 2015). Additionally, those students who only participated in the Freedom Schools program for two years saw a 1.4 grade equivalent increase.

Those who only participated for one year saw an increase of 0.2 grade equivalent (CDF, 2015). Regardless of tenure in the program, students saw measurable gains. These numbers are comparatively higher than other student counterpart groups, who only witnessed less than one grade equivalent each year (CDF, 2015).

On a regional level, data from Kansas City, Oakland, and Charlotte provide contextual data that illustrates the mezzo-level impact that Freedom Schools had on students. In Kansas City, a study was conducted comparing Freedom School students' grade-level increases. In comparison to students not attending, Freedom School students witnessed double grade-level gains over three years (CDF, 2015).

Similarly, in a Charlotte study, students' Basic Reading Inventory (BRI) was tested in a pre- and post-test format. This study assessed students at the beginning and end of the summer. This BRI assessment informally tracks reading inventory, reading ability, and comprehension (Taylor, Medina, & Lara-Cinisomo, 2010). Out of 132 students, 50.8 percent of students showed an improvement in reading, 38.6 percent maintained reading ability, and a small percentage—10.6 percent—showed a decline in reading after the Freedom School experience. This displays that 89.4 percent of students either maintained or improved in reading ability after six weeks (Taylor et al., 2010).

In addition to the aforementioned descriptive data, an Oakland study explored changes in student attitudes. The Freedom School students reported improvements in attitudes toward critical topics, such as African American culture, social skills, and student desires to participate in social action activities (Bethea, 2012). In light of standardized testing, which has purged nontestable subjects out of the curriculum, it is useful to note that Freedom Schools offer intellectual space to talk about civic, democratic, and introspective topics. Each of these attitudes, including knowledge of self, social skills, and social action, are necessary for critical education (Akbar, 1998; Freire, 2000; Woodson, 1977).

When considering that the majority of low-income students experience summer learning loss, programs such as Freedom Schools become increasingly important (Alexander, Entwisle, & Olson, 2007). The Freedom Schools program provides low-income students learning opportunities that extend beyond what traditional public schools offer during the school year (Kim & White, 2011).

Bridging the gap over the summer is critical for all learners, especially those students in low-income, urban, or rural environments. Overwhelmingly, opportunities are available for suburban or middle-class students because of social affluence and economic access (Lareau, 2011). This ignores traditionally underserved African American and Latino(a) student populations. Thus, Freedom Schools help to remove gaps in opportunity, which are traditionally unavailable to low-income students.

It is important to remember that effective summer programming is most beneficial when schooling involves more than rudimentary learning as found in traditional summer school. The aforementioned national and regional data from the CDF, Kansas City, Charlotte, and Oakland substantiate the positive impact of the Freedom Schools program on student readers, both cognitively and socially. This supportive data demonstrates the necessity to explore recommendations and implications for widespread implementation.

RECOMMENDATIONS

Today, schools must raise informed citizens. Racial turmoil that engulfed the Civil Rights Movement in the South is no longer in distant past. News reports in Charleston, Baltimore, Ferguson, and Oakland, for example, bring to remembrance the role education plays in reversing social conditions. Voting and literacy are unsympathetically important. Thus, similar to 1964, Freedom Schools—or "third spaces" for critical inquiry—are imperative.

Educators

In the elementary school setting, it is important to ensure classrooms are spaces of inquiry, discovery, and critical thinking. This is especially important for urban schools. Even when considering state curriculum standards mandated by local governments, lesson planning and teaching should rely on as much critical questioning as possible (Freire, 2000).

Instead of using the "banking" model, where teachers deposit information for students to regurgitate back on standardized assessments (Freire, 2000), it is important to venture into "non-testable" subjects and topics. Like Freedom Schools, explore topics like citizenship, race, gender, poverty, and equality. These are the transformative moments that are liberating and affirming for students.

Consistent throughout research are the stagnant, lifeless, and robotic practices found in today's schools—especially in urban settings (Chenoweth, 2007, 2009; Kozol, 2005). It is recommended that educators implement some of the strategies found in the Freedom Schools program, such as Harambee, civic engagement, or community read aloud, which allows students to center themselves within their own education.

Also related to the Freedom Schools model, it is important that coursework and classroom lessons have cultural relevance and share multicultural perspectives, especially ones that expound on the rich cultural diversity found in today's classrooms (Gay, 2000; Ighodaro & Wiggan, 2011; Ladson-Billings, 1994; Nieto, 1992). One of the most important aspects of critical theory is the elevation of students to a place of importance (Freire, 2000). Education, likewise, should build on the cultural competencies that students bring to classrooms every day.

Policymakers

It is important for district- and state-level policymakers to reform best practices in schools. This is accomplished through macro-level policy change. Policymakers should reform the curriculum to better reflect the growing, multicultural, multinational, and multilingual needs of today's students. Although teachers are encouraged to adapt culturally relevant pedagogical techniques, it is important for the overarching curricula to be adaptable and diverse.

FINAL THOUGHTS

Freedom Schools is not a prescribed solution to educational problems. Yet, the benefits of the program are noteworthy, and the supportive data confirms its usefulness for students. To ameliorate social problems, education must be critical and transformative. Additionally, it is important for educational policies to buttress critical thinking and inquiry versus irrelevant testing procedures.

The 1964 Freedom School movement provides an excellent example, both historically and contemporarily, of how free thinking and democratic education are important. As Freire (2000) suggests, this is how pedagogy becomes liberating for students. The significance of the 1964 Freedom Schools movement can be documented through the successful passing of the Voting Rights Act of 1965 and subsequent Civil Rights victories. Although Freedom Schools began more than fifty years ago in Mississippi, there are uncanny similarities in schools today. Students of the twenty-first century must also navigate governmental policies to gain increased social mobility. Whereas students in 1964 sought citizenship and equal voting rights, students today also seek equal opportunities in the midst of standardized testing and punitive discipline procedures. It is markedly important to consider the role of literacy in equalizing education attainment. Likewise, it is chiefly important to consider the role of education in equalizing social access.

REFERENCES

Akbar, N. (1998). *Know thy self.* Tallahassee, FL: Mind Productions and Associates.

Alexander, K. L., Entwisle, D. R., & Olson, L. S. (2007). Lasting consequences on the summer learning gap. *American Sociological Review, 72,* 167–80.

Anderson, J. (1988). *Education of blacks in the South, 1860–1935.* Chapel Hill, NC: University of North Carolina Press.

Bell, D. (2004). *Silent covenants:* Brown v. board of education *and the unfulfilled hopes for racial reform.* New York: Oxford.

Bethea, S. L. (2012). The impact of Oakland Freedom School's summer youth program on the psychological development of African American youth. *Journal of Black Psychology, 38*(4), 442–54. DOI: 10.1177/0095798411431982.

Chenoweth, K. (2007). *"It's being done": Academic success in unexpected schools.* Cambridge, MA: Harvard Education Press.

Chenoweth, K. (2009). *How it's being done: Urgent lessons from unexpected schools.* Cambridge, MA: Harvard Education Press.

Chilcoat, G. W., & Ligon, J. A. (1998). "We talk here. This is a school for talking." Participatory democracy from the classroom out into the community: How discussion was used in the Mississippi Freedom Schools. *Curriculum Inquiry, 28*(2), 165–93.

Chilcoat, G. W., & Ligon, J. A. (2001). Discussion as a means for normative change: Social studies lessons from the Mississippi Freedom Schools. *The Social Studies, 92*(5), 213–19.

Children's Defense Fund. (2005). *Children's Defense Fund Freedom Schools, Ella Baker Child Policy Training Institute Manual and Action Guide 2005.* Washington, DC: Children's Defense Fund.

Children's Defense Fund. (2011). *Children's Defense Fund Freedom Schools, Program Operating Principles 2011.* Washington, DC: Children's Defense Fund.

Children's Defense Fund. (2015). CDF Freedom Schools program: Program impact. Retrieved from http://www.childrensdefense.org/programs/freedomschools/.

Cobb, C. (2012). Freedom struggle and Freedom schools. *Monthly Review, 64*(3), 104–13.

Darling-Hammond, L. (2010). *The flat world and education: How America's commitment to equity will determine our futures.* New York: Teachers College Press.

Draper, S. (2006). *Copper sun.* New York: Antheneum Books for Young Readers.

Freire, P. (2000). *Pedagogy of the oppressed.* New York: Continuum International Publishing Group.

Gay, G. (2000). *Culturally responsive teaching: Theory, research and practice.* New York: Teachers College Press.

Hale, J. (2007). Early pedagogical influences on the Mississippi Freedom Schools: Myles Horton and critical education in the deep south. *American Educational History Journal, 34*(2), 315–29.

Hale, J. (2011). The student as a force for social change: The Mississippi Freedom Schools and student engagement. *The Journal of African American History, 96*(3), 325–47.

Ighodaro, E., & Wiggan, G. (2011). *Curriculum violence: America's new civil rights issue.* New York: Nova Science Publishers.

Jackson, T. O. (2009a). "Making the readings come to life": Notions of the language arts at Freedom Schools. *The New Educator, 5*(4), 311–28.

Jackson, T. O. (2009b). Towards collective work and responsibility: Sources of support within a Freedom School teacher community. *Teaching and Teaching Education, 25*(8), 1141–49.

Kim, C. Y., Losen, D. J., & Hewitt, D. T. (2010). *The school-to-prison pipeline.* New York: New York University Press.

Kim, J. S., & White, T.G. (2011). Solving the problem of summer reading loss. *Phi Delta Kappan, 92*(7), 64–67.

Kozol, J. (2005). *The shame of the nation: The restoration of apartheid schooling in America.* New York: Crown Publishing Group.

Kumaravadivelu, B. (2012). *Language teacher education for a global society: A modular model for knowing, analyzing, recognizing, doing, and seeing.* New York: Routledge Publishers.

Ladson-Billings, G. (1994). *The dreamkeepers: Successful teachers of African American children.* San Francisco, CA: Jossey-Bass.

Lareau, A. (2011). *Unequal childhoods: Class, race, and family life.* Berkeley, CA: University of California Press.

Mickelson, R. (2001). Subverting Swann: First and second generation segregation in the Charlotte-Mecklenburg Schools. *American Educational Research Journal, 38*, 215–52.

Milner, H. R., & Hoy, A. N. (2003). A case study of an African American teacher's self-efficacy, stereotype threat, and persistence. *Teaching and Teacher Education, 19*, 263–76.

Mitchell, M. K. (1998). *Uncle Jed's barbershop.* New York: Aladdin Paperbacks.

Mora, P. (1997). *Tomás and the library lady.* New York: Dragonfly Books.

Nieto, S. (1992). *Affirming diversity: The sociopolitical context of multicultural education.* White Plains, NY: Longman.

Pellegrini, N. (1991). *Families are different*. New York: Holiday House.

Ransby, B. (2003). *Ella Baker and the black freedom movement: A radical democratic vision*. Chapel Hill, NC: University of North Carolina Press.

Rodriguez, C. M. (2013). Saving the nation's expendable children: Amending state education laws to encourage keeping students in school. *Family Court Review, 51*(3), 469–84.

Schott Foundation. (2012). *The urgency of now: The Schott 50 state report on public education and black males (2012 Report)*. Cambridge, MA: The Schott Foundation for Public Education. Retrieved from http://www.schottfoundation.org/urgency-of-now.pdf.

Smith, K. (2010). Fostering regimes of truth: Understanding and reflecting on the Freedom School way. *Pedagogy, Culture and Society, 18*(2), 191–209.

Span, C. (2009). *From cotton field to schoolhouse: African American education in Mississippi 1862–1875*. Chapel Hill, NC: University of North Carolina Press.

Sturkey, W. (2010). I want to become a part of history: Freedom summer, freedom schools, and the freedom rides. *Journal of African American History, 95*(3), 348–68.

Taylor, D. B., Medina, A. L., Lara-Cinisomo, S., Children's Defense Fund (U.S.), Freedom School Partners (Charlotte, NC), & University of North Carolina at Charlotte. (2010). Freedom School Partners Children's Defense Fund Freedom Schools© Program Evaluation Report. Charlotte, NC: Center for Adolescent Literacies at UNC Charlotte.

U.S. Department of Education. (2014). Data snapshot: School discipline. Civil Rights Data Collection. Retrieved from http://www2.ed.gov/about/offices/list/ocr/docs/crdc-discipline-snapshot.pdf.

Watson, M. J. (2014). Freedom Schools: A transformative approach to learning. *Journal for Critical Education Policy Studies, 12*(1), 170–90.

Winter, J. (2009). *Nasreen's secret school: A true story from Afghanistan*. New York: Beach Lane Books.

Woodson, C. G. (1977). *The miseducation of the Negro*. New York: AMS Press.

Chapter Five

Beyond Basic Instruction

Effective Civic Literacy Instruction in Urban School Settings

Barbara Purdum-Cassidy and Karon LeCompte

According to Goldman (2012), "to be literate today means being able to use reading and writing to acquire knowledge, solve problems, and make decisions in academic, personal, and professional arenas" (p. 90). However, as a result of No Child Left Behind (NCLB) mandates, teachers have spent more time on skills focused reading instruction, less time on content area instruction, and have neglected the reading and writing of informational text (Duke, 2000; Duke & Block, 2012; Halvorsen et al., 2012; Jeong, Gaffney, & Choi, 2010).

Colleges of education are now faced with preparing pre-service teachers educated within the parameters of NCLB to teach both content and content literacy, when they have neither had those experiences nor much instruction on strategies for reading and writing informational text (Duke, 2014). Research on teachers' instructional practices reveals that teachers' practices are related to their beliefs or theories about learning and instruction (Graham & Harris, 2002).

When pre-service teachers enter teacher education programs, they have experienced a wide variety of pedagogical approaches. As a result, these approaches have shaped their skills and attitudes of reading and writing, as well as their beliefs about the nature of literacy, literacy development, and literacy instruction (Norman & Spencer, 2005).

This chapter describes a fieldwork experience designed to provide pre-service teachers with an opportunity to develop and implement civic literacy projects in their urban elementary school placements. First, the chapter will provide a short overview of civic literacy and a specific civic literacy project called Connecting Content. Next, we will provide the Connecting Content Framework that enabled urban elementary students to identify a community issue of interest, research the issue, write persuasive texts, and advocate for the issue.

The chapter will also share results from the study regarding two pre-service teachers' perceptions and enactment of the Connecting Content project within their placements in urban elementary school settings.

CIVIC LITERACY

The vision guiding the National Council of Teachers of English and International Reading Association's (1996) Standards for the English Language Arts states that "all students must have the opportunities and resources to develop the language skills they need to pursue life's goals and to participate fully as informed, productive members of society" (p. 3). As such, the integration of social studies and literacy can lead to powerful and effective instruction (Halvorsen et al., 2012). Although there are many ways to integrate social studies content and literacy, civic literacy lends itself well to integrating literacy processes for elementary learners.

According to Epstein (2010, 2014), civic literacy projects create a venue for content integration that builds students' civic knowledge and skills, addresses various state and national content and literacy standards, and improves schools and communities. The school-based practice of civic literacy can be broadly defined as a "student-centered, project-based approach to civics education that allows students to select a social problem, explore the problem to reveal its complexity, and to take action by publicly addressing the problem, seeking to ameliorate it" (Epstein, 2014, p. 3).

Research has outlined the positive impact of project-based approaches on students' achievement and attitudes (Hertzog, 2007; Kaldi, Filippatou, & Govaris, 2011), motivation and engagement (Hernandez-Ramos & De La Paz, 2009), and content literacy (Halvorsen et al., 2012). In addition, Lattimer and Riordan (2011) purported that thoughtfully designed project-based units of study are more effective than traditional instruction for teaching concept mastery in core academic disciplines, improving students' twenty-first-century literacy skills, and increasing student performance on standardized tests (Geier et al., 2008; Strobel & Van Barneveld, 2008; Walker & Leary, 2008).

CONNECTING CONTENT PROJECT

As content faculty who provide support for elementary Professional Development Schools (PDS), the authors of this chapter collaborated with four elementary PDS to design and implement the Connecting Content project.

The project took place in an initial teaching certification program at a university in central Texas. The pre-service teachers were assigned to an elementary professional development school for a junior-level literacy practicum course during either the fall or spring semester. Pre-service teachers planned and taught a one-hour literacy lesson four days each week for thirteen weeks to a small group of kindergarten through fourth-grade students.

The Connecting Content project required pre-service teacher candidates to develop and implement a minimum of ten lessons integrating language arts and social studies instruction within their urban elementary PDS placements. The candidates received both content and pedagogical instruction through coursework to support the development of the lesson plans and teaching related to civic literacy projects.

The Connecting Content lessons focused on identifying community issues, researching and interviewing peoples' opinions on the issues, writing persuasive texts to various audiences, and finally creating projects that advocated support for attention to the issues. The lesson plans executed by the pre-service teachers fit the scope and sequence for the school districts and were aligned to the state English language arts and social studies standards for each grade level.

CONNECTING CONTENT FRAMEWORK

Step 1: Identifying a Community Issue

In this step, pre-service teachers engaged students in identifying problems in their community, state, or world and then led them in selecting one to focus on for the project. Topics selected by the elementary students included issues in public safety and school (crime prevention, safe driving, and bullying), health (smoking, lack of exercise and recess), community (homelessness, veterans, and animal rights), and the environment (littering, recycling, and global warming).

The pre-service teachers used different approaches to engage their students in problem identification. For example, Mandy (pseudonym) wanted her students to pick a topic they were "passionate about in order to raise awareness about the issue and to come up with reasons that they should advocate for it." Thus, Mandy designed her issues lesson to engage students in an examination of the local newspaper, cutting out topics or issues that were of interest to them. Students then engaged in a discussion of the selected issues and debated which topic would be "the most interesting to research."

Near the end of this lesson, Mandy's students selected the topic of poverty. At that point, Mandy suggested that the students "narrow their research focus" and select one idea within the topic of poverty to study. As a result, the third-grade students decided to focus their project on the impact of poverty on children.

As part of a larger unit of study on veterans, Jennifer's (pseudonym) fifth-grade students were engaged in a literature circle of Richard Peck's (2008) *On the Wings of Heroes*. The entire fifth grade was writing a play focused on the elements they read in the book and a local World War II hero, Doris Miller.

For her issues lesson, Jennifer led a discussion on the issues faced by the survivors of World War II as they returned home. During this discussion the students became interested in how various Texas communities had honored their decorated U.S. war heroes from WWII, particularly those who had survived the attack at Pearl Harbor.

During this step the pre-service teachers learned the importance of student voice in the selection of topics though democratic processes and deliberation. In her reflection Mandy stated, "After today I am so excited to get to work on this project. My English Language Learners (ELLs) got so into deciding what issue they wanted to study. It was awesome to see my third-grade students get so passionate about community issues."

Jennifer recognized the importance of helping students make meaningful connections to the curriculum. She said the following, "This lesson was a success. We discussed what an issue was, what issues affect veterans, and the impact of veterans issues on our community and nation. My students were much more interested in the topic of veterans issues that I thought they would be."

Step 2: Research

In the second step, pre-service teachers designed research lessons to build conceptual understanding and awareness regarding their selected issue and to propose what could be changed (Epstein, 2014). To teach the lessons, pre-service teachers were required to integrate both print and visual texts within their lessons and engage students in collecting community-specific information through interviews of community members or by collecting and analyzing surveys about the issue. Pre-service teachers and students worked together to examine texts and think critically about the multiple perspectives they encountered regarding their selected issues.

To teach about the impact of poverty on children, Mandy engaged students in photo and video analysis, asking students to describe poverty based on what they saw in the picture or learned from the video. Students also examined statistical information on local poverty levels and read print and online articles about the impact of poverty on children. Mandy's students then developed a survey and interviewed classmates about their view of the impact of poverty on children.

After viewing video clips of the attack on Pearl Harbor and conducting a search of Texas Pearl Harbor veterans, Jennifer's fifth-grade students learned of another local hero, Vic Lively, who was alive and living in the local area. Students located and read articles about his service both during and after the bombing at Pearl Harbor, comparing and contrasting his military record with that of Doris Miller.

During this step, Mandy and Jennifer recognized the challenges associated with students' reading and vocabulary levels and the texts they were encountering. Both pre-service teachers noted that some texts they chose to use during the project were above those of the English-language learners in their groups, which required them to "scaffold" them appropriately for their students. To interact with texts that were above their reading levels, Mandy and Jennifer used read-alouds. To support concept and vocabulary development, the pre-service teachers chose to incorporate research mini-lessons on identifying important points, summarizing, and expanding their notes into sentences (Hoyt & Boswell, 2012).

Mandy combined interactive read-alouds with vocabulary activities to support her third-grade students' concept development during their "poverty" project. Mandy realized quickly that she needed to provide differentiated support for her students. To assist students who struggled to identify important information they heard in text, Mandy shortened the length of the passages read to students so that they "would not be overwhelmed by all the information." To scaffold students who experienced difficulty in distinguishing the most important information in a text, Mandy conferred individually with them, asking open-ended questions to help students determine "Which information is most important in helping us understand poverty?" or "What information would help us get our point across?"

To support students' vocabulary development during her "veterans" project, Jennifer first taught students how she identifies key words from a passage through think-alouds and how those words could be used to summarize what she had read. During remaining research lessons, Jennifer's students used the key word strategy during independent reading time and then shared their key words in order to determine what words needed to go onto their group word wall (Hoyt & Boswell, 2012).

Jennifer shared her insights about the benefits of teaching key words and word walls with her learners: "Teaching students to identify key words, then listing them on word walls helped my students remember important vocabulary. It was amazing to hear them recall all the information an entire week after reading it."

Step 3: Taking Informed Action

During this step, pre-service teachers required students to use their "pens as agents" (Robinson, 1998, p. 23) to determine relevant audiences for their issue and develop evidence-based arguments that encouraged their target audiences to adopt a particular view and act in a particular way (Epstein, 2014). To determine relevant audiences, pre-service teachers led discussions on how citizens take action to address civic problems and how to identify individuals in authority that have the ability to correct the problems that students had identified during their research. To support students as they wrote evidence-based arguments, pre-service teachers used a writing work-shop approach and mentor texts as students crafted a wide variety of persuasive texts.

To increase awareness on the impact of poverty, Mandy's students identified their peers as their "target audience." To do this, students wrote a variety of persuasive texts, including morning announcements, posters for the hallways, and a letter to the principal, advocating for a food and toy drive. After a meeting with the building principal to further advocate for the food and toy drive, the students received permission to "go public" with their project.

While comparing and contrasting the war records of Doris Miller and Vic Lively, Jennifer's fifth-grade students discovered that there was no memorial in Vic's Lively's honor in his hometown of Palestine, Texas. While searching the City of Palestine's website, students discovered that the city had a Historical Landmark City Council Board. The students chose a member of that board to write to, asking the board to consider erecting a memorial in honor of Lively's service during World War II.

As Jennifer's students drafted their letters they began discussing their "vision" for the memorial, advocating that their "argument would be stronger" if they created models of the memorial and took pictures of the models to send with the letters they wrote. Jennifer reflected on how students benefited from the creation of the models saying, "They wanted to show their models to EVERYONE that passed by. They were intrinsically motivated to create these models and they began sincerely caring about getting a memorial made in Vic Lively's honor. They thrived in creating these projects."

Step 4: Going Public

In the last step of the project, students shared their advocacy projects with others and reflected on the effectiveness of their actions (Epstein, 2014). As a result, both pre-service teachers and their students recognized the power of their civic actions.

After receiving permission to host a food and toy drive at their school, Mandy's students created posters and morning announcements to raise awareness about the drive. They also organized all aspects of the drive including contacting the local agency to arrange delivery of the donated food and toys.

Mandy reflected on the impact of the food and toy drive on her students. "I am very proud of my students for the advocacy project they created. Not only did they create posters and announcements to raise awareness about poverty and our food and toy drive, they also became concerned about the needs and feelings of others. We were able to donate the food and toys were collected to a local charity organization. They were so proud!"

After the fifth-grade students sent persuasive letters to the Palestine Historical Landmark City Council Board asking the board to consider erecting a memorial in Vic Lively's honor, the students received an e-mail from the board letting them know that the board was currently considering their proposal. Reflecting, Jennifer's students said, "We wrote letters and took action. We have learned that we can make a difference!"

FINAL THOUGHTS

Teaching and learning citizenship must be a critical conversation in education, one that involves critical thinking, the development of literacy skills, and active learning opportunities. Civic literacy projects advance notions of social justice by allowing students to tackle difficult subjects and transcend contexts to better understand the perspectives of others. This chapter illustrated how pre-service teachers and their students learned that meaningful curriculum, purposeful inquiry, and informed action are key elements in developing engaged citizens.

The Connecting Content project provided avenues in which students learned to read and write toward specific genres effectively through planning and implementing real-world civic literacy projects. The authors realized that at times, pre-service teachers struggled with curriculum and the call to develop lesson plans based on topics chosen by students and not available in a commercialized format. As a result, additional support was needed to assist pre-service teachers in locating appropriate resources and applying disciplinary tools and concepts.

In addition, pre-service teachers learned to teach literacy and social studies in motivating ways that promoted civic ideals and practices, whereas elementary students learned to advocate for a cause through civic action. Students felt empowered by the ability to have their voices heard, learned important research skills, proposed solutions to their community issue, and took action. How much students progressed in moving toward a justice-oriented citizen is yet to be determined.

Nonetheless, pre-service teachers engaged in planning, developing, and teaching the kinds of civic-based integrated instructional units that illuminate critical intersections in their own development as teachers who are committed to promoting grassroots community improvement. In essence, through their Connecting Content projects students came one step closer to becoming the kind of action-oriented, informed citizen that we want in our twenty-first-century communities.

At the heart of social justice lies both the belief in the equal worth of every person as well as the readiness to act from a place of both morality and care in supporting that belief. As Wade (2001) states, "in a socially just society, every person is treated according to their need toward the goal of growing into contributing members of society" (p. 25).

REFERENCES

Duke, N. K. (2000). 3.6 minutes per day: The scarcity of informational texts in first grade. *Reading Research Quarterly, 35*, 202–24.

Duke, N. K. (2014). *Inside information: Developing powerful readers and writers of informational text through project-based instruction.* New York: Scholastic.

Duke, N. K., & Block, M. K. (2012). Improving reading in the primary grades. *Future of Children, 2*(2), 55–72.

Epstein, S. E. (2010). Activists and writers: Student expression in a social action literacy project. *Language Arts, 87*(5), 363–72.

Epstein, S. E. (2014). *Teaching civic literacy projects: Student engagement with social problems.* New York: Teachers College Press.

Geier, R., Blumenfeld, P. C., Marx, R. W., Krajcik, J. S., Fishman, B., Soloway, F., & Clay Chambers, J. (2008). Standardized test outcomes for students engaged in inquiry-based science curricula in the context of urban reform. *Journal of Research in Science Teaching, 45*, 922–39.

Goldman, S. R. (2012). Adolescent literacy. *Future of Children, 2*(2), 89–117.

Graham, S., & Harris, K. R. (2002). Primary grade teachers' theoretical orientations concerning writing instruction: Construct validation and a nationwide survey. *Contemporary Educational Psychology, 27*, 147–66.

Halvorsen, A.-L., Duke, N. K., Bruger, K. A., Block, M. K., Strachan, S. L., Berka, M. B., & Brown, J. M. (2012). Narrowing the achievement gap in second-grade social studies and content area literacy: The promise of a project-based approach. *Theory and Research in Social Education, 40*, 198–229.

Hernandez-Ramos, P., & De La Paz, S. (2009). Learning history in middle school by designing multimedia in a project-based learning experience. *Journal of Research on Technology in Education, 42*(2), 151–73.

Hertzog, N. B. (2007). Transporting pedagogy: Implementing the project approach in two first-grade classrooms. *Journal of Academic Achievement, 18*, 530–64.

Hoyt, L., & Boswell, K. (2012). *Crafting nonfiction: Lessons on writing process, traits, and craft.* Portsmouth, NH: Heinemann.

Jeong, J. S., Gaffney, J. S., & Choi, J. O. (2010). Availability and use of informational text in second, third, and fourth grades. *Research in the Teaching of English, 44*, 435–56.

Kaldi, S., Filippatou, D., & Govaris, C. (2011). Project-based learning in primary schools: Effects on pupil's learning and attitudes. *Education 3–13: International Journal of Primary, Elementary and Early Years Education, 39*(1), 35–47.

Lattimer, H., & Riordan, R. (2011). Project-based learning engages students in meaningful work. *Middle School Journal, 43*(2), 18–23. http://dx.doi.org/129.62.21.173.

National Council of Teachers of English and International Reading Association. (1996). *Standards for the English language arts*. Retrieved from http://www.ncte.org/standards/ncte-ira.

Norman, K. A., & Spencer, B. H. (2005). Our lives as writers: Examining preservice teachers' experiences and beliefs about the nature of writing and writing instruction. *Teacher Education Quarterly, 32*(1), 25–39.

Peck, R. (2008) *On the wings of heroes*. New York: Penguin Group.

Robinson, J. (1998). Literacy and lived lives: Reflections on the responsibilities of teachers. In C. Fleisher & D. Schaafsma (Eds.), *Literacy and democracy: Teacher research and composition studies in pursuit of habitable spaces* (pp. 1–27). Urbana, IL: National Council of Teachers of English.

Strobel, J., & Van Barneveld, A. (2008). When is PBL more effective? A meta-synthesis of meta-analyses comparing PBL to conventional classrooms. *Interdisciplinary Journal of Problem-based Learning, 3*(1), 44–58.

Wade, R. (2001). Social action in the social studies: From the ideal to the real. *Theory into Practice, 40*(1), 23–28.

Walker, A., & Leary, H. (2008). A problem based learning meta analysis: Differences across problem types, implementation types, disciplines, and assessment levels. *Interdisciplinary Journal of Problem-based Learning, 3*(1), 12–43.

Chapter Six

Affirming the Identities of English Learners through Purposeful, Project-Based Literacy Instruction

Catherine Reischl and Debi Khasnabis

Standards for academic literacy are becoming increasingly demanding. The challenges are especially great for young people in the United States who are new to the English language. The Common Core State Standards (CCSS) place increasing language and disciplinary demands on all learners, and everyday life requires that both children and adults listen, speak, read, write, and represent our ideas in new and persistently changing sets of modalities across multiple contexts.

Early adolescent English learners (ELs) are faced with the dual task of developing both social and academic language and literacy in English and the need to draw on all of their social, linguistic, and cultural resources to do so. Given these challenges, how do teachers create high-quality literacy instruction for upper elementary aged ELs? What bodies of research can support us in conceptualizing this work? What constitutes equitable, imaginative, and effective pedagogical approaches to literacy instruction—and especially the teaching of writing in multimodal contexts—for these learners?

This chapter offers a set of research-based principles for effective pedagogical practices in the teaching of literacy to early adolescent ELs. These principles draw on current research in the areas of culturally responsive pedagogies, project-based writing instruction, the teaching of writing, and multimodal literacies for ELs. The chapter illustrates these principles in action through a detailed narrative example of a culturally responsive, project-based (CRPB) unit of instruction in a summer ESL program for low-income, fifth- to eighth-grade ELs.

In this unit of study, titled "Making a Living—Making a Life," ELs built relationships with local immigrant business owners, used a range of multi-modal tools to document what they were learning about the businesses and their owners' histories, used graphics programs to create brochures for the businesses to use on site, and began to ponder and represent their own possible future trajectories using graphics and written language. The description of this CRPB unit offers a context for discussion of possible applications of these pedagogies across teaching settings for a range of students.

To contextualize this discussion, consider the following vignette that describes the experiences of a group of ELs in the Making a Living—Making a Life unit.

A group of six ELs, a university teaching intern, and their teacher visit Golam Market, a grocery store just six blocks from their school. The store specializes in foods from Bangladesh, Pakistan, and Middle Eastern countries and is owned by the Khans, who are Bangladeshi immigrants and the family of two students.

The Khans lead the students throughout the aisles and stop in front of counters stocked with hummus and curries. They tell stories of family members sharing responsibilities for preparing foods, ordering products from around the world, ensuring that Halal meat preparation routines are followed, and serving local customers. They describe the process of learning how to run a business in a new country and about Mr. Khan's fifteen years of work at a local grocery store in the United States where he worked his way up to a manager position and eventually was able to start his own business.

Students video record these conversations and revisit these videos when they returned to the classroom to check their comprehension and generate questions for further information gathering. Often, their conversations about the Khans' experiences included reference to their own lives—points of connection or difference regarding their own families' own experiences with immigration, work, and family life.

Over time, they build relationships with the Khans—and with each other—and knowledge about this community business and the people who are so invested in making it work. They return several times to the store during their three-week summer school program, checking with the owners about the content of a promotional brochure they are creating for the owner (see figure 6.1) and editing their graphics and text in response to the owners' preferences.

The students' Golam Market trifold brochure displays vivid multigenre text and graphics including biographical information about the owners, practical information about the products and store hours, and carefully chosen persuasive graphics and text designed to promote the business as a setting where customers could find the tastes of their countries of origin.

The Khan family attends the final family evening celebration and graciously accepts a framed certificate thanking them for their participation in the program. They linger at the event, chatting with students, their families, teachers, and administrators and express their gratitude and interest in continuing to support any future school efforts. Students have tapped this family's funds of

Figure 6.1.

knowledge; this family has served as resource as ELs develop their identities as learners within a particular community context.

The vignette represents one set of experiences that took place in the summer ESL academy (SESLA). The reader is invited to hold these images in mind while reading the following discussion of the theoretical underpinnings of this CRPB approach to the teaching of literacy to EL.

PRINCIPLES OF PRACTICE

Research on the teaching of literacy to early adolescent ELs is limited and often driven by national educational policies and ideologies (Bunch, Kibler, & Pimentel, 2012; Enright & Gilliland, 2011; Harklau, 2011). Prior scholarship has tended to focus on skills and rules, rather than language use within meaningful contexts that require "deep engagement and interaction around disciplinary practices called for at the heart of the new [Common Core State] standards" (Bunch, 2013, p. 301).

The CRPB approach is situated within a theory of language development that frames literacy as socially constructed and situated in social contexts (Gee, 1992; Vygotsky, 1934/1962). CRPB units are designed in a project-based format, which is a pedagogical approach in which students have been shown to develop knowledge, skills, and improved attitudes about learning (Filippatou & Kaldi, 2010; Halverson et al., 2012; Hernandez-Ramos & De La Paz, 2009). Four key research-based principles frame the structure, content, and teaching of these "culturally responsive project-based" units. The following section describes each of these principles.

Principle 1: Draw on Community Resources

CRPB units are deliberately designed to draw on the social, linguistic, cultural, and content resources of students, their families, and their communities. To construct social contexts that make it possible for *all* students to fully participate in learning, teachers must learn to "recognize and learn the community-based knowledge held by socially, culturally and linguistically marginalized children before curriculum can be developed that is culturally relevant for such children" (Purcell-Gates, 2013, p. 69).

Such a stance requires that teachers act as ethnographers and learn to perceive the aspirational, navigational, social, linguistic, familial, and resistant capital that families possess (Yosso, 2005) and draw on these resources as part of the curriculum. In CRPB units, this principle is enacted through design of curriculum content, home visits, participation in community events, involvement with family and community members in school events, and design of family-centered "homework" that links the curriculum with family knowledge bases. Thus, these structures and activities must be integral to the planning of the curriculum.

Principle 2: Integrate Multigenre Texts and Purposeful Writing

CRPB units are multigenre and include a range of forms of narrative and informational reading and writing. Students write purposefully for highly defined, actual readers. Recent research shows that the use of real-world texts that are used for real-world purposes results in students' higher literacy learning, as compared to the use of traditional reading and writing school-based tasks where the teacher is the primary audience (Purcell-Gates, Duke, & Martineau, 2007).

ELs, who typically have age-appropriate oral proficiency in their home languages and some native language literacy skills as well, benefit from writing about meaningful ideas and information that require them to draw on their existing knowledge. Through such activity, ELs can be guided to learn linguistic and rhetorical patterns found in a range of narrative and informational genres (Bunch et al., 2012, Schleppegrell, 2004).

CRPB instruction focuses on project-based writing that integrates reading and writing with purpose (Duke, Caughlan, Juzwik, & Martin, 2012; Duke, 2014) to create instruction that offers students experience writing "real" genres such as handbooks, brochures, or memoirs for real audiences, such as visitors to a nature center, customers at a store, or younger peers. Engaging in such tasks "creates real opportunities to communicate rather than mechanical exercises for text production" (Bunch et al., 2012, p. 6).

Although notions of "authenticity" vary in the research literature (Dworin, 2011), CRPB units emphasize creating multigenre pieces, often based on mentor texts from daily life, that serve to communicate meaning with people who the writers will actually encounter.

Principle 3: Create Opportunities for Rigorous and Meaningful Academic Learning

CRPB units offer ambitious exploration of academic language and content and create opportunities for meaningful interactions between ELs, peers, and adults around this content. Academic language and content instruction, based on key standards such as the Wisconsin, Delaware, and Arkansas (WIDA) standards for English Language Learners (2012) and CCSS, must support students to develop the skills to fully participate in both social and academic life, using all of their language resources. Language used in school settings to engage in academic content is distinct from the language of home or other social settings for children (Filmore & Snow, 2000; Schleppegrell, 2004).

Specific oral and written discourse practices—the decontextualized language used in school—presents extra challenges for ELs. ELs benefit from explicit teaching of academic discourse and literacy practices and opportunities to engage in multiple forms of interaction with peers and adults to grow in their academic language and content knowledge (Bunch, 2006).

Principle 4: Engage Students in Multimodal Literacies

CRPB units incorporate multimodal literacies, using a broad range of media, technology, symbol systems and integrating reading, writing, listening, speaking, viewing, and representing. ELs' lives are varied and rich—like all learners. Learning to use video, graphics, and other forms of text and technology allows ELs to extend their written communication and more fully represent their ideas. By using technologies as "composing spaces" that integrate multimodal literacies (Vasudevan, 2010, p. 47), teachers offer students opportunities for imaginative expressions of learning and affirm the lived, in- and out-of-school experiences of our students.

In a review of ten years of research specifically addressing possibilities and challenges of multimodal literacy practices in learning and teaching English to adolescent ELs, Yi (2014) notes a variety of possible affordances of multimodal literacy practices, including the development of multimodal communicative competence; exploration and expression of identities; improvement of academic learning; development of critical literacy and perspectives; and connection of in- and out-of-school knowledge and experiences.

In CRPB units, ELs benefit from opportunities to use both visual and written materials in both concrete and digital forms to link their ideas with others and design and redesign a range of texts to communicate meaning (Bomer, Patterson Zoch, David, & Ok, 2010).

MAKING A LIVING—MAKING A LIFE: A CRPB UNIT

The application of these principles to practice can be illustrated through the Making a Living—Making a Life unit that was designed and taught in the summer of 2014 in a three-week SESLA. SESLA is a Title III funded program that is part of a partnership between the University of Michigan School of Education (SOE) and the Ann Arbor Public Schools (AAPS). SESLA is taught by a collaborative group of educators: six ESL teachers, six ESL interns, and the two coauthors, who are university-based ESL teacher educators.

Throughout this joint work, interns from the SOE learned to apply their ESL teaching skills, while also building fourth- to eighth-grade students' language and academic skills who attended AAPS schools. This chapter focuses on the teaching and learning of fifth- to eighth-grade students in this program, the majority of whom were Spanish-fluent Hispanic/Latino students. Other predominant language groups represented included children who spoke Arabic, Vietnamese, Chinese, Bengali, and Hindi. Students' families had recent histories of immigration and refugee experiences, and 80 percent or more qualified for free or reduced lunch.

The seeds of this unit were planted when school district and university collaborators began looking for a way to draw on the community-based knowledge among immigrant business owners in a commercial area within walking distance from the school. This strip mall, where teachers, neighbors, and drivers passing by stopped for a quick lunch, haircut, or to pick up groceries, was well known by many in the area. The small business owners served as important assets to the community by providing services, meeting places, and regular contact for families and other community members.

Through one-to-one conversations between the educators and the business owners, the educators explained the purpose of the unit and, although many were initially puzzled about how such an activity could serve a school, nine business owners agreed to work with the students. These included owners of two beauty salons, three grocery stores (Arabic, Mexican, and Bangladeshi), a pizza store, a taquería, an Indian restaurant, and a resale automotive business. Each grade-level class worked with a set of these stores and students chose to work in a small group with one business.

Students walked to the businesses and talked with the owners about their personal histories and about details of their work lives, including the products and services offered, clientele, logistical issues, and challenges that owners had experienced in their work. These conversations often took place in several languages, with students, business owners, teachers, and interns drawing on all of their language resources to understand each other. Students used video, still photos, and written notes to document their learning and frame their own developing aspirations in multimodal forms.

When they returned to school, through mini-lessons and modeling, they were guided to revisit these resources multiple times to glean content and the language that accompanied it. In addition, students worked on questioning skills and interviewed a range of adults who visited the school, both immigrants and others, who were pursuing a variety of other careers.

As a culminating project, students created multigenre promotional brochures for the businesses, highlighting the narratives of the owners, business services, and information about products. The brochures were given to the storeowners as marketing materials that they could share with the public and were highlighted in an evening where families, students, educators, and the business owners gathered to display their products and the brochures, eat, and celebrate together.

As they engaged in this CRPB unit, students learned not only about the lives of the business owners and their businesses, but also reflected on their own lives and how they might make steps toward their own goals. Students read biographical texts to learn about varied life paths and participated in a field trip to the local university to learn about pursuing a career through university study. They also created visual displays that mapped their ambitions for their futures onto a timeline. Throughout the three weeks, students, educators, and community members were fully engaged in examining the ways that people make their livings and construct their lives.

APPLYING THE PRINCIPLES

The four guiding principles for CRPB units of instruction were exemplified in the design and instruction of this unit. The following section takes a second more focused look at Making a Living—Making a Life to emphasize the ways that the unit illustrates the principles.

Principle 1: Drawing on Community-Based Resources

From its inception, Making a Living—Making a Life was situated within the students' communities. The unit designers' (teachers, interns, and university faculty) imaginations were sparked by the knowledge that some Scarlett students' families owned local businesses. This recognition led the planning team to wonder what knowledge bases these families possessed as they had made their livings and their lives in the United States. In addition, the planning team immediately saw the potential for the students to be excited to learn about the businesses that they frequented within their own community.

For example, students were impacted by their interactions with the owner of Tmaz Taquería, a diner that was highly frequented by community members, especially by Mexican families. When students walked down for a visit to Tmaz, they enthusiastically talked about what they liked to order with their families and relished the opportunity to share their favorite dishes with other students. They excitedly sampled foods that they were offered. Learning about the restaurant's owner, Cesar, was meaningful to the students because many already knew him as a fixture in the community. However, they did not know his personal or professional life stories.

When Cesar explained the origins of the restaurant's name, that it was named in honor of his hometown in Mexico, this struck a chord with many students whose families empathized with Cesar's feelings of homesickness. Cesar shared a range of knowledge with the students: historical knowledge of his hometown, Aztec cultural knowledge that influenced the design of the restaurant's logo, economic knowledge that contributed to the restaurant's business plan, and social knowledge of his clientele and their food preferences.

As they listened to Cesar, students video recorded and took notes on their interactions and then revisited these materials and discussed key points with each other back at school. As they built a relationship with Cesar, students made connections with their own developing identities and those of their families.

Principle 2: Integration of Multigenre Texts and Purposeful Writing

During the Making a Living—Making a Life unit, students' final project was to create a multigenre brochure that the storeowners could ultimately use as marketing materials. Although in-school writing genres are often taught as explicit categories of text, in real-world settings, writers rarely engage in genre writing in isolated, discrete ways.

For example, newspaper articles often use persuasive and informative genres simultaneously. Online blogs often include cross-cutting genres of narrative and informational writing. Even online recipes sometimes include narrative stories of the origin of a particular dish before providing a step-by-step procedural recipe. Throughout the unit, teachers and interns taught mini-lessons, using multigenre mentor texts—real brochures, drawn from multiple businesses in the area—and highlighted key features of these texts that students could emulate in their own writing.

The students created authentic texts that cut across multiple genres. In their brochures, they wrote biographical narratives to tell the stories of the storeowners' lives. They wrote informational text to inform customers about the products and services offered, as well as logistical information about the store's hours and location. They also wrote persuasively to convince customers to take advantage of all that these businesses had to offer. They wrote with their audience—potential customers including their own families—in mind, drawing on mentor texts as models, and using graphics, photos, and other visual elements to complete their message.

At the final culminating celebration event, each storeowner was publicly thanked on stage with a certificate presented by a student and then given a set of the brochures for use in their stores. Over subsequent months, when children visited the stores for a taco or a haircut with their families, they saw their brochures on display and customers picking up a copy as they waited at the cash register.

Principle 3: Creating Opportunities for Rigorous and Meaningful Academic Learning

The educators that work together in SESLA bring a wide range of skills to the table. For example, experienced mentor teachers tend to bring knowledge about the school settings, awareness of sociocultural assets of the community, and pedagogical knowledge to the table. Interns are particularly adept at drafting unit plans, because of recent coursework they have completed in their teacher education programs. Thus, interns take the lead in drafting plans that anchor the units in teaching and learning standards and that seek to align goals, assessments, and instructional activities.

Planners draw on both the WIDA performance standards (2012) and the CCSS. WIDA provides a structure for teachers to plan unit activity for ELs at each of the six stages of language development, and a primary tool for ensuring that CRPB units are academically robust is the CCSS.

For example, core standards that were used to anchor instruction in the Making a Living—Making a Life unit can be seen in table 6.1. The foci of the unit span across the literacy standards, ensuring that students have opportunities to develop writing, reading, speaking, listening, and language goals. It is noteworthy that for ELs, opportunities to integrate aspects of English literacy are particularly critical. Attending to the speaking and listening standards noted in table 6.1 helped teachers to deliberately design activities in which students learned to ask business owners questions and use elaboration prompts to ask for more details.

Through interaction, EL students gained confidence in communication and began to negotiate oral, written, and visual aspects of the English language. Likewise, honing in on several writing standards helped teachers to deliberately design activities that focused on the purpose of the informational brochures, as well as integrating revision processes and an orientation to the complexity of the content that was conveyed in the brochures.

Principle 4: Engaging Students in Multimodal Literacies

ELs in Making a Living—Making a Life had opportunities to develop their English language skills using a range of forms of language and symbol systems and a variety of tools to use these systems. Although students did practice traditional reading and writing through the reading of books, they read these texts as mentor texts that supported their writing of the multigenre brochures that "went public" upon completion. While they worked in class on structures for asking questions, they did this to satisfy their curiosities and learn more about a person they were truly interested in.

For example, an Iraqi student who had listened to the owner of a Mexican grocery store talk about how he tried to offer a broad range of foods for people from Latin America, asked, "What products do you have to offer the Muslim community?" The owner responded in detail, describing how he stocked a particular type of squash that he knew his Muslim customers liked to use in cooking.

Through such conversations, students were not simply asking questions. They were structuring the visit—and their own forays into language use—in ways that were personally *and* academically meaningful. Further, they were deepening connections to both people and places in their community. On a subsequent trip to the area, the same Iraqi student made sure to return to the grocery to purchase chips that her family loved.

Table 6.1.   Common Core Standards Addressed

Writing	Speaking and Listening	Language	Reading
CCSS.ELA-LITERACY.CCRA.W.2 Write informative/ explanatory texts to examine and convey complex ideas and information clearly and accurately through the effective selection, organization, and analysis of content. CCSS.ELA-LITERACY.CCRA.W.4 Produce clear and coherent writing in which the development, organization, and style are appropriate to task, purpose, and audience. CCSS.ELA-LITERACY.CCRA.W.5 Develop and strengthen writing as needed by planning, revising, editing, rewriting, or trying a new approach. CCSS.ELA-LITERACY.CCRA.W.6 Use technology, including the Internet, to produce and publish writing and to interact and collaborate with others.	CCSS.ELA-LITERACY.CCRA.SL.1 Prepare for and participate effectively in a range of conversations and collaborations with diverse partners, building on others' ideas and expressing their own clearly and persuasively. CCSS.ELA-LITERACY.CCRA.SL.5 Make strategic use of digital media and visual displays of data to express information and enhance understanding of presentations.	CCSS.ELA-LITERACY.CCRA.L.1 Demonstrate command of the conventions of standard English grammar and usage when writing or speaking. CCSS.ELA-LITERACY.CCRA.L.2 Demonstrate command of the conventions of standard English capitalization, punctuation, and spelling when writing. CCSS.ELA-LITERACY.CCRA.L.3 Apply knowledge of language to understand how language functions in different contexts, to make effective choices for meaning or style, and to comprehend more fully when reading or listening.	CCSS.ELA-LITERACY.RI.7.5 Analyze the structure an author uses to organize a text, including how the major sections contribute to the whole and to the development of the ideas.

In addition to practicing oral language, some students were assigned to take notes while others recorded video of interviews or took photos. These materials were pooled and analyzed by the group members when they returned to school. They used all of this material to inform their writing on the computer and to prepare follow-up questions for subsequent visits. Students used the graphics program Pages to document their work, a tool well suited to supporting multigenre writing, as it includes options for students to include captions, photos, and text and to easily shift the layout of a document.

In these ways, the use of multimedia tools was a generative resource for the whole multimodal project and also a resource that allowed the experience to be personally meaningful, instead of a school assignment alone. Students were able to exercise voice and choice throughout the process, and they had flexible options that suited their needs. For example, the students who were least proficient in English often took the lead on taking photographs and writing captions rather than composing the lengthiest paragraph of informational texts. They often also led efforts to translate the work into their home languages.

FINAL THOUGHTS

The work of educating multilingual students is complicated; research-based principles of practice and vivid examples of how to enact such practices offer common ground from which a broad range of educators may build an engaging and equitable literacy curriculum for ELs—and for other students.

This chapter has detailed the ways that one unit of instruction was steeped in the principles of CRPB. During other summers, CRPB units developed for SESLA have been situated in a center for rescued raptors, an art museum, local businesses, and at a teen community center. All of these spaces offered people and projects that enriched the learning of ELs and their teachers. Educators interested in initiating this model in their own contexts may wish to identify an educational "space," such as a summer program or after school program for a first foray into this kind of teaching. Often, these spaces offer fewer curricular constraints and flexible time frames.

Consider ways of collaborating with local teacher education programs or with adult volunteers who can amplify opportunities for interaction between ELs and English speakers and support their multigenre, multimodal, multimedia efforts.

Be sure that early on in the process, a meaningful writing product with a real audience becomes central to the work, and consult with community organizations to be sure that this product fills an authentic need in the setting. Plan for a final "reveal" of students' work where students, family members, community members, and educators can revel in the accomplishments of the students, and make sure that this event includes food and opportunities for students to informally share their work.

Align the unit with content and language standards that are valued in school settings and be sure that administrators, families, and community members understand how work on the CRPB project supports ELs academic growth. These efforts, undertaken in a principled manner, can lead to personally and academically rich teaching and learning for all involved.

REFERENCES

Bomer, R., Patterson Zoch, M., David, A. D., & Ok, H. (2010). New literacies in the material world. *Language Arts, 88*(1), 9–20.

Bunch, G. C. (2006). "Academic English" in the 7th grade: Broadening the lens, expanding access. *Journal of English for Academic Purposes, 5*, 284–301.

Bunch, G. C. (2013). Pedagogical language knowledge: Preparing mainstream teachers for English Learners in the New Standards Era. *Review of Research in Education, 37*, 298–341.

Bunch, G. C., Kibler, A. K., & Pimentel, S. (2012). Realizing opportunities for English learners in the Common Core English Language Arts and Disciplinary Literacy Standards. Paper presented at the Understanding Language Conference, Stanford, CA. Retrieved February 3, 2015 from http://ell.stanford.edu/papers.

Duke, N. K. (2014). *Inside information: Developing powerful readers and writers of informational text through project-based instruction*. New York: Scholastic.

Duke, N. K., Caughlan, S., Juzwik, M. M., & Martin, N. M. (2012). *Reading and writing genre with purpose in K–8 classrooms*. Portsmouth, NH: Heinemann.

Dworin, J. (2011). The family stories project: Using funds of knowledge for writing. *The Reading Teacher, 59*(6), 510–20.

Enright, K. A., & Gilliland, B. (2011). Multilingual writing in an age of accountability: From policy to practice in U.S. high school classrooms. *Journal of Second Language Writing, 20*, 182–95.

Filippatou, D., & Kaldi, S. (2010). The effectiveness of project-based learning on pupils with learning difficulties regarding academic performance, group work and motivation. *International Journal of Special Education, 25*, 17–26.

Filmore, L. W., & Snow, C. (2000). *What teachers need to know about language*. Available: http://www.cal.org/ericcll/teachers/teachers.pdf.

Gee, J. P. (1992). *The social mind: Language, ideology and social practice*. New York: Bergin & Garvey.

Halverson, A., Duke, N. K., Brugar, K. A., Block, M. K., Strachan, S. L., Berka, M. B., & Brown, J. M. (2012). Narrowing the achievement gap in second-grade social studies and content area literacy: The promise of a project-based approach. *Theory and Research in Social Education, 40*, 198–229.

Harklau, L. (2011). Adolescent L2 writing research as an emerging field. *Journal of Second Language Writing, 20*, 227–230.

Hernandez-Ramos, P., & De La Paz, S. (2009). Learning history in middle school by designing multimedia in a project-based learning experience. *Journal of Research on Technology in Education, 42*, 151–73.

Purcell-Gates, V. (2013). Literacy worlds of children of migrant farmworker communities: Participating in a migrant Head Start program. *Research in the Teaching of English, 48*(1), 68–97.

Purcell-Gates, V., Duke, N. K., & Martineau, J. (2007). Learning to read and write genre-specific text: Role of authentic experience and explicit teaching. *Reading Research Quarterly, 42*(1), 8–45.

Schleppegrell, M. (2004). *The language of schooling: A functional linguistics perspective*. Mahwah, NJ: Erlbaum.

Vasudevan, L. (2010). Literacies in a participatory, multimodal world: The arts and aesthetics of web 2.0. *Language Arts, 88*(1), 43–50.

Vygotsky, L. S. (1962). *Thought and language* (A. Kozalin, Trans.). Cambridge, MA: MIT Press (Original work published in 1934).

WIDA. (2012). 2012 Amplification of the English language development standards, kindergarten–grade 12. Board of Regents of the University of Wisconsin System.

Yi, Y. (2014). Possibilities and challenges of multimodal literacy practices in teaching and learning English as an additional language. *Language and Linguistics Compass, 8*(4), 158–69.

Yosso, T. (2005). Whose culture has capital? A critical race theory discussion of community cultural wealth. *Race, Ethnicity, and Education, 8*(1), 69–91.

Chapter Seven

Using Critical Pedagogies for Increasing English Language Learners' Reading and Writing Achievement

Cherese Childers-McKee, Libra N. Boyd, and Corliss Brown Thompson

Drawing on critical language teaching research, this chapter explores ways in which the tenets of critical pedagogies might be integrated into the teaching of reading, writing, and content instruction for English language learners (ELLs). This chapter draws from the ideas of critical pedagogy (Freire & Macedo, 1987), culturally relevant pedagogy (Ladson-Billings, 2006), critical literacy (Morrell, 2002), critical applied linguistics (Pennycook, 2001), and other critical pedagogies that help students critique and act against the status quo while at the same time helping them learn about the world around them.

ELLS IN URBAN SCHOOLS

Large numbers of ELLs are educated in U.S. public schools. Of the 4.4 million ELLs in K–12 public schools across the nation, 42 percent attend schools where more than 50 percent of students qualify for Free or Reduced Lunch (National Center for Educational Statistics [NCES], 2012a, 2012b). Fifty-one percent of language minority students who spoke English with difficulty failed to complete high school (NCES, 2004), five times higher than the rate for students who spoke English at home. Also, according to the National Assessment of Educational Progress (NAEP) score data, ELLs reading scores continue to lag behind their non-ELL peers with a thirty-eight-point achievement gap for fourth graders and a forty-five-point gap for eighth graders (NCES, 2015).

ELLs face numerous challenges in urban school settings. Many urban schools are unprepared or poorly resourced to address the complex needs of their second-language learners (Fix & Capps, 2005). Despite increases in second-language acquisition training and professional development, students are still likely to be in classrooms with teachers who have limited training in working with ELLs (Horwitz, et al., 2009; McKeon, 2005).

Urban schools also lack adequate numbers of bilingual teachers and tutors, have high numbers of teachers inexperienced in delivering effective and culturally relevant instruction to ELLs, and struggle to address the increased numbers of students dealing with issues such as poverty and transiency (Fix & Capps, 2005; Nevárez-La Torre, 2011).

USING CRITICAL PEDAGOGIES TO INCREASE ELL ACHIEVEMENT

Of the myriad inequalities that ELLs often face, the most alarming continues to be the predominance of functional literacy-oriented curriculum across U.S. public schools, particularly in schools with large numbers of race or ethnic minority and poor or working-class students (Cadiero-Kaplan & Smith, 2002). Cadiero-Kaplan and Smith (2002) state that "a functionally literate person is generally considered an individual who can read and write 'well enough' . . . [and] reading focuses on decoding words and analyzing text by answering specific reading comprehension questions orally and in writing" (p. 374).

Although these skills are important and necessary building blocks to literacy, they stop short of encouraging students to think critically, see multiple perspectives of text, challenge text, and use literacy to transform their social worlds. In essence, ELLs are trapped by a never-ending ideology of "learning to read" instead of "reading to learn" (Cadiero-Kaplan & Smith, 2002, p. 377).

The influence of critical pedagogies has been profound and its roots are evident in critical and social justice-oriented education (Hytten & Bettez, 2011). Yet, a critique launched at critical teaching in general is that it lacks relevance and applicability (Ewald, 1999), particularly in the elementary grades where there is an increased focus on foundational literacy skills. Confronted with the realistic challenges of reading, language, and content instruction, teachers ponder the practicality of implementing instruction that reflects the ideals of critical pedagogies in a classroom of students with a range of academic and linguistic abilities.

TEACHING LITERACY FROM A CRITICAL PEDAGOGICAL LENS

The implementation of critical literacy into reading instruction enhances existing approaches for ELLs in that it guides students beyond basic comprehension skills and language acquisition. Critical literacy moves students into more engaging learning experiences that connect to their everyday lives (Scorza, Mirra, & Morrell, 2013). As such, it serves to not only enhance language skills but to arouse their critical consciousness (Abednia & Izadinia, n.d.).

Critical literacy for ELLs deepens comprehension of the text at hand as well as the environments which surround them. As the Ontario Ministry of Education (2006) describes it, critical literacy

> involves looking beyond the literal meaning of texts to observe what is present and what is missing, in order to analyze and evaluate the text's complete meaning and the author's intent. Critical literacy goes beyond conventional critical thinking in focusing on issues related to fairness, equity, and social justice. Critically literate students adopt a critical stance, asking what view of the world the text advances and whether they find this view acceptable. (p. 152)

In other words, not only does critical literacy teach students to deeply understand the text, but it also guides students in thinking beyond the text to address issues of fairness and justice in their communities and elsewhere.

CRITICAL LITERACY: ENGAGING ELLS AS ACTIVE COMMUNITY CITIZENS

Critical literacy connects ELLs with culture and context in a way that affords them multidimensional learning opportunities. Beyond merely learning a second language, ELLs learn to examine issues of privilege, power, oppression, and difference to acquire a robust understanding along with a vision to "disrupt existing power relations" (Morrell, 2005, p. 4) within their societal contexts by challenging mainstream ideologies that marginalize them. Other rationales for critical literacy are highlighted herein.

Social Practice

Many ELLs are challenged with learning a new language as well as the cultural norms of U.S. schools. Through critical literacy, teachers can help ELLs question and interpret norms of mainstream culture, thus building skills that help students to negotiate new multicultural contexts (Daniel & Lenski, 2007). Consequently, language learning and text interpretation do not become a means of culturally assimilating ELLs. Instead, teachers make space for their students' perspectives, cultures, voices, and identities to move from margin to center. More importantly, teachers can then empower ELLs to enact change within their mainstream social settings.

Texts in Context

Teachers who use critical literacy look for texts that students find meaningful. These texts may contain characters, geographic settings, or cultural practices that students find personally relevant and relatable. For ELLs, texts within context provide a frame of reference, but perhaps more importantly, such texts let them know their cultures are recognized and valued in their present academic setting. Provision of relevant texts also helps deepen students' comprehension.

Harvey and Goudvis (2000) suggest the purpose of teaching reading comprehension is to help students construct meaning. More specifically, they suggest that teachers should help students "enhance their understanding, acquire and use their knowledge, monitor their understanding, and develop insight" (p. 8). Interesting texts with which ELLs can connect allow them to recount experiences, which helps make their learning meaningful.

Engagement

Daniel and Lenski (2007) propose, "Engaging ELLs in provocative dialogues sets up a classroom society that is not centered on the majority culture's viewpoint, nor is it centered on the interpretation of words from an author's perspective or the teacher's stance" (p. 34). Critical literacy engages learners in a number of ways. Not only are students able to make connections between their lives and social structure, but they are also allowed to do what is sometimes discouraged in American classrooms—challenge intent and content, as well as express opposing ideas. This climate of support and inclusivity is appealing to ELLs.

Classroom Practice for All Learners

Teachers can help their students develop a critical literacy lens as early as kindergarten (see Vasquez, 2014; Wood, 2005), by using strategies that promote a critical perspective in their students. The strategies are applicable across grade level and learning style. As Ladson-Billings (1995) suggests, learning should promote "collective empowerment." This means that all students regardless of their academic strengths or challenges should be actively engaged in the learning process. Therefore, it is important for teachers of critical literacy to employ strategies to help differentiate and provide learning opportunities according to the needs of the students.

Multimedia Texts from a Variety of Genres

Teaching literacy from a critical pedagogy lens lends itself to the integration of multimedia texts from a variety of genres. Teachers can use magazines, song lyrics, graphic novels, and movies, for instance, to help students interrogate societal norms (Behrman, 2006). Multimedia texts that students already connect to in one way or another increase students' motivation, enhance their engagement, and improve their general attitude about reading itself (Strangman & Dalton, 2006).

Negotiation

Teachers who employ a critical literacy approach teach students to not only read a text, but to reflect on it and ask questions. Consequently, ELL students are empowered to raise their social consciousness as they read, listen, and write in the target language. It is notable that a primary goal of critical literacy is not merely interrogating issues of privilege, power, and difference in texts, but seeking to improve one's surroundings as a result. Negotiation can be summed up as praxis (Freire, 2007). Students read texts to understand new concepts and then they act on their new knowledge (Ladson-Billings, 1995).

CONTENT-BASED LITERACY INSTRUCTION

In recent years, second-language researchers and policymakers have increasingly emphasized the importance of teaching academic language to ELLs and encouraging reading and writing across the curriculum. Although there are many types of English-language instruction delivery models, the pullout model continues to be one of the most common, particularly for younger learners. In the pullout model, ELLs spend most of their day with their primary classroom teacher and may only be pulled out for instruction by their English as a second language teacher once a day or as little as once a week.

Thus, for many ELLs the largest amount of their exposure to language and literacy instruction occurs within the mainstream classrooms with content area teachers. In the following sections, the specifics of incorporating critical pedagogies with researched-based best practices for ELLs are delineated. Then, more concrete examples are given about how project-based learning and youth participatory action research represent effective instructional strategies for fostering critical thinking, critical literacy, writing, and a greater awareness of societal issues that face disenfranchised communities of students.

Despite a plethora of recommendations and techniques for second-language acquisition, young ELLs (as well as many of their English-speaking peers) still experience challenges that prevent them from fully accessing even the best of instructional strategies. Many ELLs are beleaguered by curriculum that lacks cultural relevance and applicability to students of diverse backgrounds, fails to excite their motivation to learn, and focuses too heavily on process and rote skills without enough focus on quality language and literacy instruction. When ELL teaching occurs through the lens of critical pedagogies,

> students should study the world around them, in the process, learning who they are and what has shaped them. In this context students as odd as it might sound become epistemologically informed scholars. As such, they are challenged to analyze and interpret data, conduct research, and develop a love for scholarship that studies things that matter to the well-being of the people of the world. (Kincheloe, 2008, p. 11)

Stated differently, critical teachers work to instill a love and passion for learning, help students discover how it relates to their everyday lives, and encourage them to think creatively about how through learning one might improve the lives of the poor, oppressed, or disenfranchised.

The Institute of Education Sciences (2014) provides four research-based recommendations for working with ELLs in the content area (figure 7.1). These recommendations are based on empirical studies of English-language acquisition and considered by many language teachers as crucial for successful second-language acquisition. These recommendations, when infused with the components of critical pedagogies, become powerful tools for transforming the learning and achievement of ELLs.

Recommendation 1: Teaching of Academic Vocabulary

Language-acquisition researchers find that explicit teaching of academic vocabulary using engaging texts contributes to ELLs' learning outcomes. One approach is to choose an informational text, identify important academic vocabulary, and create lessons to explicitly teach these terms (Baker et al., 2014). Sample activities include generating pictorial representations of the word, finding cognates in the student's native language, and mapping the word's common uses.

Recommendations 2 and 3: Integration of Oral and Written Language Instruction with Content/Regular, Structured Opportunities to Develop Written Language Skills

ELLs are likely to spend most of their school day in content area classrooms and are expected to achieve at faster rates. Consequently, expectations of who holds responsibility for English-language instruction has shifted. Con-

Teaching Academic Content and Literacy to English Language Learners in Elementary and Middle School

- Recommendation 1: Teach a set of academic vocabulary words intensively across several days using a variety of instructional activities.

- Recommendation 2: Integrate oral and written English language instruction into content area teaching.

- Recommendation 3: Provide regular, structured opportunities to develop written language skills.

- Recommendation 4: Provide small-group instructional intervention to students struggling in areas of literacy and English language development

Figure 7.1. Teaching Academic Content and Literacy to English Language Learners in Elementary and Middle School. Source: Institute of Education Sciences, http://ies.ed.gov/ncee/wwc/PracticeGuide.aspx?sid=19.

tent teachers work with second-language teachers to ensure ELLs receive language instruction throughout the day. Therefore, learning literacy, oral, and written language often occur through the core content areas (Baker et al., 2014).

To ensure ELLs can access the academic language of the content as well as acquire English, language-acquisition researchers recommend scaffolding to increase comprehension by using videos, media, and graphic organizers. ELLs need regular opportunities to engage with content orally and in writing. Word walls and bilingual resources are particularly useful for written responses.

Recommendation 4: Small-Group Instruction as an Intervention for Struggling Readers

Language-acquisition researchers suggest that small-group instruction for struggling readers improves learning outcomes. According to the IES report (Baker et al., 2014), ELLs with reading difficulty typically fall within two categories—those with decoding or phonemic awareness issues and those with comprehension issues. Suggested strategies include text walkthroughs, word attack strategies, sequencing, and discussing story elements (Baker et al., 2014).

INCORPORATING THE RECOMMENDATIONS WITH CRITICAL PEDAGOGIES

Although the strategies discussed represent often-used, research-based strategies, none of them address the challenge of motivating students or making content engaging or culturally relevant and affirming. Teaching using critical pedagogies contributes meaningfulness and relevance to curriculum. Using the word radical to denote critical teaching that fights oppressive societal forces, Crookes (2009) suggests that

> there is [nothing] completely different in classroom practices, curriculum, or learning theory that sets off radical language teaching absolutely from other approaches to language teaching; it is the values of the curriculum, the philosophy of the teachers and students, and the long-term aims of programs of this kind which are different. (p. 604–5)

A critical pedagogical curriculum values student perspectives, engages them in understanding academic language from multiple perspectives, and has the long-term goal of encouraging students to see learning as a life-long journey, as a source of empowerment, and as a vehicle to transform students' social worlds. (Additional qualities of critical teaching are listed in figure 7.2.)

Thus, in critical classrooms, when informational articles are chosen to teach academic vocabulary (as mentioned in recommendation 1), they are not chosen arbitrarily, but they are chosen to engage students' ideas about social issues and connect to their cultures and prior experiences. Then, these topics are further developed in small groups as students practice reading and engaging one another through oral and written discussions, debates, and writing.

Improving Literacy through Participatory and Project-Based Learning

One tenet of critical pedagogical teaching is that students become able to read the word and the world (Freire & Macedo, 1987). Therefore, teaching English and literacy occurs through context-rich, engaging, relevant, content-based activities as students become passionate about societal issues. An approach in which these principles have been applied is participatory action research with youth (PAR or YPAR).

YPAR's ideology borrows from critical theory, critical race theory, and critical pedagogical traditions in challenging dominant narratives and engaging in praxis (Kincheloe, McLaren, & Steinberg, 2011). McIntyre (2000) outlines three major components of participatory action research (PAR): "(1) the collective investigation of a problem, (2) the reliance on indigenous knowledge, and (3) the desire to take individual and/or collective action to deal with the stated problem" (p. 128).

Tips for Teaching from a Critical Pedagogical Lens

Critical Teachers…

- Realize that teaching is not structure less and done at a whim—but complex, child-centered, serious engagement of real life learning.
- Acknowledge and negotiate the reality of standards and school constraints. Critical teachers cannot hide the fact that these things exist, but instead work creatively to transform the instructional constraints that they confront.
- See teaching and learning as an interconnected journey and as a collaborative process.
- Resist the harmful practice of attaching labels to their students.
- Recognize the importance of context.
- Seek to uncover the wealth of prior knowledge that students bring to their classrooms.
- View education as a journey—instead of a product to be attained.
- See themselves as teacher, facilitator, guide, leader, coach, and encourager.

Figure 7.2. Tips for Teaching from a Critical Pedagogical Lens

YPAR develops student literacy skills (Morrell, 2006) and provides a relevant, empowering approach to allowing youth to "seek the wide, deep, and thoughtful engagement with high-quality literary and informational texts that builds knowledge, enlarges experience, and broadens worldviews" (Common Core State Standards Initiative, 2012, para. 6).

In studying the effects of critical pedagogies on urban youth, Scorza et al. (2013) found youth were transformed in their learning, level of empowerment, and engagement with civic issues. Strategies and activities included using pop culture sources to promote critical literacy and greater understanding of world issues; teaching youth to uncover, describe, and transform social issues facing their schools and communities through YPAR; and using multiple forms of print and media to raise awareness of social justice.

The section that follows describes the specifics of a concrete lesson infused with the qualities of critical pedagogies and intended to teach both content and literacy.

CRITICAL LITERACY UNIT DESCRIPTION

Francisco Jimenez's (1998) *La Mariposa* (The Butterfly) is a book that can be used as the foundation for a critical literacy unit for third-grade elementary students. *La Mariposa* is a fictional text, although based on the author's lived experiences, which tells the story of a young boy from a family of migrant workers. The story describes his challenges adjusting to a new language, culture, peers, and the hardships that he faces at school. Selecting a rich text, such as *La Mariposa*, allows for consideration of social practice and engagement, while using the text in context for all learners.

Classroom Practices for All Learners

La Mariposa, as the foundation of a critical pedagogical unit, provides the engaging text needed to provide structure for reading and writing growth in ELLs. As previously mentioned, the Institute of Education Sciences (2014) recommends that teaching for ELLs include the teaching of academic vocabulary, integrating oral and written language instruction with content, structured opportunities to develop written language skills, and small-group instruction.

These strategies can be used to further the development of critical literacy practices in addition to grade-level specific reading and writing curricular objectives. As the tenets of critical literacy are described, these strategies for ELL instruction will be included.

Social Practice

Critical pedagogical lessons for ELLs help them understand and adjust to cultural differences in their school settings. In *La Mariposa*, Francisco, the main character, has to adjust to a new culture. Francisco grapples with adjusting to new norms, such as clothing, language, school rules, and relating to other children who challenge him. Children will be able to perceive the frustration Francisco feels at his new school.

After children are familiar with the book and the overall plot, during a reread of the book, students can help the teacher create a list of the social events and norms that make Francisco feel uncomfortable. Depending on the level of the students, this could be done independently or with a group.

Organizing and thinking about information from books accomplishes two goals: First, students are reading, using skills to help them read, and engaging in the thought processes involved in reading. Simultaneously, students engage with meaningful content which allows them to not only learn about social practices, but to question the fairness of taken-for-granted social practices.

For example, dealing with bullies or people who are difficult to get along with is another social practice that Francisco encounters. Students can use their reading comprehension skills to understand the bully's perspective, Francisco's perspective, and imagine a new way forward. In doing so, students begin to think of themselves as change agents able to transform inequalities in their schools, homes, and communities.

Texts in Context

La Mariposa is an example of a text that students, especially ELL students, will find meaningful. *La Mariposa* includes characters with which students can relate. The use of a language other than English interspersed throughout the text is another space of connection for students, particularly students who speak Spanish. Like the story's characters, students will be able to relate to being in a new culture with few family or friends nearby.

Using a text such as *La Mariposa*, which may be familiar to some ELLs, has the potential to activate students' prior knowledge. Selecting a book such as this allows the teacher to help students find connections to the text thereby aiding in their comprehension.

A strong foundation in understanding the context and the feelings expressed in a book can help support ELLs in learning a crucial reading comprehension skill: making inferences. Making inferences, determining implied meaning based on what is said and left un-said by the author, is a skill that students are asked to do across multiple grade levels (Common Core State Standards Initiative, 2012).

There are multiple instances throughout *La Mariposa* where students can be guided to make inferences or they can make inferences independently. For example, Francisco has one friend in his class who speaks Spanish, but whenever his teacher hears them speaking Spanish she tells them to stop and they must only speak English.

The author does not say how this makes Francisco feel, and the author does not say the types of challenges that not being able to speak or be spoken to in Spanish causes for him. This provides an opportunity for students to infer information that the author did not include using clues from the text and their own knowledge.

Engagement

Inferring is a skill that helps students understand the text, but it can also help them connect their own lives to the text and understand the world around them. For example, in regard to Francisco not being allowed to speak Spanish, students can engage in a discussion about their own experiences learning English. Students can also discuss whether or not it is fair for the teacher to prevent Francisco from communicating in Spanish.

Teachers can guide students in expanding this conversation to include a discussion of privilege and discrimination related to language. For instance, teachers could share information about the implications of Arizona's ELL policies (Lawton, 2012) for elementary students. Then, students can describe their own personal experiences with privilege or language discrimination.

Multimedia Texts from a Variety of Genres

Through a deeper analysis of Francisco's family's social status as migrant farm workers, students can engage in discussions of social structures and issues. There are resources, appropriately leveled for elementary children, about migrant farm workers. Teachers can couple *La Mariposa*, a fictional text, with nonfictional texts about migrant farm workers and their children. An example of a book with similar themes would be *Esperanza Rising* by Pam Munoz Ryan (2000). Reading *Esperanza Rising*, a chapter book, would be a way to differentiate instruction for advanced younger elementary readers, or it would be appropriate for an upper-elementary, whole-class book study.

Additional resources from the Internet can be used to further students' understanding of the plights of migrant workers. Also, community members can be invited to tell stories or share experiences about migrant farm work, farming, labor, or other related topics to help deepen students' comprehension. Based on Francisco's experience and the additional information about migrant farm children, students will be able to develop more empathy toward children who live in poverty and difficult situations.

Not only will students be able to make connections between their lives and social issues, but they are allowed to do what is sometimes discouraged in U.S. classrooms—challenge intent and content, as well as voice opposing ideas. Not only can they develop empathy, they can also discuss ways that they as a class would be able to help a student, such as Francisco, in their class or in other spaces. They can also begin to learn about pay distribution associated with various jobs to consider the hardships that a lack of financial resources can create.

Negotiation

Based on their reading and discussion of *La Mariposa* and related texts, students will have a foundation from which they can begin to suggest answers and actions for the inferences they made and questions they asked. Based on YPAR principles, students' actions should emerge from their own thinking and preferences.

For instance, if students determine they need to create a more inclusive environment where multiple languages are encouraged and spoken, they can brainstorm and create a plan to do this. Other students may be more interested in migrant farm workers. They could create a plan to further research the topic to find a way that they can be supportive or bring larger awareness to the issues.

Action and creating awareness lend themselves nicely to writing in the elementary setting. All plans need to be communicated and captured, and writing is a way for students to do this. Writing should be modeled and supported by the teacher. Students will have different writing projects depending on their ability level. For example, some students may be read to fully transcribe the plans of the group. Other students may take a leadership role in helping to verbally plan and communicate ideas. Group projects can allow students to practice new skills that are developmentally appropriate.

Even though the projects are student-driven, teacher planning and guidance is an important part of student growth and development. Students would discuss their projects and areas of interest and communicate ideas to the teacher. The teacher would then need to take time to plan and determine how student project goals, curricular goals, and individual student needs can be met within the group project. After the teacher has time to plan, each group should be given the guidance and structures they need to develop their projects.

Additional Activities and Content

La Mariposa is a beginning resource to help students experience critical pedagogies, more specifically critical literacy, and there are many ways the content in this text can be expanded. To expand literacy instruction, students should have the opportunity to engage in guided reading texts that are at their appropriate level.

Books that share similar themes (e.g., new school, growth) or similar topics (e.g., language, farming, bullying at school) should be selected for guided reading. Independent reading can also help further students' literacy skills. A variety of texts including nonfiction books, magazines, Internet articles, poetry, and other fiction books can be included in a classroom library for students to read. Students can be encouraged to develop compositional skills by writing personal narratives about their experiences moving to a new place, or they could write about a time they experienced discrimination.

La Mariposa also creates a starting place for math and science instruction. Migrant farm workers make $10,000 per year (National Farm Worker Ministry, n.d.). Third graders can be given a monthly migrant farm worker salary and create their own budgets. Budgeting lessons can include practice with multiplication, addition, subtraction, and division skills. Students can solve multistep word problems or write their own.

Third graders following the North Carolina Essential Science Standards (North Carolina Department of Public Instruction, n.d.) learn about plants. Integrating *La Mariposa* with a unit on plants will help students gain a deeper understanding of the work migrant farmers do to keep plants alive and growing. Third-grade social studies includes a focus on people, events, and ideas in local communities. A social studies lesson prompted by *La Mariposa* might include inquiry into the local community, particularly an examination of agriculture, where the community buys its food, and how this may have shifted over time.

Critical pedagogies can be used to help students examine their own surroundings and experiences in a deeper way while supporting the required curriculum. Although it may require additional planning time on the part of the teacher, it will also require additional thinking from the students. Learning additional reading and writing skills, deepening the ability to understand and critique societal issues, and beginning to think of themselves as change agents can result in enriching learning experiences for ELLs.

FINAL THOUGHTS

Elementary ELLs in urban settings face a unique set of challenges. They may confront a marginalized position in the school by virtue of their English proficiency and cultural difference. Particularly in communities experiencing poverty, ELLs may be in educational settings dealing with limited resources and high teacher turnover.

Although it is not the intention of this chapter to propose that critical pedagogical instructional approaches represent the sole answer to challenges ELLs face in urban schools, it does represent an approach to teaching and learning intended to empower and make content area instruction more relevant, purposeful, and connected to students' prior knowledge and experiences.

REFERENCES

Abednia, A., & Izadinia, M. (n.d.). Five steps to practice critical literacy in second language reading. Retrieved from https://www3.aucegypt.edu/auctesol/Default.aspx?issueid= 1d8f85d0-1f98-4cd7-9f2c-fc7790380b31&aid=541447a1-b1fd-4bb6-8715-227ce250c44c.

Baker, S., Lesaux, N., Jayanthi, M., Dimino, J., Proctor, C. P., Morris, J., . . . Newman-Gonchar, R. (2014). *Teaching academic content and literacy to English learners in elementary and middle school* (NCEE 2014-4012). Washington, DC: National Center for Education Evaluation and Regional Assistance (NCEE), Institute of Education Sciences, U.S. Department of Education. Retrieved from the NCEE website: http://ies.ed.gov/ncee/wwc/publications_reviews.aspx.

Behrman, E. H. (2006). Teaching about language, power, and text: A review of classroom practices that support critical literacy. *Journal of Adolescent & Adult Literacy, 49*(6), 490–98.

Cadiero-Kaplan, K., & Smith, K. (2002). Literacy ideologies: Critically engaging the language arts curriculum. *Language Arts, 79*(5), 372–81.

Common Core State Standards Initiative. (2012). *English Language Arts Standards.* Retrieved from http://corestandards.org/the-standards.

Crookes, G. (2009). Radical language teaching. In M. H. Long & C. J. Doughty (Eds.), *The handbook of language teaching* (pp. 595–609). Oxford, UK: Wiley-Blackwell.

Daniel, M., & Lenski, S. (2007). The importance of critical literacy for English language learners. *Illinois Reading Council Journal, 35*(2), 32–36.

Ewald, J. (1999). Comments on Graham Crookes and Al Lehner's, "Aspects of process in an ESL critical pedagogy teacher education course": A plea for published reports on the application of a critical pedagogy to "language study proper." *TESOL Quarterly, 33*(2), 275–85.

Fix, M., & Capps, R. (2005). Immigrant children, urban schools, and the no child left behind act. Migration Information Source. Retrieved from http://lwvindy.org/files/MigrationInformationSource_-ImmigrantChildrenUrbanSchoolsAndTheNCLB.pdf.

Freire, P. (2007). *Pedagogy of the oppressed* (30th Anniversary Ed.). New York: Continuum.

Freire, P., & Macedo, D. (1987). *Literacy: Reading the word and the world. Critical studies in education series.* South Hadley, MA: Bergin & Garvey Publishers.

Harvey, S., & Goudvis, A. (2000). *Strategies that work: Teaching comprehension to enhance understanding.* Portland, ME: Stenhouse.

Horwitz, A., Uro, G., Price-Baugh, R., Simon, C., Uzzell, R., Lewis, S., & Casserly, M. (2009). *Succeeding with English language learners: Lessons learned from the Great City Schools.* Washington, DC: Council of the Great City Schools. Retrieved from http://www.cgcs.org/cms/lib/dc00001581/centricity/domain/4/ell_report09.pdf.

Hytten, K., & Bettez, S. C. (2011). Understanding education for social justice. *Educational Foundations, 25*, 7–24.

Institute of Education Sciences. (2014). Teaching academic content and literacy to English learners in elementary and middle school. Retrieved from http://ies.ed.gov/ncee/wwc/PracticeGuide.aspx?sid=19.

Jimenez, F. (1998). *La Mariposa.* New York: Houghton Mifflin Company.

Kincheloe, J. L. (2008). *Knowledge and critical pedagogy: An introduction.* Dordrecht, Netherlands: Springer.

Kincheloe, J. L., McLaren, P., & Steinberg, S. R. (2011). Critical pedagogy and qualitative research. In N. K. Denzin & Y. S. Lincoln (Eds.), *The SAGE handbook of qualitative research* (pp. 163–77). Thousand Oaks, CA: Sage Publications Inc.

Ladson-Billings, G. (1995). But that's just good teaching! The case for culturally relevant pedagogy. *Theory into practice, 34*(3), 159–65.

Ladson-Billings, G. (2006). From the achievement gap to the education debt: Understanding achievement in U.S. schools. *Educational Researcher, 35*(7), 3–12.

Lawton, S. B. (2012). State education policy formation: The case of Arizona's English language learner legislation. *American Journal of Education, 118*(4), 455–87.

McIntyre, A. (2000). *Inner-city kids: Adolescents confront life and violence in an urban community.* New York: University Press.

McKeon, D. (2005). *Research talking points on English language learners.* Washington, DC: National Education Association. Retrieved from http://www.nea.org/home/13598.htm.

Morrell, E. (2002). Toward a critical pedagogy of popular culture: Literacy development among urban youth. *Journal of Adolescent & Adult Literacy, 46*(1), 72–77.

Morrell, E. (2005). Critical English education. *English Education, 37*(4), 312–21.

Morrell, E. (2006). Critical participatory action research and the literacy achievement of ethnic minority groups. *National Reading Conference Yearbook, 55,* 1–18.

National Center for Educational Statistics. (2004). *The condition of education.* Washington, DC: U.S. Department of Education. Retrieved from http://nces.ed.gov/programs/coe.

National Center for Educational Statistics. (2012a). *The condition of education* (NCES Publication No. 2012045). Washington, DC: U.S. Department of Education. Retrieved from http://nces.ed.gov/programs/coe/indicator_cgf.asp.

National Center for Educational Statistics. (2012b). *Fast facts.* Washington, DC: U.S. Department of Education. Retrieved from http://nces.ed.gov/fastfacts/display.asp?id=96.

National Center for Education Statistics (NCES). (2015). *The condition of education 2015* (NCES 2015-144), English Language Learners. Washington, DC: U.S. Department of Education.

National Farm Worker Ministry. (n.d). Low Wages. Retrieved from http://nfwm.org/education-center/farm-worker-issues/low-wages/.

Nevárez-La Torre, A. (2011). Transiency in urban schools: Challenges and opportunities in educating ELLs with a migrant background. *Education and Urban Society, 44*(1), 3–34.

North Carolina Department of Public Instruction. (n.d.). NC Essential Standards. Retrieved from http://www.dpi.state.nc.us/acre/standards/new-standards/.

Ontario Ministry of Education. (2006). *The Ontario curriculum, grades 1–8: Language.* Retrieved from http://www.edu.gov.on.ca/eng/curriculum/elementary/language18currb.pdf.

Pennycook, A. (2001). *Critical applied linguistics: A critical introduction.* Mahwah, NJ: Routledge.

Ryan, P. M. (2000). *Esperanza rising.* New York: Scholastic.

Scorza, D. A., Mirra, N., & Morrell, E. (2013). It should just be education: Critical pedagogy normalized as academic excellence. *The International Journal of Critical Pedagogy, 4*(2), 16–34.

Strangman, N., & Dalton, B. (2006). Improving struggling readers' comprehension through scaffolded hypertexts and other computer-based literacy programs. In M. C. McKenna, L. D. Labbo, R. D. Kieffer, & D. Reinking (Eds.), *International handbook of literacy and technology,* Volume II, 75–92. Mahwah, NJ: Lawrence Erlbaum Associates.

Vasquez, V. M. (2014). *Negotiating critical literacies with young children.* New York: Routledge.

Wood, J. W. (2005). Moses's story: Critical literacy and social justice in an urban kindergarten. *Voices of Practitioners.* Online: http://journal.naeyc.org/bt/vp/VoicesWood.pdf.

Chapter Eight

How Does Your Garden Grow?

Using Nature to Bridge the Language Gap with Young English Learners

Elena King and Michelle Plaisance

Teachers who work with English learners approach each new school year a bit like a treasure hunt, often without a map. How many students will there be this year? Will there be children who have just arrived from their native countries? How will students' needs be met without a common language? With the transient nature of the typical ESL student population, all of these questions and more are answered in the form of young children from around the world, full of energy and curiosity, entering classrooms across the country with the common expectation of learning.

Projections from the National Center for Education Statistics (2013) suggest that the percentage of students of color is expected to grow from 48 to 52 percent by 2021. Currently, English learners comprise 9.1 percent of the total student population, nearly 4.4 million students, during the 2011–2012 school year; in urban schools, the average enrollment of English learners was 14.2 percent (U.S. Department of Education, 2014).

Despite this increased diversity, the majority of schools continue to deliver instruction from a curriculum infused in a Eurocentric perspective, casting aside or paying merely surface attention to the perspectives and contributions of culturally diverse student populations (Ladson-Billings, 1995a, 1995b; Nieto & Bode, 2012). In response to this incongruence, literature illustrates the connection between culture and learning (Ariza, Marales-Jones, Yahya, & Zainuddin, 2010; Bartone, 2010; Cummins, Chow, & Schecter, 2006), and a call for culturally affirming considerations to be taken in the instruction of diverse students (Delpit, 2006; Gay, 2002; Ladson-Billings, 1995a).

Although the name for aligning instruction with students' cultural background may vary depending on the scholar—and certain peripheral concepts may be incorporated or omitted depending on the context—there is generally a shared consensus that culturally responsive teaching improves learning outcomes for minority students, including English learners.

Finding pathways to connect with students with varying degrees of English proficiency can be a daunting task. Multiple linguistic backgrounds result in the absence of a common language to use as a platform for learning, which inevitably creates a difficult challenge for even veteran teachers (Calderón & Minaya-Rowe, 2011).

Working with English learners requires teachers to think outside the confines of the traditional classroom and to develop alternative ways of engaging students in learning. Presenting students with an arena for exploration that is both practical and culturally appropriate supports learning and school community (Blair, 2009; Cutter-Mackenzie, 2009; Williams & Brown, 2012). In addition, it is essential that students feel secure and safe to take risks when acquiring language skills. Fortunately, every school in the United States has the potential to create such a place right outside their classroom doors, in the form of a school community garden.

LIVING EXAMPLES OF CULTURALLY AFFIRMING PEDAGOGY IN THE CLASSROOM: LEARNING GARDENS

There are programs and strategies that successfully employ culturally relevant pedagogy with improved learning outcomes for culturally and linguistically diverse students (Chamot & O'Malley, 1996; Cohen 1994; Delpit, 2006; Traoré & Lukens, 2006). According to Quintero (2007), for learning to occur in these contexts, three conditions must be met: respect for students and knowledge of their unique backgrounds; involvement in the learning community in the form of dialogue; and transformative learning which asks the learner to "make the world a better place" (p. 158).

Learning gardens implement all three of these categories. In addition, research suggests that they provide opportunities for increased student learning and achievement (Blair, 2009; Lieberman & Hoody, 1998; Passy, 2014).

Learning gardens encourage the stimulation of all senses through first the rudimentary element of earth and gardening, and then expanding those ideas to integrate learning about the community and holistic life interactions (Williams & Brown, 2012). Experiential education in this manner incorporates more than seeing and hearing; students must use all their senses to create natural inquiry and develop new knowledge in this arena outside of the classroom (Williams & Brown, 2012).

Learning gardens are not a new phenomenon; they have been sprouting up in schools for decades (Trelstad, 1997). However, in this age of standardized testing and budget cuts, it seems as though cultivating seeds has been replaced by cultivating strong test takers. A more extensive look at the research on learning gardens suggests that they could propagate both.

Lieberman and Hoody (1998) provided one of the first analyses of learning gardens in which they found that "students learn more effectively within an environment-based context than within a traditional educational framework" (p. 2). The environment-based framework resulted in standardized test scores and grade point averages that were higher in 92 percent of the comparisons—particularly in the areas of language arts, social studies, science, math, and higher-order thinking skills.

In a more recent review of school programs specifically using learning gardens, Blair (2009) found nine out of the twelve quantitative studies explored "revealed a positive difference in test measures between gardening students and non-gardening students" (p. 20). In addition, all nine qualitative studies "unanimously reported positive learning and behavior effects of school gardening or garden involvement" (p. 33).

Similarly, Passy (2014) found that gardens led to learning beyond the standardized curriculum and created a feeling of calmness and sense of pride within students. Williams and Dixon's (2013) meta-analysis of learning garden research also yielded positive results in both academics and social outcomes for students who were exposed to a learning garden curriculum.

Although researchers have found success with learning gardens in the mainstream classroom, these spaces have also afforded a natural teaching environment for teachers of English learners. Aubrecht and Eames-Sheavly (2012) suggest two reasons to invest time and money into extension spaces such as learning gardens. First, they found that many immigrants expressed feeling disconnected from the land within new urban surroundings.

In addition to creating opportunities to connect to the land, learning gardens create potential language-sharing spaces for both English speakers learning Spanish and immigrant students learning English. The spaces of a learning garden are often more relaxed and create an arena in which language sharing can be cultivated along with the cultivation of plants. In summary, learning gardens create a space in which to connect to the environment and to each other (Aubrecht & Eames-Sheavly, 2012).

Cutter-Mackenzie's (2009) study followed the development of a multicultural school garden in an Australian elementary school in which the school's ESL teacher used the garden to create an authentic speech arena. She described students reading, writing, speaking, and listening to create recipes, follow instructions, and communicate their own cultural norms, creating a shared space that "facilitated a strong sense of belonging among students who were formerly dislodged from their birthplaces" (Cutter-Mackenzie, 2009, p. 133).

Similarly, Tangen and Fielding-Barnsley (2007) observed greater communication, class participation, and feelings of involvement when teachers used school gardens as a conduit for learning. This type of experiential learning benefits English learners as they make academic gains and find their place within the school community.

Multiple books (Gaylie, 2011; Thorp, 2006; Williams & Brown, 2012), anecdotal articles (Bang-Jensen, 2012; Hebert, Martin, & Slattery, 2014; Kirby, 2008; Reeves & Emeagwali, 2010), and websites (see the websites provided at the end of this chapter) are devoted to the benefits and implementation of learning gardens in schools. This chapter explores practical considerations for using a learning garden in a multilingual elementary school context. Specifically, the inception of learning gardens and how to incorporate the lessons with English learners will be discussed.

CREATING A SCHOOL GARDEN

A school garden is an affordable and realistic project that can be taken on by school personnel, either individually or collectively. Parent volunteers and community partners are additional assets that can be used when possible. Ideally, a team of teachers who perceive the garden as being useful to their students join forces to obtain the funding and labor necessary to have the garden installed and maintained.

School gardens are useful for making connections across the curriculum, in every subject area including math, social studies, science, and language arts. Nature provides boundless opportunities for engaging young children in hands-on lessons, providing them with the visual and contextual support they need to comprehend the curriculum.

To utilize the garden to its fullest potential, it is important to first conduct research to find plants appropriate for the current season and regional climate. By partnering with local hardware or farming stores, schools can create opportunities for community support. In addition, teachers can involve students in research and planning, furthering the learning opportunities inherent in investigating a meaningful topic.

Garden Journals

A garden journal is an essential component of any garden lesson because it facilitates the incorporation of language instruction throughout each lesson and provides a vehicle for dialogue between teachers and students. Dialogue journals (Cloud, Genese, & Hamayan, 2009; Peregoy & Boyle, 2008; Wright, 2010) have often been encouraged as a strategy for working with

English learners, and creating a specific garden journal aids students in initial writing and communication in a new language.

Begin by creating a model journal so that students can conceptualize the finished product. Give each student time to design and decorate the cover so that this core component of the garden classroom is a personal representation of their experience with nature and gardening concepts. The journal can be divided into three sections: lessons, writing, and a glossary.

The student-maintained glossary gives the students a space to record new words as they are encountered and explored. Students can write the words in English, as well as their native language, write a definition, and draw an illustration showing their comprehension of the word's meaning.

Younger students can simply draw a picture of their conceptualization of the meaning and perhaps supply a beginning phoneme while a teacher writes the word for them in English. Students with intermediate proficiency can draw the picture and provide the beginning sounds of each new word they learn. As proficiency develops, students are encouraged to use the new garden vocabulary in sentences or to show relationships between words by providing synonyms or antonyms.

The writing portion of the journal should be used in each lesson, giving the students an opportunity to express their thoughts and ideas in written English, as well as providing a place where students can ask questions or seek clarity without negative input from their peers. The teacher can then respond to the students' writing in an informal fashion, answering and asking additional questions for clarification while modeling correct spelling and grammar forms. The following lesson plans can be used in conjunction with the garden journals to aid in language acquisition for English learners.

Lesson Ideas

Science instruction is perhaps the most traditional use of the garden classroom. Lessons focus on a variety of objectives including animal habitats, weather concepts, physical properties of matter, needs of plants and the plant cycle, rocks and minerals, water cycle, animal life cycle, plant adaptations, animal adaptations, the food pyramid, ecosystems, and recycling, just to name a few. However, the learning garden should also be used as a space to practice literacy and language instruction.

A sampling of lesson ideas across grade levels and content areas that are enriched by a garden setting follow. These lessons can be expanded into full, garden-based unit plans, or used as mini-lessons to integrate learning gardens into already established traditional classroom lessons.

Common Core math and literacy standards are found with each lesson, but these lessons also align with multiple states' Science, English Language Arts, and Social Studies Standards as well. Adaptability suggestions are provided, as flexibility is essential when working with linguistically diverse students. All lessons are designed to encourage language production and literacy skills in English learners through authentic reading, writing, speaking, and listening activities.

SAMPLE LESSONS

Garden Scavenger Hunt

This activity is suitable for kindergarten students. In the lesson, students will be able to connect the information found in the text to experiences by describing or identifying vocabulary from the text. This activity addresses the following Common Core State Standards (CCSS) of Speaking and Listening by allowing students to: (1) describe familiar people, places, things, and events and, with prompting and support, provide additional detail; and (2) speak audibly and express thoughts, feelings, and ideas clearly.

This lesson begins by the introducing the story, *A Tiny Seed*, by Eric Carle (1970) and conducting a picture walk with students to build background and assess prior knowledge. Students will describe what they see on each page, with the teacher eliciting unfamiliar vocabulary. The teacher then conducts a read aloud of the selection, emphasizing elements related to the garden and making phonemic connections such as pea pod and potato both begin with initial phoneme [*p*]. Ideally, the teacher reads the story aloud in the garden.

The students are then asked to find realia that represents new vocabulary in the story (i.e., leaf, stem, soil, etc.) within the garden indicating their learning of the new vocabulary. The students will then participate in a speaking and listening exercise in which they share aloud with their peers, describing the item they found, reinforcing vocabulary, and practicing oral language skills. To develop spatial awareness the teacher opens the book and students place the realia on the corresponding picture in the book. Students then illustrate the new vocabulary in their garden journals and add developmentally appropriate corresponding sounds or spellings.

There are a few modifications that can be made for this lesson. For students in the silent phase of second language learning, the teacher can call out elements from the story while the student finds and points to them. For students with advanced language skills, opportunities can be given for students to describe how the item they have located was addressed in the story.

Treasure Maps

This activity is suitable for first-grade students. In the lesson, students will investigate the key features of a map and use features learned to create a map guiding other students to a specified location. This activity addresses CCSS of Reading by allowing students to know and use various text features (e.g., headings, tables of contents, glossaries, maps, icons) in a text.

In this lesson, the teacher can use a selection such as Joan Sweeney's *Me on the Map* (1996) to introduce the topics of maps. While previewing the book, the teacher points to key vocabulary and asks students to read it aloud. The meanings of the new vocabulary words should be discussed. Students can look at world maps and share where they are from. The teacher will point out the features of a map and assist students in adding key terms (i.e., directions, compass, etc.) to their garden journals.

Students can then work in small groups to create a map of the garden, adding map details such as a scale, compass rose, and a key to symbols. Students can then hide a coin somewhere in the garden, mark its location on the map, and invite other students to find their "treasure." The student who finds the treasure may then narrate how he found this treasure while the teacher writes words on a white board for the class to see. Making such text to speech connections is indicative of the Language Experience Approach (Herrell & Jordan, 2012).

Students with limited English skills can work with a more proficient partner and can be given a word bank to use when creating the map. More proficient students can write step-by-step directions to instruct peers as to the location of the coin.

Measuring the Garden: Inch by Inch

This activity is suitable for second-grade students. In the lesson, students will estimate and measure the length of a garden object using appropriate units and express their findings by producing a written report. This activity addresses CCSS of Writing by allowing students to participate in shared research and writing projects. Additionally, CCSS of Mathematics are also covered by allowing students to: (1) generate measurement data by measuring lengths of several objects to the nearest whole unit, or by making repeated measurements of the same object; and (2) estimating lengths using units of inches, feet, centimeters, and meters.

In this lesson, the teacher will introduce the concept of measurement and supply the students with appropriate vocabulary and standard tools used to measure (i.e., ruler, inch, meter, centimeter, etc.). The teacher will then conduct a read aloud of the story *Inch by Inch* by Leo Leoni (1960). Emphasis should be placed on words and concepts related to both the garden and measurement. Students will add these words to their garden journals. Students will then work in pairs to create an "inch" worm or a paper worm of any standard measurement unit.

The teacher will then give each team a sheet of paper listing ten objects found in a garden. Students will first be responsible for estimating the number of units each will be and recording these predictions in their journals with the sentence structure "I predict that the measure of the _____ will be _____ inches." Then the students will find and measure each item with their measurement instrument. Students will reconvene and compare predictions as well as measurement results. They will then record their measurement results in their journals comparing them to their original predictions.

Students in need of additional language support can be given a drawing of each garden element they are to measure and can be allowed to work with a more proficient peer. Students with advanced language skills can write sentences comparing the measurement of each object with another object in the garden, reinforcing comparison vocabulary.

Graphing Data in the Garden

This activity is suitable for third-grade students. In the lesson, students will be able to collect, organize, analyze, and display data by creating a picture graph and describing the data. This activity addresses CCSS in Literacy by allowing students to write informative/explanatory texts to examine a topic and convey ideas and information clearly. This lesson also aligns to CCSS in Mathematics by allowing students to draw a scaled picture graph and scaled bar graph to represent data sets with several categories.

In this lesson, students may work in small groups on this project to promote collaboration and increase oral language development. The teacher will display various types of charts and graphs, naming each and asking students to share ideas about what they might be used to illustrate. Students will then be given a written "research" question that can be carried out in the garden (i.e., Are there more brown, tan, or grey rocks in the third bed of the garden? How many of each vegetable plant is in the garden?).

Students work in the garden to collect the necessary data, recording their findings in a table provided by the teachers. Finally, students will work together to create three different types of graphs illustrating their finding on a poster. Students will then present their results to their peers. The teacher will ask questions such as "how many more grey rocks are there than brown rocks?" to encourage the development of the language of math. Finally, students will write paragraphs describing the graphs and answering their research questions.

Students with lower English language skills can be given predrawn tables or graphs and be responsible for recording data and labeling the data fields in each one. Students with more advanced skills can be required to write predictions and summaries of their findings.

Tracking Weather in the Garden

This activity is suitable for fourth-grade students. In the lesson, students will use common tools to measure weather including a thermometer, rain gauge, and wind vane and be able to graph this data. They will then use the data collected to create a story modeled after the mentor text. This activity addresses CCSS in Literacy by allowing students to use technology, including the Internet, to produce and publish writing as well as interact and collaborate with others. This lesson also aligns to CCSS in Mathematics by allowing students to make line plots to display datasets of measurement in fractions of a unit.

In this lesson, the teacher will share the story *Rain* by Manya Stojic (2001) and discuss the impact of precipitation on the environment. Evidence of its impact will be emphasized and pointed out in the garden (lack of rain causes the ground to dry out; too much rain creates puddles; etc.). The teacher will explain that tools are used to measure the weather that affects plant growth and the teacher will show pictures of these instruments.

The class will work together to build a weather vane and a rain gauge. Each day, students will go to the garden to record the data collected from these tools in their garden journals. After a set number of days, students will transfer the data to create a line plot of the rain and wind speeds. Finally, the students will use the mentor text *Rain* and the data collected in the garden to create and publish an original story about weather using creative writing software such as Storybird.com.

All students should be able to participate in this activity because it can be done whole group. Students who need extension activities can write daily descriptions of the weather patterns and predict the impact they will have on the garden.

Composting in Our School

This lesson is designed for fifth-grade students. In the lesson, students will describe how some materials are recycled in nature through research and participate in a composting project. They will then use the data collected to create a story modeled after the mentor text. This activity addresses CCSS in Literacy by allowing students to integrate information from several texts on the same topic to write or speak about the subject knowledgeably. This lesson will also help students to demonstrate independence and proficiency in reading a range of texts and leveling their complexity.

With the guidance of the teacher, students will read multiple books, articles, and websites about composting. They will then discuss the benefits of composting and generate a list of materials that are good candidates. Horticulture websites often provide detailed instructions for creating compost piles with children. A large barrel can be placed in the garden area and the students can use it to dispose of garden clippings and weeds.

Students can also invite peers to contribute to the composting pile and collect appropriate food waste from meals served at the school. They can do this in the form of creating newsletters, posters, or school announcements encouraging compositing. Students will observe the compost bin and write predictions and observations in their garden journals. Students can use the final compost product to provide nutrients to future plants.

The compost research can be done as a whole group led by the teacher if English proficiency levels are too low to allow students to work independently. For intermediate students, a cloze activity or Internet scavenger hunt could be created in advance to facilitate the retrieval of necessary information.

Fables in the Garden

This lesson is designed for sixth-grade students. In the lesson, students will convert an existing fable into an original dramatic production using the garden as a setting. This activity addresses CCSS in Literacy by allowing students to compare and contrast texts in different forms or genres in terms of their approaches to similar themes and topics. The lesson also addresses CCSS in Writing by having students to write narratives to develop real or imagined experiences of events using effective technique, relevant descriptive details, and well-structured even sequences.

In this lesson, the teacher begins by reading examples of multiple fables with the students. In pairs, students are then given a fable to read and work with. They work together to convert the fable to a play by including dialogue and rewriting much of the narrative as stage directions or asides. Students are then given time to practice their short plays using the garden for inspiration by adding props and backdrops. Students' final products are performed for the rest of the class.

There are modifications that can be made to this lesson. Students can create their own fable rather than adapt an existing one. They could also type the script for other students to perform. Students with beginning English proficiency can use their scripts as support during the productions.

FINAL THOUGHTS

The lessons given in this chapter address the core content areas and literacy, but there are many other subjects that can be enriched through a garden setting, such as art, music, and basic English language instruction. By focusing instruction on the physical environment, students will feel they are in a safe place to take the linguistic risks necessary to advance their level of proficiency. In addition, the act of being outdoors and involved in hands-on learning will provide English learners the relief they need from the intense setting of the monolingual classroom. Finally, garden learning provides the rich contextual support necessary for English learners to gain a deeper understanding of the concepts being taught.

ADDITIONAL RESOURCES ON LEARNING GARDENS

Web Resources

The Texas A & M Department of Horticultural Sciences: The university maintains a page specifically for children that provides a wealth of information about gardening, composting, and nutrition, including a slide show that can be shared with students to assist in the comprehension of composting concepts. http://aggie-horticulture.tamu.edu/kindergarden/

KidsGardening.org: This organization supports the use of classroom and school gardens. Interested school personnel can research grant and funding opportunities. Teachers can collaborate online with other teachers through their open garden discussion forum. There is also a monthly newsletter specifically designed to assist in the use of a garden in classroom instruction. http://www.kidsgardening.org/

University of Florida School Gardens: This site contains a comprehensive list of resources from funding a school garden to how to incorporate it into content-area lessons. http://gardeningsolutions.ifas.ufl.edu/schoolgardens/school_gardens/index.shtml

Written Resources

Jurenka, N. A., & Blass, R. J. (1996). *Beyond the bean seed: Gardening activities for grades K–6*. Englewood, CO: Teacher Ideas Press. This book was written by two educators with a mission to connect gardening with children's literature. It is packed full of lesson ideas and enrichment activities for use with primary school students.

Jurenka, N. A., & Blass, R. J. (1996). *Cultivating a child's imagination through gardening*. Englewood, CO: Teacher Ideas Press. Similar to their other work, this book takes central garden themes and provides activities that assist students in making connections to the world around them.

White, H. (2004). *The edible garden*. Menlo Park, CA: Sunset Books. This book is an excellent resource for determining which plants are seasonally and geographically appropriate for school gardens. Important information about plants and their needs is given, and the author also supplies teachers with some suggestions for garden projects in the classroom.

REFERENCES

Aubrecht, A., & Eames-Sheavly, M. (2012). From translation to cultural responsiveness: A garden program evolution in understanding educators' perceptions of Spanish-language resources. *Journal of Extension, 50*(4). Retrieved from http://www.joe.org/joe/2012august/rb3.php.

Ariza, E. N., Marales-Jones, C. A., Yahya, N., & Zainuddin, H. (2010). *Why TESOL?: Theories & issues in teaching English to speakers of other languages in K–12 Classrooms* (4th ed.). Dubuque, IA: Kendall Hunt.

Bang-Jensen, V. (2012). Reading a garden. *Educational Leadership, 69(9),* 1–5. Retrieved from http://www.ascd.org/publications/educational-leadership/summer12/vol69/num09/Reading-a-Garden.aspx.

Bartone, M. (2010). Cultural applications: Ideas for teacher education programs. *Perspectives on Urban Education, 7*(1), 91–95.

Blair, D. (2009). The child in the garden: An evaluative review of the benefits of school gardening. *Journal of Environmental Education, 40*(2), 15–38.

Calderón, M., & Minaya-Rowe, L. (2011). *Preventing long-term ELs: Transforming schools to meet core standards.* Thousand Oaks, CA: Corwin.

Carle, E. (1970). *A tiny seed.* Natick, MA: Picture Book Studio.

Chamot, A., & O'Malley, J. (1996). The cognitive academic language learning approach: A model for linguistically diverse classrooms. *The Elementary School Journal, 96*(3), 259–73.

Cloud, N., Genese, F., & Hamayan, E. (2009). *Literacy instruction for English language learners: A teacher's guide to research-based practices.* New York: Heineman.

Cohen, E. G. (1994). *Designing groupwork: Strategies for the heterogeneous classroom.* New York: Teachers College Press.

Cummins, J., Chow, P., & Schecter, S. (2006). Community as curriculum. *Language Arts, 83*(4), 297–307.

Cutter-Mackenzie, A. (2009). Multicultural school gardens: Creating engaging garden spaces in learning about language, culture, and environment. *Canadian Journal of Environmental Education, 14*(1), 122–35.

Delpit, L. (2006). *Other people's children: Cultural conflict in the classroom.* New York: The New Press.

Gay, G. (2002). Preparing for culturally responsive teaching. *Journal of Teacher Education, 53*(2), 106–16.

Gaylie, V. (2011). *Roots and research in urban school gardens.* New York: Peter Lang.

Hebert, T., Martin, D., & Slattery, T. (2014). Growing gardens, growing minds. *Science and Children, 51*(7), 52–59.

Herrell, A., & Jordan, M. (2012). *Fifty strategies for teaching English language learners.* Upper Saddle River, NJ: Pearson Education.

Kirby, T. (2008). A garden of learning. *Science and Children, 45*(9), 28–31.

Ladson-Billings, G. (1995a). But that's just good teaching! The case for culturally relevant pedagogy. *Theory into Practice, 34*(3), 159–65.

Ladson-Billings, G. (1995b). Towards a theory of culturally relevant pedagogy. *American Education Research Association, 32*(3), 465–91.

Leoni, L. (1960). *Inch by inch.* New York: Astor-Honor.

Lieberman, G. A., & Hoody, L. L. (1998). *Closing the achievement gap: Using the environment as an integrating context for learning.* Paper presented at the State Education and Environmental Roundtable, San Diego, CA. Retrieved from http://www.seer.org/extras/execsum.pdf.

National Center for Education Statistics. (2013). *Projections of education statistics to 2021.* Washington, DC: U.S. Department of Education Institute of Education Sciences.

Nieto, S., & Bode, P. (2012). *Affirming diversity: The sociopolitical context of multicultural education.* Boston: Pearson Education.

Passy, R. (2014). School gardens: Teaching and learning outside the front door. *International Journal of Primary, Elementary and Early Years Education, 42*(1), 23–38. doi: 10.1080/03004279.2011.636371.

Peregoy, S. F., & Boyle, O. (2008). *Reading, writing and learning in ESL: A resource book for K–12 teachers* (6th ed.). Boston: Pearson Education.

Quintero, E. (2007). Can literacy be taught successfully in urban schools? In S. R. Steinberg, & J. L. Kincheloe (Eds.), *19 Urban Questions: Teaching in the City* (pp. 157–71). New York: Peter Lang Publishing, Inc.

Reeves, L., & Emeagwali, N. S. (2010). Students dig for real school gardens. *Techniques: Connecting Education and Careers, 85*(4), 34–37.

Stojic, M. (2001). *Rain.* New York: Dragonfly Books.

Sweeney, J. (1996). *Me on the map.* New York: Crown.

Tangen, D., & Fielding-Barnsley, R. (2007). Environmental education in a culturally diverse school. *Australian Journal of Environmental Education, 23*, 23–30.

Thorp, L. (2006). *The pull of the earth: Participatory ethnography in the school garden.* Lanham, MD: Rowman & Littlefield Publishers, Inc.

Traoré, R., & Lukens, R. J. (2006). *This isn't the America I thought I'd find: African students in the urban US high school.* Lanham, MD: University Press of America.

Trelstad, B. (1997). Little machines in their gardens: a history of school gardens in America, 1891 to 1920. *Landscape Journal, 16*(2), 161–73.

U.S. Department of Education. (2014). *The condition of education 2014* (NCES 2014-08). Washington, DC.

Williams, D. R., & Brown, J. D. (2012). *Learning gardens and sustainability education: Bringing life to schools and schools to life.* New York: Routledge.

Williams, D. R., & Dixon, P. S. (2013). Impact of garden-based learning on academic outcomes in schools: Synthesis of research between 1990 and 2010. *Review of Educational Research, 83*(2), 211–35. doi: 10.3102/0034654313475824.

Wright, W. (2010). *Foundations for teaching English language learners: Research, theory, policy and practice.* Philadelphia: Caslon.

Chapter Nine

Culturally Relevant Texts and Urban English Language Learners

Jessica Meehan

Tamara is a teaching associate (TA) at Pine Creek Elementary School. She is completing her final field experience in an urban school setting in Texas. She cares about her students and sincerely wants them to succeed. While teaching at Pine Creek Elementary, Tamara works with culturally and linguistically diverse students (CLDS). Ninety-three percent of the students at Pine Creek are recognized by the state as economically disadvantaged, and 51 percent are identified as Limited English Proficient (LEP) (Texas Education Agency [TEA], 2009).

As Tamara's field experience requirements intensify, she and her mentor teacher become increasingly aware of a significant phenomenon. Despite the fact that Tamara is well organized, knowledgeable about the content areas, and well equipped with instructional strategies, she is frustrated. For the most part, she is successful in executing her lessons and in promoting academic achievement. However, on several occasions, there was a disconnect between her instructional materials and examples, and English-language learners (ELLs) in which she will teach.

During some of these lessons, her examples and materials served as stumbling blocks and actually hindered the concept being introduced to the class. When checking for understanding many of the students were not "getting it," whereas others did not seem to be engaged at all. Tamara is not alone.

Tamara is one of many pre-service and novice teachers that will be confronted with understanding how to teach students from linguistically diverse backgrounds. The Migrant Policy Institute (Ruiz Soto, Hooker, & Batalova, 2015) reports that western states such as California, New Mexico, Nevada, Texas, and Colorado have the highest density of ELLs enrolled in public schools, ranging from 13 to 24 percent. However, eastern states such as Florida, New York, and the District of Columbia are not far behind with 9 to 10 percent of their enrollment identified as ELLs (see figure 9.1).

Urban school districts such as Los Angeles Unified School District (LAUSD), New York City public schools, Nevada's Clark County School District (CCSD), Florida's Miami-Dade County Schools (M-DCS), Dallas Independent School District (DISD), and Houston Independent School District (HISD) are accountable for the education of the highest number of ELLs in the nation (Ruiz Soto et al., 2015). ELLs enrolled in urban school settings are a trend across the United States (see table 9.1).

Historically, the U.S. public school system has struggled to meet the needs of the ELL demographic, emphasizing the development of oral language proficiency rather than content and academic achievement (Wright, 2010). However, federal policies are explicit in stating that ELLs must have equitable access to all educational opportunities (González, 2008; Menken, 2009). Recent National Assessment of Educational Progress (NAEP) scores demonstrate that this charge has yet to be fully realized.

Of particular concern is the development of literacy for ELLs. According to NAEP (2013), the average scores for ELLs on reading assessments in grades 4, 8, and 12 were significantly lower than the average scores for non-

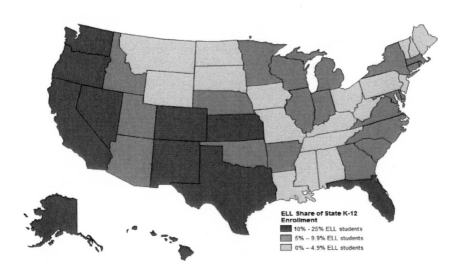

Figure 9.1.   English Language Learner representation in the United States.
Source: Ruiz Soto, A.G., Hooker, S., & Batalova, J. (2015). *States and districts with the highest number and share of English language learners.* Washington, DC: Migration Policy Institute.

Table 9.1.   U.S. School Districts with Highest ELL Representation

District/Agency Name	State	ELL Enrollment	Total K–12 Enrollment	Share of ELLs among K–12 Students (%)
Los Angeles Unified	CA	152,592	659,639	23.1
New York City	NY	142,572	968,143	14.7
Clark County	NV	68,577	313,398	21.9
Dade County	FL	66,497	350,239	19.0
Dallas Independent	TX	56,650	157,575	36.0
Houston Independent	TX	54,333	203,066	26.8
City of Chicago	IL	53,786	403,004	13.3
Fairfax County	VA	36,551	177,606	20.6
San Diego Unified	CA	36,453	131,044	27.8
Santa Ana Unified	CA	32,170	57,250	56.2
Orange County	FL	28,311	180,000	15.7
School District 1 County of Denver	CO	25,417	80,890	31.4
Hawaii Department of Education	HI	24,750	182,706	13.5
Broward County	FL	24,143	258,478	9.3
Hillsborough County	FL	22,474	197,041	11.4
Fort Worth Independent	TX	21,913	83,109	26.4
Austin Independent School District	TX	21,751	86,528	25.1
Long Beach Unified	CA	20,746	83,691	24.8
Garden Grove Unified	CA	20,743	47,999	43.2
Montgomery County	MD	20,580	146,459	14.1
Gwinnet County	GA	18,968	162,370	11.7
Palm Beach County	FL	18,698	176,901	10.6
Fresno Unified	CA	17,536	74,235	23.6
San Bernardino City Unified	CA	17,488	54,379	32.2
San Francisco Unified	CA	17,083	56,310	30.3

Source: Ruiz Soto, A. G., Hooker, S., & Batalova, J. (2015). *States and districts with the highest number and share of English language learners.* Washington, DC: Migration Policy Institute.

ELLs. Delpit (2012) asserts that schools can overcome this opportunity gap through the integration of cultural connections.

According to Gay (2000), teachers need to be equipped to create democratic classrooms with a culturally responsive and inclusive curriculum. Robledo (2013) states that teacher preparation and professional development should include strategies for making information relevant and comprehensible to ELLs.

In the case of Tamara and Pine Creek Elementary, the adoption of culturally responsive teaching and culturally relevant texts can improve the academic achievement of her students (Gay, 2002). When selecting classroom texts, Tamara can select books that are culturally compatible and that contain content familiarity for her students (Teale, 2009). These culturally relevant texts provide *identity affirmation*, assist in addressing the ELLs need for *belonging and self-esteem*, and *activate prior knowledge*. The benefits of culturally relevant texts are worth exploring.

CULTURALLY RELEVANT BOOKS

It is important to debunk the myth that culturally relevant books are synonymous with multicultural books. Although both types of texts are essential for the classroom, it is important to distinguish their fundamental differences. Lynch-Brown and Tomlinson (1999) define multicultural literature as any trade book, regardless of genre, that has as a main character "who is a member of a racial, religious or language micro culture other than the Euro-American one" (p. 188). Similarly, Mitchell (2003) elaborates that multicultural literature calls attention to peoples and voices not traditionally written about or included in the body of literature most frequently taught.

According to Gopalakrishnan (2010), "multicultural children's literature is about the sociocultural experiences of previously underrepresented groups" (p. 5). These multicultural books can serve as a window into a different culture or they may mirror the culture of a classroom (Bishop, 2012).

Culturally relevant books are primarily used as mirrors and reflect the cultural identity of a classroom. A culturally responsive curriculum uses "cultural characteristics, experiences, and perspectives of ethnically diverse students as conduits for teaching" (Gay, 2002, p. 106). Culturally relevant books should reflect the lives of the students (Gay, 2002). Freeman, Freeman, and Freeman (2003) assert that students should be able to connect and relate to culturally relevant texts. Ebe (2010) asserts that "culturally relevant texts draw on the schema that ELLs bring to reading" (p. 196). Rodriguez (2009) states that books are culturally relevant when the characters, experiences of the characters, settings, events, and language of a given text are similar to the lives and experiences of the students in the classroom.

Given that each school and classroom is unique in its ELL population, teachers must be mindful of their specific students when selecting texts. Teachers can select culturally relevant texts that are appropriate for their classrooms but must be critically reflective in examining the content of the texts.

Teachers can do this by (1) examining the similarities between characters and students; (2) interrogating the relationships between students' experiences and the stories told; (3) questioning if students are familiar with places and/or significant events mentioned in the story; and (4) asking if the language and contexts used in the story resemble the students' lived experiences and world view (Ebe, 2010; Freeman, 2000; Rodriguez, 2009).

Furthermore, ELLs should not be subjected to a narrow library of only culturally relevant texts. However, far too often, culturally relevant books are not emphasized enough in the classroom. For example, in an informal interview with a Mexican American student in south Texas, when asked, "How often do you read stories like these?" the student responded with, *"Nunca"* (Never) to the question (Freeman & Freeman, 2004, p. 10). This student, like many others in U.S. public schools, could benefit from the multiple purposes of culturally relevant books.

Advocates of culturally relevant books stress that these types of stories promote student engagement, interest, and cause the reader to connect to the text (Delpit, 2012; Freeman & Freeman, 2004; Gay, 2007). Freeman (2000) states, "culturally relevant books connect to students' lives" (p. 8). Similarly, Gay (2007) asserts that curriculum should be relevant to students to promote engagement and interest. However, the instructional value of using culturally relevant books is much more educationally profound when examined closely; culturally relevant books have the power to shape and transform a student's cultural and academic identity beyond classroom walls.

Identity Affirmation

Culturally relevant texts can serve to affirm the identities of ELLs. When students are able to connect to the curriculum via culturally relevant books, "teachers and administrators focus on and celebrate what students do know and can do" (Cowan Pitre, 2014, p. 215). By being exposed to story elements that are similar, students can develop a positive affirmation of their ethnic identity. Cummins (1996) elaborated: "when students' developing sense of self is affirmed and extended through their interactions with teachers, they are more likely to apply themselves to academic effort and participate actively in instruction" (p. 2).

Similarly, Giroux (1997) emphasized that "how we understand and come to know ourselves cannot be separated from how we are represented and how we imagine ourselves" (p. 15). Therefore, the culturally sensitive classroom must be mindful of the manner in which students come to know themselves (Hunsberger, 2007). Fountas and Pinnell (2006) state that students "should see illustrations with people like themselves in books, and have their cultures reflected in the food, celebrations, customs, dress, holidays, and events they encounter in the stories" they read (p. 506).

Educators who work in urban settings and have ELLs can foster an environment that is supportive, inclusive, and affirming by incorporating culturally relevant texts into their classrooms and lessons. When an individual is affirmed he/she is validated as a member of the group and further enhances his/her sense of belonging and self-concept.

Belonging and Self-Esteem

CLDS often feel disenfranchised and are "placed at the margins of classroom interactions" (Teale, 2009, p. 699). Students that have experienced classroom environments that are not inclusive of their culture and language backgrounds express a deep desire to be accepted and to belong. In the landmark case *Castañeda v. Pickard* (1981), the Castañeda family sued the Raymondville Independent School District (RISD) and sought equity in the classroom for CLDS and ELLs. Like many children in the United States the students of RISD faced linguistic profiling and a hegemonic school curriculum (Meehan, 2013).

Despite the many years that have passed, the Castañeda children are still able to recall the emotions that CLDS and ELLs experience while in school. Pam and Kathy stress that while in school they felt that they were "not accepted or welcome and expressed some level of discomfort in relation to school" (Meehan, 2013, p. 140). Similarly, when Eloise, a former ELL student, was asked to recall her overall feelings about her early education, she shared, "I remember being afraid and thinking that I would really rather be at home" (Meehan, 2013, p. 19).

Teacher education programs can nurture pre-service teachers to exercise compassion with ELLs and urge them to consider not just the students' everyday academic struggles but to also acknowledge their social and emotional needs. According to Gorman (2010), "Belongingness is achieved through affiliation with a group, a process that is very much impacted by cultural values and beliefs about what is acceptable to the group" (p. 27).

Additionally, Gorman (2010) shares: "self-esteem is attained through recognition or achievement, both of which can only be attained through meeting, or exceeding, the expectations of society; expectations based on the values and beliefs determined by culture" (p. 27). When students feel a sense of belonging and have self-esteem, they are more likely to achieve.

According to Ferkany (2008), "self-esteem is importantly connected to the confidence and motivation children need in order to engage in and achieve educational goals and can and should be facilitated socially, i.e. not just, or even primarily, through the interactions between teacher and student, but between student and the social environment of the school itself" (p. 120).

Through the use of culturally relevant books, teachers can meet these significant needs (Rubie, Townsend, & Moore, 2004). Teachers not only affirm their students but also communicate that cultural identity and language backgrounds are not simply accepted but also valued. In addition to meeting ELLs' affective needs, culturally relevant texts have the potential to meet their cognitive needs as well.

Activating Prior Knowledge

The process of activating prior knowledge has been researched extensively, particularly in the field of literacy. According to Campbell and Campbell (2008) prior knowledge "is the raw material that conditions learning. It acts as mental hooks for the lodging of new information and is the basic building block of content and skill knowledge" (p. 9). Research indicates that activating prior knowledge has a positive effect on reading fluency and comprehension (Shapiro, 2004).

It is considered an instructional best practice for teachers to activate prior knowledge as an appropriate entry point for instruction. Teachers that use texts that mirror the lives of their ELL students will find that these students "can more easily construct meaning from a text that contains familiar elements because their background knowledge helps them make predictions and inferences about the story" (Freeman & Freeman, 2004, p. 7). Similarly, these students are able to picture the events read in stories because they have had similar situations in their own lives (Freeman & Freeman, 2004). The activation of prior knowledge can be particularly helpful in the development of language and literacy.

ELL students are confronted with multiple obstacles in the classroom. The ELL students' disconnect from the content being taught is two-fold. They face their language barrier and then they are further alienated by their unfamiliarity with the characters, themes, and experiences found within their texts.

According to Krashen (2008), language learners need learning experiences that are applicable to their real lives as well as have a need for sufficient exposure to comprehensible input. Krashen (2008) asserts that learning experiences should be interesting so that the learner is focused on the content rather than focused on the correctness of the language being used. It is through these learning experiences the learner will develop comprehensible input. This input will later facilitate the student to produce oral or written language.

Culturally relevant books can assist in exposing students to comprehensible input and serve as a medium for classroom instruction. Culturally relevant texts can function as the link between what students already know and new knowledge.

In addition to promoting language development, research indicates that culturally relevant books used within literacy instruction promote high achievement among culturally and linguistically diverse students (Gay, 2000; Ladson-Billings, 1994). Herrero's (2006) research indicates that using culturally relevant texts not only encourages student participation but also promotes success in specific reading tasks. In a more recent study, Ebe (2010) examined student reading proficiency levels by investigating miscue analysis and story retelling of culturally relevant texts compared to nonculturally relevant texts. Ebe (2010) found that

> When analyzing the retellings and the types of miscues participants made during the reading of the two stories, they were more proficient in their reading of the story they identified as being more culturally relevant. For example, the readers made more high quality miscues that made sense and were grammatically correct when reading the story to which they related. (p. 208)

It is evident that using culturally relevant books to activate student prior knowledge has incredible worth and results in a multitude of educational benefits. Despite these validations, culturally relevant books are not used enough in the classroom. It is up to schools of education and school districts to facilitate the use of culturally relevant books in the classroom.

FINAL THOUGHTS

Classroom teachers need to be equipped to create democratic classrooms with a culturally and linguistically responsive and inclusive curriculum (Gay, 2000). Schools of education need to coach pre-service teachers as well as in-service teachers on how to appropriately select and use culturally relevant books for instructional purposes. This knowledge can be incorporated into ESL certification programs, literacy methods courses, or into multicultural education classes. In doing so, graduates of such programs become critical, culturally responsive, and compassionate teachers.

REFERENCES

Bishop, R. S. (2012). Reflections on the development of African American children's literature. *Journal of Children's Literature, 38*(2), 5–13.

Campbell, M., & Campbell, B. (2008). *Mindful learning: 101 proven strategies for student and teacher success*. Thousand Oaks, CA: Corwin Press.

Castañeda v. Pickard, 648 F. 2d 989 (5th Cir. 1981).

Cowan Pitre, C. (2014). Improving African American student outcomes: Understanding educational achievement and strategies to close opportunity gaps. *The Western Journal of Black Studies, 38*(4), 209–17.

Cummins, J. (1996). *Negotiating identities: Education for empowerment in a diverse society*. Ontario, CA: California Association for Bilingual Education.

Delpit, L. (2012). *Multiplication is for white people: Raising expectations for other people's children*. New York: The New Press.

Ebe, A. (2010). Culturally relevant texts and reading assessment for English language learners. *Reading Horizons, 50*(3), 193–210.

Ferkany, M. (2008). The educational importance of self-esteem. *Journal of Philosophy of Education, 42*(1), 119–32.

Fountas, I. C., & Pinnell, G. S. (2006). *Teaching for comprehension and fluency: Thinking, talking, and writing about reading, K–8*. Portsmouth, NH: Heinemann.

Freeman, Y. (2000). *Considerations for the selection of culturally relevant text*. Unpublished article. University of Arizona, Tucson.

Freeman Y., & Freeman, D. (2004). Connecting students to culturally relevant texts. *Talking Points, 15*(2), 7–11.

Freeman, Y. S., Freeman, A., & Freeman, D. (2003). Home run books: Connecting students to culturally relevant texts. *NABE News, 26*(3), 5–12.

Gay, G. (2000). *Culturally responsive teaching: Theory, research, and practice*. New York: Teachers College Press.

Gay, G. (2002). Preparing for culturally responsive teaching. *Journal of Teacher Education, 53*(2), 106–16.

Gay, G. (2007). The importance of multicultural education. In A. C. Ornstein, E. F. Pajak, & S. B. Ornstein (Eds.), *Contemporary issues in curriculum* (4th ed., pp. 273–78). Boston: Allyn and Bacon.

Giroux, H. A. (1997). *Channel surfing: Racism, the media, and the destruction of today's youth*. New York: St. Martin's.

González, J. (2008). A brief history of bilingual education in the United States. In J. M Gonzalez (Ed.), *Encyclopedia of Bilingual Education* (pp. 545–49). Los Angeles, CA: Sage.

Gopalakrishnan, A. (2010). *Multicultural literature: A critical issues approach*. Thousand Oaks, CA: Sage Publications.

Gorman, D. (2010). Maslow's hierarchy and social and emotional wellbeing. *Aboriginal and Islander Health Worker Journal, 34*(1), 27–29.

Herrero, E. A. (2006). Using Dominican oral literature and discourse to support literacy learning among low-achieving students from the Dominican Republic. *International Journal of Bilingual Education & Bilingualism, 9*(2), 219–32.

Hunsberger, P. (2007). Where am I? A call for connectedness in literacy. *Reading Research Quarterly, 42*(3), 420–24.

Krashen, S. D. (2008). Language education: Past, present, and future. *Regional Language Centre Journal, 39*(2), 178–87.

Ladson-Billings, G. (1994). *The dreamkeepers: Successful teachers of African American children*. San Francisco, CA: Jossey-Bass.

Lynch-Brown, C., & Tomlinson, C. M. (1999). *Essentials of children's literature*. Boston: Allyn and Bacon.

Meehan, J. P. (2013). Castañeda v. Pickard: *The struggle for an equitable education: One family's experience with resistance* (Doctoral dissertation). Retrieved from proquest. (3593319).

Menken, K. (2009). No child left behind and its effects on language policy. *Annual Review of Applied Linguistics, 29*, 103–17. doi: 10.1017/S0267190509090096.

Mitchell, D. (2003). *Children's literature: An invitation to the world.* Boston: Allyn and Bacon.

National Assessment of Educational Report. (2013). *A first look: 2013 mathematics and reading* (NCES-2014 451). Washington, DC: U.S. Department of Education.

New York Department of Education. (2013). *Office of English language learners 2013 demographic report.* New York: New York City Department of Education's Division of Students with Disabilities and English Language Learners.

Robledo, B. (2013). The importance of preparing teachers for vulnerable populations. *Harvard Journal of Hispanic Policy, 25*, 97–115.

Rodríguez, A. D. (2009). Culturally relevant books: Connecting Hispanic students to the curriculum. *GiST Colombian Journal of Bilingual Education, 3*, 11–29.

Rubie, C. M., Townsend M., & Moore, D. (2004). Motivational and academic effects of cultural experiences for indigenous minority students in New Zealand. *Educational Psychology, 24*(2), 143–60. doi: 10.1080/0144341032000160119.

Ruiz Soto, A. G., Hooker, S., & Batalova, J. (2015). *States and districts with the highest number and share of English language learners.* Washington, DC: Migration Policy Institute.

Shapiro, A. (2004). How including prior knowledge as a subject variable may change outcomes of learning research. *American Educational Research Journal, 41*(1), 159–89.

Teale, W. (2009). Students learning English and their literacy instruction in urban schools. *Urban Literacy, 62*(8), 699–703. doi: 10.1598/RT.62.8.9.

Texas Education Agency. (2009). *Enrollment in Texas public schools, 2008-09* (Document No. GE10 601 02). Austin TX: Author.

Wright, W. (2010). *Foundations for teaching English language learners: Research, theory, policy, and practice.* Philadelphia: Caslon, Inc.

Chapter Ten

Moving beyond Apartheid Schooling and "Adequate Education"

Empowering the Minoritized through Critical Media Literacy

Elena M. Venegas

Though the passage of the Civil Rights Act of 1964 outlawed discrimination based on race, color, religion, sex, and/or national origin, contemporary society within the United States is all but free from discrimination. The Supreme Court *Brown v. Board of Education* (1954) ruling and other landmark legislation passed during the Civil Rights Movement pushed our country toward a path of tolerance and the end of discrimination. Yet, despite these tremendous gains, discrimination still occurs not only at a societal level, but also in terms of schooling (Bakari, 2003; Ferguson, 2003; Harris & Schroeder, 2013; Mackinney & Rios-Aguilar, 2012.)

Through critical media literacy, youth—particularly those who are minoritized—can be participatory in debunking discriminatory rhetoric. Critical media literacy provides youth the skills to combat marginalizing societal norms by equipping them with the tools necessary to create a counternarrative to discriminatory practices.

This chapter will expose discriminatory educational policies and practices that stand to make U.S. schooling highly detrimental for minoritized student populations as well as give examples of how to use critical media literacy to empower minoritized students.

APARTHEID SCHOOLING AND AN "ADEQUATE EDUCATION"

Within the United States, groups who share a particular racial identity have often been subjected to prejudicial treatment in both law and practice. However, race is a social—not biological—construct (Coates, 2013). The term *minoritized* refers to such groups who are socially subjected to deferential treatment (Benitez, 2010). In the United States, people identifying as Asian American, Black, Latino, Native American, and Pacific Islander comprise racially minoritized groups (Stewart, 2013).

Despite a national history of minoritizing various groups of people through colonization and proselytizing, many Americans claim that the contemporary United States is devoid of racism (Wise, 2011). Some may consider the election and reelection of Barack Obama, the first African American president in U.S. history, as evidence of "living in a post-racial society"; however, this is simply not the case. Voter identification laws, for example, are veiled attempts at once again limiting the voting rights of minoritized groups (Childress, 2014).

The Supreme Court's *Shelby County v. Holder* (2013) ruling inherently nullified the Voting Rights Act of 1965. Consequently, many of the states and counties previously under the jurisdiction of the Voting Rights Act of 1965 have enacted voter identification laws. Supporters claim such laws prevent voting fraud, yet they are intended to prevent people of low socioeconomic status, racially minoritized groups, college students, and women from voting (Childress, 2014).

The enactment of voter identification laws illustrates that we are in fact not living in a post-racial society. Author and anti-racism activist Tim Wise refers to the notion that racism in our contemporary society has been eradicated as "Racism 2.0" (Wise, 2009). Racism 2.0 refers to white supremacist notions that undergird our "post-racial" society. Unfortunately, many current educational policies and practices illustrate the prevalence of Racism 2.0.

Public schools are becoming increasingly racially segregated (Rothstein, 2013), and linguistically minoritized students are neglected in terms of differentiation. For example, English learners in Texas and Massachusetts are denied accommodations on the state exit-level standardized exam (Texas Education Agency, 2010; Massachusetts Department of Elementary and Secondary Education, 2015).

Some U.S. neighborhoods and school districts stand in stark contrast to the societal advancements toward eradicating prejudicial policies and practices made during the Civil Rights Movement. *Brown v. Board of Education* (1954) was monumental in that it mandated the integration of U.S. public schools. Conversely, educational activist Jonathan Kozol (2005) asserted that many schools operate under the antiquated U.S. Supreme Court *Plessy v.*

Ferguson (1896) ruling, which stated that whites and non-whites are to be separate but equal.

Apartheid schools have come into being as a result of white flight, inequitable school funding, and increased accountability standards. Kozol (2005) coined the term *apartheid schools* to refer to the many low socioeconomic, "failing" schools composed of a 90 to 100 percent non-white student body. Students attending apartheid schools are often taught by teachers lacking full certification, receive fewer curricular and extracurricular resources and opportunities, and attend school in unsafe and unsanitary conditions.

Parents of students attending apartheid schools, concerned citizens, and educational activists have worked to make them more equitable. Though the plaintiffs of many court cases have worked to improve the state of apartheid schools, courts have responded by stating that education is not a constitutional right and students are entitled only to an "adequate education." An adequate education is defined as: "the preparation of students to function productively as capable voters, jurors, and citizens of a democratic society and to be able to compete effectively in the economy" (Nelson, Palonsky, & McCarthy, 2013, p. 74). However, an adequate education does not suffice to truly prepare low socioeconomic and other minoritized students for academic and vocational success.

Minoritized students are not only subjected to poor school conditions and novice teachers, but also frequently receive the brunt of stereotypic ideologies from those who are supposed to educate them (Ferguson, 2003). Teachers are prone to harboring racial bias (Ferguson, 2003). Perceptual bias refers to the tendency of teachers to evaluate students based on their preconceptions of their students (St. C. Oates, 2003).

Unfortunately, teachers' descriptions of the ideal student do not match their characterizations of Black students (Bakari, 2003). Consequently, teachers often negatively perceive racially minoritized students, evaluate them in accordance with stereotypic beliefs, and subsequently fail to empower these students for success both in and out of the classroom.

The consequences of minoritizing racially and linguistically diverse students speak to limited opportunities for success. Non-white students, particularly Blacks, are overrepresented in special education (Taylor & Whittaker, 2009). Whereas non-white students disproportionately comprise the number of students enrolled in special education, Black and Brown children are vastly underrepresented in Gifted & Talented and enrichment programs (Taylor & Whittaker, 2009). Black and Latino students are negatively represented at both ends of the achievement spectrum, and the opportunities of linguistically diverse students are also hindered.

Aside from limiting educational opportunities to minoritized students, policymakers have attempted to suppress students' language and culture. Many of these policies are enacted under a deficiency orientation, which negatively views persons who do not conform to the dominant language or culture (Harris & Schroeder, 2013).

Arizona is one of five states with the highest concentrations of English learners (ELs), yet has enacted restrictive language policies in its schools such as mandating content to be taught in English only as well as for EL students to read and write only in English (Mackinney & Rios-Aguilar, 2012). These policies limit ELs by refusing to capitalize on their first language literacy.

The consequences of deficiency-oriented language policies are particularly evident in secondary schools. ELs must demonstrate their academic competence on state standardized tests to graduate. Expectedly, many ELs lack the language proficiency to demonstrate their academic knowledge on standardized assessments given only in English. Though demonstrating their academic aptitude in their coursework, some ELs become so discouraged by their failure to pass the exit-level state standardized assessment that instead of becoming high school graduates they become high school dropouts (Valenzuela, 2000).

In response to the current societal and educational policies designed to hinder participation in exercising one's citizenship as well as opportunities for educational and vocational success of minoritized people, critical media literacy provides a means for raising awareness of such issues.

As activist Tim Wise asserts, it no longer suffices to simply raise awareness of discriminatory practices—people must also write a counternarrative to current socially unjust practices (Wise, 2011). Critical media literacy enables both minoritized students and students wanting to change discriminatory policies and practices to author such a counternarrative.

CRITICAL MEDIA LITERACY

Media literacy is the ability to access, analyze, evaluate, and create media messages (Schwarz, 2014). In the contemporary United States, media saturates our society. Though quite often media are approached with an uncritical eye, educator Marshall McLuhan famously stated, "The media is the message" (McLuhan, 2003). McLuhan's quote is rich because it asserts that media are not neutral but rather that all media exist to communicate a message, whether or not the audience is privy.

As educators, media literacy is of the utmost importance because we must not only prepare students to think critically about the various media they encounter each day but also help students further develop their literacy as the nature of literacy continues to evolve in the twenty-first century. The Common Core State Standards for English/Language Arts may be addressed through media literacy (Common Core State Standards Initiative, n.d.).

Media literacy presents an engaging and interesting alternative to more conventional pedagogical approaches. Apart from addressing curriculum standards, teaching media literacy to students is imperative because their lives are inundated with media. Today's students readily access print, social media, websites, television, radio, and films both inside and outside of school.

Media literacy education empowers individuals so that they no longer passively receive media messages (Considine, Horton, & Moorman, 2009). Rather, media literacy requires examining an author/producer as well as his or her purpose for communicating. Through media literacy, the choice of medium is also analyzed in terms of not only how it facilitates communication but also in terms of how the chosen medium contributes to the message because as McLuhan (2003) asserted the medium and the message are inextricably intertwined.

The impact of the message on the audience is analyzed along with the author's credibility and the various means by which the message may be interpreted. Media-literate students become critical of media messages that they encounter meanwhile gaining necessary skills for English/Language arts. For example, through their analysis of media messages students begin to understand important writing concepts such as: understanding the author's purpose, writing for an audience, and using persuasive rhetorical devices. They can then begin to author their own media messages, which can further a counternarrative to racism, discrimination, and prejudice.

Critical media literacy involves the critique of media messages particularly in regard to portrayals of race, class, gender, sexual orientation, and power in media (Kellner & Share, 2007). As previously mentioned, media are not without bias. Thus, advertent or inadvertent messages that are prejudicial or seek to minoritize others can be communicated to respective audiences. Kellner and Share (2007), however, hold that media can be a tool of empowerment through which minoritized groups can express their concerns.

The Black Lives Matter movement that arose in response to the tragic and controversial murder of Trayvon Martin in 2012 is just one example of critical media literacy in action. Advocates of this movement brandished the hashtag #BlackLivesMatter and engaged in critical conversations about the minoritizing of Blacks in the United States via social media sites such as Twitter, Facebook, and Instagram.

Though the Black Lives Matter movement grew organically this does not mean that critical media literacy is beyond the scope of our nation's schools. Critical media literacy, in fact, is an avenue by which teachers can seek to empower all students, but especially minoritized students to express their concerns about current prejudicial and discriminatory practices that affect their daily lives.

EMPOWERING MINORITIZED STUDENTS THROUGH CRITICAL MEDIA LITERACY

As previously mentioned, media literacy education can be used to creatively and engagingly address Common Core Standards. Whereas media literacy education as a whole engages people in critical analysis of media messages, teachers can foster a more democratic classroom as well as engage students in praxis through critical media literacy.

Critical Media Literacy as Praxis

Brazilian educator and activist Paulo Freire is a strong proponent of a demo-cratic education, which entails the teacher and students being coauthors of learning. As co-learners the teacher and students dialogue and engage in problem-posing education, which requires individuals to critically think about a real-world issue and actually seek to resolve the issue through praxis, which is reflection and action on a real-world problem (Freire, 2014).

Critical media literacy, in particular, allows educators to engage their students in problem-posing education. Through critical media literacy educa-tion, students participate in a democratic education by actively discussing why a media message may be alienating as well as how it contributes to the minoritizing of others. Subsequently, students and teachers engage in praxis as they begin to create their own media messages of empowerment.

Critical Media Literacy in Action

A prime opportunity exists for students to engage in critical media literacy through the intersection of English/language arts and social studies learning. Upper-elementary and middle school students, for example, can make cross-curricular connections by examining media from the Civil Rights Movement. In particular, students can listen to Dr. Martin Luther King Jr.'s speech at the conclusion of the march from Selma to Montgomery on March 25, 1965. Students might also watch the award-winning 2014 motion picture titled *Selma* (Winfrey, Gardner, Kleiner, & Colson, 2014), which portrayed events leading up to the march, including Bloody Sunday.

Dr. King and other Civil Rights leaders organized the march to draw attention to the egregious denial of Blacks' constitutional right to vote in many southern states. Students can analyze Dr. King's speech for its content, the rhetorical devices that he employs, as well as how the utilization of audio recording influenced the message or audience.

Students can then analyze media messages from today's contemporary political arena concerning voter identifications laws. Once analyzing both sides of the spectrum, students can then take a position and create their own media messages (e.g., website, Tweet, Instagram, infographic, public service announcement, meme, etc.) by which to convince their fellow Americans of their viewpoint.

Many elementary students enjoy popular films produced by the Walt Disney Company. Some of these beloved children's films present a prime opportunity for engaging young children in critical media literacy. For example, the film *Peter Pan* (Disney, 1953) features a song titled "What Makes the Red Man Red?" The song portrays Native Americans in a stereotypical manner, and they are referred to as "savages" by the film's characters. Teachers can use *Peter Pan* (1953) in teaching critical media literacy by asking children to describe the characteristics that the filmmakers attribute to Native Americans.

Children can then compare the negative portrayal of Native Americans in the film to a more accurate portrayal in *Greet the Dawn: The Lakota Way* (Nelson, 2012). The teacher and students can then discuss how they would rather be portrayed—in a manner that pokes fun at their cultures or in a manner that showcases how their cultural heritage and the larger American culture intermingle.

Though some may claim that *Peter Pan* (1953) is outdated, Disney again portrayed Native Americans as savages (either noble or ignoble) in the film *Pocahontas* (Pentecost, 1995). *Pocahontas* (1995) presents an opportunity to discuss cultural invasion, and teachers can supplement this discussion with a reading of *Fatty Legs: A True Story* (Jordan-Fenton & Pokiak-Fenton, 2010). In *Fatty Legs*, the main character is a Native American girl who realizes that her education is meant to strip her of culture. Again, elementary teachers can use *Pocahontas* (1995) and *Fatty Legs* (2010) to discuss minoritization of racially and ethnically diverse people.

In encouraging students to participate in praxis, elementary teachers can have their students brainstorm ways in which they want to change the portrayal of Native Americans in popular culture. For example, students may choose to write to the Walt Disney Company to discuss the importance of portraying diverse cultural heritages in a culturally affirming and accurate manner.

During the month of November, which is Native American Heritage Month, students may elect to host an event in which they educate the community on the importance of resisting cultural invasion and appreciating diverse cultures.

Elementary students in particular can watch a popular film such as *Remember the Titans* (Bruckheimer & Oman, 2000), which showcases racial tension on a fictional 1960s-era football team. After watching the film, the students can discuss how Blacks were minoritized during and before the Civil Rights era. A reading of the daily newspaper or watching of an evening television news program will undoubtedly reveal that racial tension still exists in the United States.

The teacher and students can then dialogue about ways in which the United States has changed and areas in which improvement is still needed in terms of eradicating prejudice and discrimination.

A viewing of a family-friendly popular movie set in the Civil Rights era as well as an examination of contemporary race-related issues provides the perfect avenue for not only engaging in critical media literacy, but also living out the democratic educational experience. Elementary students can author their own media messages about an issue of importance to them to counter narratives promoting inequality and discrimination.

IMPLICATIONS

Unfortunately, minoritized students are viewed as "others" within the dominant U.S. society. Critical media literacy is a means by which educators can not only equip diverse students with the English/Language Arts skills necessary for academic success but also empower traditionally marginalized students to create a counternarrative to a narrative of oppression.

As educator Paulo Freire asserts, the oppressed must institute praxis—reflection and action—to not only liberate themselves but also their oppressors (Freire, 2014). Critical media literacy allows traditionally marginalized students to exercise praxis as they seek to better our contemporary society—both for themselves and for the nation as a whole.

There are several practical implications for educators. The first is being aware of potential bias against those who identify as a different race, ethnicity, religion, sexual orientation, etc. As several studies referenced in this chapter suggest, educators are prone to bias, and it is important to have this awareness to guide interactions with one's students, families, and colleagues.

Another practical implication is that educators need to be mindful of the educational resources that they use in their classrooms. An educator should preview each resource before using it with his or her students and ask himself or herself how others may perceive that material. This is an opportunity for the educator to engage in media literacy himself or herself in contemplating what perspectives are left out and what are the (c)overt messages communicated through the medium.

Perhaps the greatest implication is to foster a democratic education by involving even young children in praxis through encouraging them to identify real-world problems of importance to them as well as take steps to actually make changes.

REFERENCES

Bakari, R. (2003). Preservice teachers' attitudes toward teaching African American students. *Urban Education, 38*(6), 640–54.

Benitez, M., Jr. (2010). Resituating culture centers within a social justice framework: Is there room for examining Whiteness? In L. D. Patton (Ed.), *Culture centers in higher education: Perspectives on identity, theory, and practice* (pp. 119–34). Sterling, VA: Stylus.

Brown v. Board of Education of Topeka, Opinion; May 17, 1954. Records of the Supreme Court of the United States, Record Group 267. National Archives.

Bruckheimer, J., & Oman, C. (Producers), & Yakin, B. (Director). (2000). *Remember the titans* [Motion picture]. United States: Walt Disney Pictures.

Childress, S. (2014, October 20). Why voter ID laws aren't really about fraud. Retrieved from http://www.pbs.org/wgbh/pages/frontline/government-elections-politics/why-voter-id-laws-arent-really-about-fraud/.

Coates, T. (2013, May 15). What we mean when we say "Race is a social construct." Retrieved from http://www.theatlantic.com/national/archive/2013/05/what-we-mean-when-we-say-race-is-a-social-construct/275782/.

Common Core State Standards Initiative. (n.d). Common Core State Standards for English language arts & literacy in history/social studies, science, and technical subjects. Retrieved from http://www.corestandards.org/wp-content/uploads/ELA_Standards.pdf.

Considine, D., Horton, J., & Moorman, G. (2009). Teaching and reading the millennial generation through media literacy. *Journal of Adolescent & Adult Literacy, 52*(6), 471–81.

Disney, W. (Producer), & Geronimi, C., Jackson, W, & Luske, H. (Directors). (1953). *Peter Pan* [Motion picture]. United States: Walt Disney Productions.

Ferguson, R. F. (2003). Teachers' perceptions and expectations and the Black-White test score gap. *Urban Education, 38*(4), 460–507.

Freire, P. (2014). *Pedagogy of the oppressed*. New York: Bloomsbury Academic.

Harris, Y. R., & Schroeder, V. M. (2013). Language deficits or differences: What we know about African American Vernacular English in the 21st century. *International Education Studies, 6*(4), 194–204. http://dx.doi.org/10.5539/ies.v6n4p194.

Jordan-Fenton, C., & Pokiak-Fenton, M. (2010). *Fatty Legs: A true story*. Toronto, Canada: Annick Press.

Kellner, D., & Share, J. (2007). Critical media literacy, democracy, and the reconstruction of education. In D. Macedo & S. R. Steinberg (Eds.), *Media literacy: A reader* (pp. 3–23). New York: Peter Lang Publishing.

Kozol, J. (2005). *The shame of the nation: The restoration of apartheid schooling in America*. New York: Broadway Paperbacks.

Mackinney, E., & Rios-Aguilar, C. (2012). Negotiating between restrictive language policies and complex teaching conditions: A case study of Arizona's teachers on English learners. *Bilingual Research Journal, 35*(3), 350–67. http://dx.doi.org/10.1080/15235882.2012.734545.

Massachusetts Department of Elementary and Secondary Education. (2015). *Requirements for the participation of English Language Learners in ACCESS for ELLs 2.0, MCAS, and PARCC: A guide for educators and parents/guardians*. Malden, MA: Massachusetts Department of Elementary and Secondary Education.

McLuhan, M. (2003). *Understanding media: The extensions of man, critical edition*. W. T. Gordon (Ed.). Berkeley, CA: Gingko Press, Inc.

Nelson, J. L., Palonsky, S., & McCarthy, M. R. (2013). Financing schools: Equity or privilege? In *Critical issues in education: Dialogues and dialectics* (8th ed.). New York: The McGraw-Hill Companies, Inc.

Nelson, S. D. (2012). *Greet the dawn: The Lakota way*. Pierre, SD: South Dakota State Historical Society.

Pentecost, J. (Producer), & Gabriel, M. & Goldberg, E. (Directors). (1995). *Pocahontas* [Motion picture]. United States: Walt Disney Pictures.

Plessy v. Ferguson, Opinion; May 18, 1896. Records of the Supreme Court of the United States, Record Group 267. National Archives.

Rothstein, R. (2013). Why our schools are segregated. *Faces of Poverty, 70*(8), 50–55.

Schwarz, G. (2014). *Rhetoric in a new key: Media literacy education for the twenty-first-century university*. In B. De Abreu & P. Mihailidis (Eds.), *Media literacy education in action* (pp. 213–18). New York: Routledge.

Shelby County v. Holder, Opinion; June 25, 2013. Records of the Supreme Court of the United States, Record Group 193. National Archives.

St. C. Oates, G. L. (2003). Teacher-student racial congruence, teacher perceptions, and test performance. *Social Science Quarterly, 84*(3), 508–25.

Stewart, D. (2013). Racially minoritized students at U.S. four-year institutions. *Journal of Negro Education, 82*(2), 184–97.

Taylor, L. S., & Whittaker, C. R. (2009). *Bridging multiple worlds: Case studies of diverse educational communities* (2nd ed.). New York: Pearson.

Texas Education Agency. (2010). English Language Learners (ELLs) and the State of Texas Assessments of Academic Readiness (STAAR) program. *House Bill 3 Transition Plan*, pp. I-67–I-74.

Valenzuela, A. (2000). The significance of the TAAS test for Mexican immigrant and Mexican American adolescents: A case study. *Hispanic Journal of Behavioral Sciences, 22*(4), 524–39.

Winfrey, O., Gardner, D., Kleiner, J., & Colson, C. (Producers) & DuVernay, A. (Director). (2014). *Selma* [Motion picture]. United States: Paramount.

Wise, T. (2009). *Between Barack and a hard place: Racism and White denial in the age of Obama*. San Francisco, CA: City Lights Publishers.

Wise, T. (2011). *White like me: Reflections on race from a privileged son*. Berkeley, CA: Soft Skull Press.

Chapter Eleven

"Started from the Bottom Now We Here"

Helping Educators to Empower Urban Students about Their Futures by Liberating Them from Cultural Past

Lakia M. Scott and Marcia Watson

This chapter will discuss the historical and contemporary contexts of education for African American students most recently highlighted and based on a song from a contemporary rap artist. Students will be reminded that adversity continues to serve as a motivating factor to achieve success, access, and opportunity.

In recognition that negative teacher perceptions, issues of racial identity, and self-concept impact how education is prescribed for African Americans, the authors will argue that urban youth should see their academic potential and success through the realization that the life history of our people have been premised in achieving against the odds.

The chapter will briefly highlight the historical importance of education as an act of emancipation by reviewing educated societies in early African civilizations and then lead into a discussion on the emergence of Black education institutions as a source of education for freedom.

Next, three imperatives for empowering Black students about their own education will be provided; these include: (1) the reteaching of Black history; (2) using relevant Black curriculum as a core tenet to learning; and (3) increasing the academic expectations of African American students through the affirmation of positive self-concept.

"STARTED FROM THE BOTTOM NOW WE HERE": HELPING EDUCATORS TO EMPOWER URBAN STUDENTS ABOUT THEIR FUTURES BY LIBERATING THEM FROM CULTURAL PAST

In 2013, contemporary rap artist Drake released a single that captivated radio airways and music media stations. "Started from the Bottom" highlights the lyricist's virtual "come-up" through the music industry. On a fast track to fame, Drake compares being at the "bottom" before stardom, to finally being "here": after hard work.

Reaching measurable financial success and fame, the message of resiliency in this song serves as a permeating drumbeat for contemporary urban youth. Truth is the ancestral lineage of African Americans within the United States who started from the bottom. The proverbial reference to "started from the bottom" references the history of a group of people uprooted from continental Africa for slavery and indentured servitude.

During slavery, reading was prohibited and African Americans were denied access to education. The historical atrocity of slavery later served as a catalyst for revolutionary figures in African American history to fight for education and freedom. Historically, education has been used for liberation and emancipation.

Historical figures such as Frederick Douglass, Harriet Jacobs, Malcolm X, Joycelyn Elders, Gwendolyn Parker, Don L. Lee, Septima Clark, Ben Carson, and Maya Angelou each started from the bottom and used education—specifically literacy—for social mobility. These models serve as historical reminders of resiliency in African Americans' quest to acquire education. Although unrecognized by many students, African Americans in a contemporary sense are now "here." The fight for freedom, equality, and educational access has been fought. Now what?

Throughout this chapter, song lyrics will be used abstractly as a guide to show the twenty-first-century relevancy of the phrase "started from the bottom." Using coupled stanzas as prequels to each section, the lyrics are purposefully placed to match each section's theme. In addition, the incorporation of the song lyrics hopes to demonstrate the connection between historical and contemporary educational victories. Just as the hip-hop song serves as the drumbeat in today's pop culture, the authors hope to demonstrate how the struggle for educational freedom has served as the drumbeat of equality for centuries.

HISTORICAL AND CONTEMPORARY CONTEXT OF EDUCATION FOR AFRICAN AMERICANS

The history of education for Blacks since the Reconstruction Period is one that is complex in nature; however, what is easy to understand is the continual denigration of educational opportunity that carries on to present day. Anderson (1988) begins an elaborate discussion that predates this period on how slaves sought education as the key to their freedom and liberation. This was done many times in secret; slaves would teach each other how to read and write in the late hours after their work of tilling fields and manual labor was done.

He extends the discussion about their educational pursuits after the Reconstruction Period as still trying to attain educational opportunity through schooling, specifically through Sabbath schools and other independent Black institutions. However, there were many debates as to how Whites would view this surge in education; mainly, Northerners saw this as an opportunity to produce a worker class that would understand their societal roles and conform to racial subordination. On the other hand, Southerners opposed the push for former slaves to be educated because they felt it would create tension among menial jobs that were designated for Blacks.

Eventually, universal education provided former slaves with educational "opportunity," but Anderson (1988) reminds us that Northern philanthropy was of false benevolence and that Blacks were educating their own children (as teachers and administrators) long before bureaucratic influences of developing school infrastructures and funding were factors to contribute to Black education.

These conceptions of race and its impact on education can be translated to present day as well. For public schooling, these issues are present through property taxation. Meyer (2000) provides a historical account of racial discrimination against Blacks in the form of property ownership. Blacks faced many hardships during the Great Depression and World War II eras with securing homes and jobs. White property owners would physically and mentally harass Blacks so that their neighborhoods could remain White.

This relegated many of the living spaces for Blacks to impoverished neighborhoods where crime, diseases, and dilapidated infrastructures all posed threats to their safety. Lipman (2004) also provides insight that gentrification in urban meccas such as Chicago continue to stratify educational opportunities for Blacks. She discusses how standardized testing provides justification to fail Black students and limit their resources at underperforming schools.

Kozol (2005) adds to the discussion that the conditions of schooling for Blacks in inner-city schools in New York are unbearable. The educational environment for Black students explicitly demonstrates racial disparities and implicitly communicates to students that they are not valued as contributing members of society, but rather second-class citizens that will always be considered working class.

Darling-Hammond (2010) provides impetus for financial resources to be allocated to schools that need additional support with educating students and evenly appropriating high-quality teachers throughout the district to increase student academic outcomes. Additionally she asserts that if measures such as these are taken into consideration, educators can harness equitable educational opportunities for all students to pass standardized tests while still providing relevant curriculum and pedagogy.

Within the context of the United States after Emancipation, education has been consistently used as a tool for freedom and opportunity, especially for African Americans. However, this triumphant past is negated in history books (such as the slaves' rebellion or freedom fighters like the Maroons) or relegated to a coincidence such as the common misconception that Rosa Parks, a Civil Rights activist, refused to give up her seat on the bus simply because she was tired of being on her feet all day.

As a result, many students do not see education as a liberating agent for increasing their social mobility. Although historical qualms depict African Americans as between the extremes of subservient or rebellious, our delicate, yet complicated past is actually a culmination of both. And as it relates to twenty-first-century students, it is necessary to share these historical pasts as a means to guide students' future aspirations. A closer look at the notion of resiliency is conceptualized in the next section.

Resiliency: A Continued Trait in Black Students

The term *resilience* is not new in referencing the tenacity of African American families, and in particular, traditionally marginalized student populations. Merriam-Webster (2013) provides two definitions for resilience: (1) the capability of a strained body to recover its size and shape after deformation caused especially by compressive stress; and (2) an ability to recover from or adjust easily to misfortune or change. In both contexts of the term, resiliency is the embodiment which has continued to propel African American students in achieving educational outcomes.

Since the 1970s, this term has been used to describe characteristics of perseverance for children from impoverished or low-income backgrounds. Recent studies continue to examine students that are labeled "at-risk," "damaged," or "poverty-stricken" and find that although students are aware of their circumstances, they still overcome nearly impossible obstacles and are able to achieve academic success (Francois, Overstreet, & Cunningham, 2011; Marsh, Chaney, & Jones, 2012).

Francois and colleagues (2011) examined the impact of exposure to community violence on academic performance. Using questionnaires to gauge the experiences of approximately 200 high school students from low-income neighborhoods, researchers found that even when students face exposure to negative environments such as criminal activities and violence, those who are involved in positive, community-based settings (such as recreational facilities, religious affiliations, traditional centers, or nontraditional facilities), they have better academic outcomes in school.

Additionally, Marsh and colleagues (2012) conducted a study to examine how Black high-achieving high school students in racially diverse academic environments navigated through racially integrated settings. They found that regardless of the setting where they experienced isolation and separation from affinity groups and social clubs in the school, students resisted their initial feelings of apprehension and worked resiliently to achieve academic success.

Based on these findings, it can be concluded that even under dire situations and daily circumstances, African American students have been known (historically and contemporarily) to overcome such obstacles to achieve their academic goals.

Factors that Impede African American Student Achievement

Negative perceptions about African American students and their ancestral roots are one of the chief factors that impact African American student achievement. Traore and Lukens (2006) discuss perceptions that African American students have on African immigrants and the perceptions that immigrants have on American students.

Their research is telling of the misconceptions and negative perceptions of Africa, language, the role of education in public schools, and the collective identity of African-born and American-born Black students. As a way to build community, the researchers employed Afrocentric curriculum to student learning; this yielded highly positive results and concluding perceptions about each cultural group.

Additionally, teacher perceptions also serve as a detriment to the learning potential of students. Kozol (2005) discusses how the structural inequalities and teacher perspectives of Black students also contribute to the negative perceptions and their resulting juxtaposition as second-class citizens in society.

Steinburg and Kincheloe (2004) provide introductory chapters that define an urban student and common perceptions about them. They elaborate on the stigma that urban students are from poor, Black, unintelligible, defiant, lower-class families. These perceptions are further heightened by their teachers and school administrators.

Ogbu (1978) also discusses the oppositional identity theory in which students depict learning and academically achieving as "acting White" and failing or dropping out of school as "acting Black." However, Wiggan (2008) quickly debunks this theory with his notion toward an engagement theory in which high-achieving students are the subjects of research as well as the voice as impetus for increasing urban student outcomes.

IMPERATIVES FOR ACADEMIC POTENTIAL AND SUCCESS

Education as an Act of Freedom

Na'im Akbar's emancipatory work *Know Thy Self* (1998) explains the benefits of personal, introspective education. Through internally realigning history and miseducation, Akbar describes a personal journey toward education as an act of freedom. Although many historical figures predate Akbar, his urgent push toward emancipatory education, centering "self" as the focal point for personal and social mobility, was paramount to his work.

Frederick Douglass, Harriet Jacobs, Malcolm X, Joycelyn Elders, Gwendolyn Parker, Don L. Lee, Septima Clark, Ben Carson, and Maya Angelou are just some of the examples of Black excellence, where literacy was seen as a liberation in the face of the oppressor (Perry, Steele, & Hilliard, 2003). Iconic figures, such as Malcolm X for example, document literacy as the catalyst for personal change. Their educational attainment was merely a reflection of the sacrifice of slaves risking their lives for educational freedom. Some of the risks and triumphs of Black education are accurately depicted by Anderson (1988).

This need for critical consciousness is not exclusive to African Americans. In fact, an entire theoretical framework centers on the need to critically examine the educational point of praxis, or change that causes liberation and mobilization. Pablo Friere (1970), a seminal critical theorist, discusses the "banking" model of education in which students are seen as empty vessels that teachers deposit and then withdraw information from.

Sadly, this popular educational practice is still used today. However, as Freire urges, this further alienates students from their learning. He asserts that only through dialogic interaction between the teacher and the student will reflection and examination of social/political/economic forms of control push for liberation of the oppressed. He also contends that liberation and social agency from oppressive forces should not be based on charity, but through an effort of solidarity for social change.

Additionally, Ladson-Billings (1994), Delpit (2006), and Gay (2000) push for culturally relevant teaching and pedagogy. This takes the critical lens popularized by Freire and intertwines the delicate relations of race, ethnicity, and cultural value. Loosely defined, this involves learning that is centered on providing meaningful curriculum and instruction for students. In this model, students reactivate their prior knowledge and experiences to make connections in learning.

Further, in this model, multiple perspectives are encouraged to foster learning. Culturally relevant pedagogy and teaching also involves allowing students to examine the social, political, economic, and cultural implications of society. In a contemporary sense, education as an act of freedom for the twenty-first-century student must intermingle this critical lens, specifically the value of education.

Reteaching Black History

From its inception, education was defined to "bring forth or bring up," stemming from the Latin word *educare* (Akbar, 1998, p. 1). Every culture has recognized the importance of education in the human condition. In addition to the aforementioned need for personal reflexivity in education, Akbar (1998) also uncovers some cultural importance that must be regained by humanity, especially the knowledge removed from Blacks' education. Omitted and committed curriculum falsities have irreversibly damaged education, both for members of the hegemonic "norm" and for others, such as African American students.

The coined term *curriculum violence* refers to "the deliberate manipulation of academic programming" in a manner that ignores or compromises "the intellectual and psychological" well-being of learners (Ighodaro & Wiggan, 2011, p. 2). Akbar (1998) assures there has to be the restoration of a child's ethnic greatness, as all European-descendent children are afforded. As a people, there must be an acknowledgment of the "African self," which encourages "self-knowledge." A child that engages in self-knowledge does not practice what Westernized education would acknowledge as an "ego"; rather, learning about oneself is put into holistic perspective.

Joyce King's *Black Education* critically examines the need for transformative education, which aims to dismantle oppression and liberate communities of people of African descent. This is not to be confused with elitism or cultural segregation. However, many of the same educational principles currently taught using Eurocentric paradigms could be better taught using African models.

As Akbar (1998) also suggests, the Kemetic principles and original teachings should be acknowledged as the founding beginnings of education. Both of these authors recognize a need for praxis in American schools, starting with a recentralization of Black people to their origin—Africa.

Undoubtedly, history has shown that Africans have valued education throughout history. Perry and colleagues (2003) show historical examples of generations of scholarship. Likewise, Peter Murrell (2002) details his journey toward African praxis and liberation through pedagogy. He also recognized the importance of education to African Americans. He notes, "Two major themes in the Black cultural experience that are central to education—double vision/consciousness and resistance through which achievement is realized" (Murrell, 2002, p. 5).

It should be noted, however, that students of African descendent are no less capable or intelligent. It is the American system of schools that has failed many of them. Furthermore, it should also be noted that intelligence is a created term with little scientific value.

A reoccurring theme throughout educational research is the importance of good teachers. However, a critical need within Black education is teachers who promote and challenge students to *excellence*, versus simply attaining hegemonic achievement measures. Meaning, the goal for all who teach African children should be to raise the level by which we measure their success.

As Asa Hilliard reiterates, the mythical "achievement gap" is based on false pretenses where "white America" is the measure for achievement. Instead, he argues, all should be measured on excellence. Murrell also challenges the role of teachers in *African-Centered Pedagogy* through the roles of teachers in creating a "community of achievement" (Murrell, 2002).

Murrell consistently advocates for teachers to culturally and historically understand their students, resist traditional pedagogy that perpetuates underachievement, and view education in a broader context of schooling. When we consider the reteaching of Black history, it is important to use the critical lens described through the lives of ancestors to invoke critical education, for both teachers and students.

Providing a Relevant Black Curriculum to Foster Learning

A major imperative for creating academic success for students is that of providing a curriculum that not only empowers students through connecting to their cultural communities, but also providing lessons that are critical and significant in propelling students to value their education. Ladson-Billings (1994) indicates the importance of understanding one's individual perspective about African American students, which is directly connected to the way in which we teach them. Ladson-Billings (1994) references "dysconsciousness" as an implication for educators who claim to "not" see color in the classroom.

In understanding how social class struggles and perceptions can preface the behavior toward African American students, Ladson-Billings (1994) exposes this cultural dilemma. She also relates comparisons among assimilationists' versus culturally relevant approaches, as noted in tables addressing self-impressions, social relations, and conceptions of knowledge.

Perhaps her most explicit point for educators is the element of parental involvement as both a necessity and a variable in helping to attain student success. It is crucially important that educators are cognizant of the type of parental structures that exist in their schools and surrounding community; placing blame on parents without fully deconstructing socioeconomic factors further perpetuate assimilationist models of teaching.

Landsman and Lewis (2006) highlight the impact of teacher perceptions and their detrimental impacts on Black students. They also provide recommendations for curriculum that is engaging, encompassing, and enriching to the lives of students.

Haberman (1995) also examines effective practices of teachers in urban school populations that can build, nurture, and sustain cultural relevance. He discusses how successful and effective teachers of urban students set high expectations for their students to learn, provide engaging curriculum, and are considerate of students' home environments and possible dysfunctional situations. He asserts that star teachers are realistic with expectations for their students and don't rely on scripted curriculums, parental involvement, or even placement to determine the success of that student.

Less emphasis on standardized measures, Haberman contends that star teachers are more concerned with the academic development and outcomes of their students. In particular, he highlights fifteen attributes of successful teachers; these features can be directly linked to implications for teacher education programs. To simply understand the differences and disconnects that exist in a classroom is not enough; one must embrace such discussions in action and practice to become truly competent in cultural relevancy.

Haberman (1995) asserts that a culturally relevant and critically conscious educator is not only aware of his or her children's environmental, social, and cultural dilemmas, but also encourages students to participate in conversations about these problems and issues to create, stimulate, and encourage change. By becoming content masters, teachers share their value and zest for life-long learning. It is suggested that teacher education programs invest heavily in providing more opportunities for future teachers to develop their content knowledge in a particular area or set of areas so that this love for learning can inherently spread to those they teach.

Lastly, Kunjufu (2002) provides strategies and solutions to improve the academic achievement of all African American students regardless of their economic class. These strategies are written to all teachers of African American students, yet, because the vast majority of teachers are White middle class, they are at the forefront of the audience. He also discusses that teachers should hold high expectations of their students and change curriculum to infuse African American cultures in to the classroom.

It is in this regard that they become master teachers. They should spend less time in the workroom and more time on developing new lessons and reading books to improve their craft. They do not subscribe to negative stereotypes and work tirelessly to dispel myths surrounding African American student achievement. Additionally, he provides the reader with a multitude of resources and research to better understand African American culture and students.

He speaks greatly about providing schools with a *relevant Black curriculum* that not only engages students, but also fosters academic outcomes and a love of learning. This fully emulates Woodson's (1977) suggestions for educating the Negro and reshaping (mis)education that societal influences juxtapose.

CONCLUSION: NOW WE HERE

In conclusion, African American's lineage within the United States literally "started from the bottom." But as the song suggests, now we're "here." The aim of this chapter was to highlight the historical significance of the African American struggle and the eventual relentless fight for education. These selfless ancestral contributions are recognized in this chapter, as the torch has now been passed for us to help future generations. The opening question, "now what?" undergirds some closing thoughts. Using two contemporary models, from Ronnie Hopkins's *Educating Black Males* (1997) and Venus Evans-Winters's *Teaching Black Girls* (2011), we offer you a "boost" for your classroom or school.

In his book Hopkins takes a critical view of what is needed to teach Black male students. Hopkins takes three major traits of proper education for African American males and explores public school examples. Early intervention is a key strategy for teaching African American males, because students often first show indicators of educational endangerment well before dropping out in high school. Also, an implementation and infusion of culturally specific curriculums are also important. Whereas school models traditionally strip cultural relevance and promote a grand narrative, it is important of African American male students to regain a sense of academic pride within their culture and heritage.

Evans-Winters (2011), likewise, reveals the need for culturally relevant curriculum and critical pedagogy for Black female students. This involves teaching within context and providing cultural connections. Like Hopkins who argues for these same sentiments for the benefit of Black male students, the reality of Black female students existing as multiple minorities magnifies their disadvantages in traditional schooling, according to Evans-Winters. Implementing self-reflexivity within the curriculum design is a way to foster the resiliency that many urban African American female students possess.

Both Hopkins and Evans-Winters advocate the need for community environments among teachers and students. Evans-Winters mentions, "Although the Black community has traditionally served as an important resource to African American families and their children, a 'community' mentality has been most critical to the development of Black females' multiple identities" (2011, p. 45). In addition, through their use of student perspectives, both authors elevate students as equally substantial in the school design process.

The need for student advocacy and support is urged to begin at the classroom level, through effective student interaction. This lends a personal responsibility for all of us (especially classroom teachers) to be a bridge between past and present, to use historical knowledge of "starting from the bottom" to encourage students to recognize the present condition of "now we're here."

REFERENCES

Akbar, N. (1998). *Know thy self.* Tallahassee, FL: Mind Productions and Associates.

Anderson, J. (1988). *Education of blacks in the South, 1860–1935.* Chapel Hill, NC: University of North Carolina Press.

Darling-Hammond, L. (2010). *The flat world and education: How America's commitment to equity will determine our future.* New York: Teachers College Press.

Delpit, L. D. (2006). *Other people's children: Cultural conflict in the classroom.* New York: New Press.

Evans-Winter, V. E. (2011). *Teaching black girls: Resiliency in urban classrooms.* New York: Peter Lang Publishers.

Francois, S., Overstreet, S., & Cunningham, M. (2011). Where we live: The unexpected influence of urban neighborhoods on the academic performance of African American adolescents. *Youth & Society, 44*(2), 307–28.

Freire, P. ([1970] 2000). *Pedagogy of the oppressed.* New York: Continuum International Publishing Group.

Gay, G. (2000). *Culturally responsive teaching: Theory, research and practice.* New York: Teachers College Press.

Haberman, M. (1995). *Star teachers of children in poverty.* Indianapolis, IN: Kappa Delta Pi.

Hillard, A. (1998). *SBA: The reawakening of the African mind.* Atlanta, GA: Makare Publishing.

Hopkins, R. (1997). *Educating black males: Critical lessons in schooling community, and power.* Albany, NY: SUNY Press.

Ighodaro, E., & Wiggan, G. (2011). *Curriculum violence: America's new Civil Rights issue.* New York: Nova Science Publishers.

King, J. E. (2005). (Ed.). *Black education: A transformative research and action agenda for the new century.* Mahwah, NJ: Lawrence Erlbaum Associates.

Kozol, J. (2005). *The shame of the nation: The restoration of apartheid schooling in America.* New York: Three Rivers Press.

Kunjufu, J. (2002). *Black students. Middle class teachers.* Chicago, IL: African American Images.

Ladson-Billings, G. (1994). *The dreamkeepers: Successful teachers of African American children.* San Francisco, CA: Jossey-Bass.

Landsman, J., & Lewis, C. W. (2006). (Eds.). *White teachers/diverse classrooms: A guide to building inclusive schools, promoting high expectations, and eliminating racism.* Sterling, VA: Stylus Publishing.

Lipman, P. (2004). *High stakes education: Inequality, globalization, and urban school reform.* New York: RoutledgeFalmer.

Marsh, K., Chaney, C., & Jones, D. (2012). The strengths of high-achieving Black high school students in a racially diverse setting. *Journal of Negro Education, 81*(1), 39–51.

Meyer, S. P. (2000). *As long as they don't move next door: Segregation and racial conflict in American neighborhoods.* Lanham, MD: Rowman & Littlefield.

Murrell, P. C. (2002). *African-centered pedagogy.* Albany, NY: State University of New York Press.

Ogbu, J. U. (1978). *Minority education and caste: The American system in cross-cultural perspective.* San Diego, CA: Academic Press.

Perry, T., Steele, C., & Hilliard, A. (2003). *Young gifted and black.* Boston: Beacon Press.

Resilience. (2013). In Merriam-Webster.com. Retrieved May 17, 2013, from http://www. merriam-webster.com/dictionary/resilience.

Steinburg, S. R., & Kincheloe, J. L. (2004). (Eds). *19 urban questions: Teaching in the city.* New York: Peter Lang.

Traore, R., & Lukens, R. J. (2006). *This isn't the American I thought I'd find: African students in the urban U.S. high school.* Lanham, MD: University Press of America.

Wiggan, G. (2008). From opposition to engagement: Lessons from high achieving African American students. *Urban Review, 40*(4), 317–49.

Woodson, C. G. (1977). *The miseducation of the negro.* New York: AMS Press.

Chapter Twelve

Teaching with Technology

Apps and Social Media for the Urban Literacy Classroom

Jason Trumble and Michael Mills

Teachers know the amazing strengths and passions in their students, and they are also finding that students are learning more differently now than ever before (Turkle, 2012). This is perhaps most apparent when, amid a discussion, a student calls out, "Oh, I saw this on YouTube." Further, "Googling" has become a verb, and connectivity is as close as the next store, coffee house, or bookstore. As digital technologies become more and more ingrained in everyday life, our students have begun to view their devices as extensions of themselves (Clayton, Leshner, & Almond, 2015).

Connectivity and access to media through the Internet and Internet-enabled devices is nearly ubiquitous. Ninety-two percent of teens reported that they access the Internet at least once a day, 6 percent reported accessing the Internet once a week, and only 2 percent of the thirteen- to seventeen-year-olds reported accessing the Internet less than once a week (Lenhart, 2015). Additionally, a 2013 study revealed that 72 percent of children ages birth to eight years have access to mobile computing devices (Holloway, Green, & Livingstone, 2013).

Students' learning has changed with Internet-enabled technology, which has created the need to change the way teachers teach. It also requires the teacher to take a fresh look at new literacies. Media literacy and digital citizenship must be embedded in the classroom as a foundational piece of K–6 education.

Media literacy is defined as the ability to access, analyze, evaluate, and create media in various forms including digital media (National Association for Media Literacy Education, 2010). Digital literacies are less exact but they include the ability to navigate, operate, and understand digital technologies for various purposes. As teachers, there is often a disconnect between students' personal uses of technology and the use of technology in the classroom.

The purpose of this chapter is to provide resources that will help the teacher connect the technology-skilled student with learning and literacy. This chapter will introduce applications that have been found to be successful in literacy instruction. The functions and potential of the technologies will be discussed, and the chapter will discuss how literacy educators can use social media to motivate and teach urban students to learn and thrive in the twenty-first century. Although the technologies can be used in many ways, this chapter focuses on K–6 students' technology interaction throughout the learning process.

The core elements of language arts are reading, writing, listening, speaking, viewing, and visual representation (Roe & Ross, 2006). To incorporate technology into the language arts is to engage the students in each of the core elements while motivating them in relevant and new ways that prepare them for using the apps in authentic contexts.

To do this, it is suggested that teachers first experiment with and learn the technology before using it with the students to understand how these digital-age learning tools can be incorporated into classroom practice. Play with the applications, brainstorm how they might compliment your teaching, and then develop a strategy that includes specific explicit instructions and expectation. It helps to start with a small group of students and scale the integration in degrees until the whole class is proficient.

SOCIAL MEDIA IN THE URBAN CLASSROOM

Many of the twenty-first-century communication trends are associated with social media platforms. During an informal visit to an urban middle school, fifteen sixth graders were asked if they had an Instagram, Twitter, or Facebook account. Nine of them replied with a positive, most of them using Instagram. Although this is not surprising and it corresponds to the report mentioned previously, the responses reinforce the understanding that students are indeed learning and communicating in different ways than ever before (Turkle, 2012).

This new form of learning is hinged on social constructivism (Vygotsky, 1978). Social media is changing how students learn and communicate. The development of literacy, in particular critical literacies, in students is a necessity for twenty-first-century curricula. To capitalize on the new learning, teachers must be able to incorporate social media into daily practice.

As previously mentioned, there is a bridge between students' personal uses of technology and the uses of technology in school. The separation is evident when students enter a school where, when it is time to learn, they put their digital expertise and devices away until they leave. Every part of students' lives outside of school are touched by technology to the point that their context of life is digitally informed (Talbert & Trumble, 2014).

There is no doubt that students are learning, especially from each other, while using technology outside of the classroom walls. What is tricky, as a teacher, is to find ways to capitalize on social media to help students learn. Fortunately, in the urban elementary literacy classroom, there are several options for incorporating social media into the learning environment.

Edublogs (edublogs.org) is a WordPress platform for blogging with a few added security features for schools and classrooms. As students log in with the teacher-provided information, they are sent to a dashboard where they can compose or edit a post. They have the ability to also create hyperlinks, add video, audio, or still pictures. When they have completed the post, they submit it for approval.

Before the blog post can be viewable on the blog site, the teacher should confer with the student and approve it for publishing. The literary benefits of classroom blogging are infinite. As an example, while in the fifth-grade classroom, students used the blog as a platform for responding to reading. They would summarize passages, predict events, respond to fact in nonfiction works, analyze the author's intent, write continued story lines, and evaluate the moral or message from the literature they read.

Employing blogging through edublogs increases students' motivation for reading and composition, as well as provides opportunities for students to collaborate with their peers. The classroom blog can also be shared with educational stakeholders including parents, families, and school and district administration.

From a prior classroom experience, sharing the class blog was an added benefit for families because it provided opportunities for parents to respond by commenting and asking questions. This real-world communication also increased students' evaluative skills when responding to reading and composing for digital publication. Instead of receiving anecdotal announcements of what students were learning, all stakeholders could see and respond to student work. School administrators also read the class blogs and saw the curriculum at work.

Integrating blogging and other social media creates the opportunity for additional communication. Teachers have been known to invite authors as guest bloggers on classroom blog sites as the class or group is reading that author's work. Although contacting authors seems like a daunting task, it can be well worth the effort as students then begin to think and communicate beyond the classroom walls and their local environment with connections to the outside world.

This is a particularly powerful benefit for the urban school setting. Many students in urban settings struggle to find references outside of their situations; using social media and blogging to provide experiences linked outside the classroom allows students to analyze different perspectives (Gebhard, Shin, & Seger, 2013).

There are a myriad possibilities with classroom blogging that have the potential to contribute to learning and literacy in the twenty-first century. Students who engage in blogging read, write, analyze text, view, and organize their understandings of literature and the world around them. These skills are all needed to traverse the digital world around them.

Additionally, the composition of blogs has become multimodal and multimedia rich. Students can create a video, screencast, or podcast their learning and post it along with text. By publishing blogs with multiple modes of expression and sharing these posts with classmates and the world, students are continually evaluating, analyzing, and adding to their literacy and creation skills that are essential in a digitally driven world.

Twitter has become one of the most popular social media apps available. Many students have it, and many people in the world get and share news through the 140-character tweets. In the classroom, this app can be used to generate classroom news and real-world opportunities for learning, even in the K–6 environment. One option is to create a classroom Twitter account and have students follow and or post directly to it depending on the age of the student.

This social media tool is most suitable for students in the third to sixth grades. Through mobile devices or tablets, students can tweet about what they learned to the classroom Twitter account and have a parent or guardian "favorite" and "retweet" it moments later. In addition to Twitter serving as a platform for increasing understanding and developing real-world communication skills, the social media tool also encourages parental involvement and engagement.

The potential of Twitter in the classroom is limitless. This tool also has the capability to be used as a collaborative repository for Web research and communication between students as they traverse projects and ideas. In this way, Twitter becomes a bank of resources for the student to return to as they begin to compose a report or develop a presentation for the class regarding the information they found. Additionally, those who follow the class Twitter account can be privy to these occurrences simply by "following."

Instagram is another Web application that allows users to post pictures or short videos with text to a social network. There are several ways teachers can incorporate Instagram into the literacy setting. Students respond differently to reading and learning, and many times in urban settings language can be a barrier to the students' authentic expression. Because Instagram is primarily focused on pictures, students can create digital images, take pictures, or create short videos in response to their learning and post them on Instagram to show their understanding and critical response to learning. Here is an example of Instagram's use in the classroom:

> A fourth-grade teacher who had a class Instagram account collaborated with a small group of students to do a novel study on Avi and Mordan's (2013) historical fiction book, *Iron Thunder: The Battle between the Monitor & the Merrimac: A Civil War Novel*. The students were instructed to read to a certain point in the story where the main character found himself in a life-threatening situation. The readers were then instructed to create a post that could be put on Instagram that explored the character's feelings in that moment. The five students each created a post separately for homework, each of the students created a drawing and commentary that related to the pivotal point in the book. The next day, the students' uploaded their posts by using the teacher's iPad and then viewed each other's pictures and commentary through the Instagram feed that sparked a rich, group discussion that led to the students' recognition and deeper appreciation for the unique perspectives of each group member.

Instagram is a fantastic tool that can enhance struggling learners' nonfiction writing and expression. This tool can also be integrated into science content by having students document each step of a science lab through pictures and short captions posted to a class Instagram account. This allows students to review each step of the scientific process for the lab experience.

This also provides an opportunity for the teacher to formatively assess student understanding throughout each step of the lab activity. Finally, as students write their report they are able to review their images and captions and build their conclusions and narrative on through multimedia documentation. Instagram offers the potential to connect the process of scientific inquiry with the development of nonfiction writing that is currently an area of need in schools today.

MOBILE APPS TO SUPPORT LITERACY

One of the most powerful mobile Web apps available to support literacy programs is **Evernote** (Evernote.com), a note-taking, annotation, and Web-clipping tool that empowers students to cultivate multimodal resources in a way to support both verbal and visual literacy. Beyond the simple (yet often underrated) task of recording written notes that can be synced among mobile devices, there are a variety of other Evernote tools that facilitate literacy instruction.

Audio notes are a powerful way to have students read their writing or to demonstrate fluency. Evernote allows for audio recording, providing teachers the opportunity to record students reading a text excerpt aloud, which is beneficial in several ways, including students being able to read and then listen to their own writing, to compare an audio recording of a teacher's lesson to written notes, and to serve as a scaffold for students reading a difficult passage.

Using Evernote in a K–6 class is simple. The teacher must set up an account with student e-mail addresses, then the students log in with their teacher-provided credentials. Simply clicking the *plus* button opens a blank note-taking space where the students can add text, visual, or audio notes directly to the page. Using this app, teachers can teach traditional note-taking skills and so much more. Through Evernote, students can record their comprehension of read-alouds or any teacher-led activity. Evernote and its connected extensions also offer powerful tools for the teacher to enhance student literacy by sharing notes, annotations, and multimedia files.

Skitch (Skitch.com) is a stand-alone app that integrates directly into Evernote. Students can annotate a photo or image from their mobile camera or the Internet with text, arrows, shapes, highlighting, and blur effects. Students can use Skitch to mark up text passages and images or even draw measurements and diagrams for math problems. Math teachers would have students take photos of everyday images and apply their knowledge of geometry to classify and measure the objects.

One way Skitch has been embedded into activities is through the enhancing school use of Instagram. Students save the images they posted to Instagram to their device's camera roll and then annotate the image using Skitch. This increased engagement for students because it added a layer of creation to simply taking standard images and annotating them. Students enjoyed using Skitch as well as applying Instagram filters in an effort to personalize the images.

This phenomenon is enhanced by asking students to apply a filter that matches the tone or mood of the concept they are trying to demonstrate. This has proven particularly useful in lessons on mood and tone in language arts.

Evernote Clearly (Evernote.com/clearly/) is a browser plugin (a built-in app that integrates into an Internet browser like Safari, Firefox, or Chrome) that allows students and teachers to simultaneously clip a Web page as a note and strip the Web page of all incidental media. The result is a clean page of only the Web page text and any multimedia directly related to the main content of the page.

Combined with Evernote's notebook and tagging capabilities, students can easily curate and organize reading and research material without the distractions associated with conventional Internet browsing. This tool has been particularly helpful with struggling readers who, as Navalpakkam, Rao, and Slaney (2011) indicate, have much difficulty reading online material that contains extraneous and irrelevant advertisements. Removing advertisements that distract from online reading has been instrumental in the literacy development of traditionally low-achieving students who struggle with higher-level reading tasks.

With Evernote Clearly K–6 teachers are able to both provide students online reading opportunities that are free from external advertisements and reading distractions. In preparation, the teacher can choose a common website or blog for his or her students to read. Then, using Evernote Clearly they can create a note that only includes the appropriate content for the elementary learner and share that note as an assignment. Additionally, using the highlighting feature, the students can mark up the text in the browser and then have that text saved with its highlighting in the Evernote notebook.

Collaboration through Evernote can be accomplished through shared notes as well as notebooks. By sharing a notebook link with students, any note added to that notebook can be accessed by students. The power of Evernote and its many add-ons fit perfectly into urban classroom settings. This application increases motivation and functionality for student learning experiences and teacher organization.

Blendspace (Blendspace.com) is a free (with tier-based fee options) portfolio Web service that allows students to post multimodal resources and evidence of learning. Students can post these resources by uploading them as digital files or by linking them through Blendspace's integration with many popular cloud and hosting services, like Google Drive, Dropbox, and YouTube.

The material in a Blendspace is organized by a blocked grid, whereby each block contains a resource or a quiz. Students can use this structure as part of an individual or collaborative portfolio assessment, and teachers can use Blendspace to provide students with multimedia lessons, which can be accessed even away from school.

The success of using Blendspace with urban students has been demonstrated through increased engagement and comprehension by combining text elements related to a lesson with relevant videos and images (Mayer, 2005). This combination has allowed teachers to scaffold material in a compelling way. Beyond this teacher-directed approach, students who have been tasked with creating their own Blendspace projects have had the option of demonstrating their comprehension multimodally, allowing for individual student differentiation.

Visual literacy is an integral component of modern textual literacy (New London Group, 1996). From media-rich Web pages to interactive eTexts, students must grasp with a multimodal understanding that goes beyond what is simply written on the page. In an effort to support this understanding, students were required to create image-rich presentations that eschewed the conventional bullet-point format of most presentation slide decks. A useful tool for this approach is **Haiku Deck**, a free (with tier-based fee options) slide deck application available through the Web and as an iOS app.

Working with a sixth-grade teacher, the author designed a lesson by which students deconstructed the poem "Oranges" by Gary Soto (2006) and created a slide for each line of the poem. Although students struggled in choosing the fonts for their text, the activities moved them into matching the tone and mood of each line of the poem to an image in Haiku Deck's built-in image library. The students learned to refine their search terms and discriminated among images that appropriately illustrated the tone and mood of each line.

Students were grouped to discuss their choices and rationale. This led to the observation of real progress, when the students started to collaborate on what constituted acceptable images to fully convey the sense of tone and mood in the poem. This lesson could easily be extended throughout the intermediate grades (3–6) as long as the textual complexity of the work matches the grade level being taught.

TodaysMeet is a free Web-based app that allows students to backchannel or have a secondary route for discussion during a lesson or project. This is particularly powerful tool for teacher-led activities like lectures and read-alouds. Here is an example of how this app was used in the classroom:

> This activity was designed for a literacy lesson on comprehension that required students to share questions about and thoughts about a text during a think-aloud. The method we used was a backchannel, which is a streaming conversation between teachers and students to mimic the think-aloud process. Noting the variety of devices students brought with them to class, the teachers had to use a discussion and collaboration tool that everybody could access regardless of the technology students had with them.
>
> TodaysMeet (todaysmeet.com) proved to be the best option to serve this purpose for urban elementary students. Setting up a class backchannel was simple. The teacher selected a name for the discussion room (that name becomes part of the URL for your chat area) and how long the backchannel stream was to exist. Students accessed TodaysMeet through a browser on their Internet-enabled devices and entered an alternate name that they were assigned. This was a great strategy because the teacher could track the content and frequency of responses from particular students, but from the student perspective the posts were anonymous.
>
> After a short orientation and chance for students to get used to the backchannel format, the teacher then performed a short think-aloud of Ray Bradbury's (1991) short story "The Pedestrian," while the students offered their thoughts and posed questions. Students were specifically asked to contribute detailed comments and questions, including their analysis, predictions, and use text excerpts to support their points.
>
> What got the students seriously engaged was that they could ask questions or add their comments without having to wait to be called on. The backchannel was projected through the teacher's projector, so students could monitor their contributions and the posts of other students. Although some of the students offered seemingly irrelevant comments, this opportunity was used to refocus

the discussion back to the text and required the students to provide evidence and reasoning to their classmates supporting their interpretations. Remarkably, the students did just that.

Another effective backchanneling tool in the literacy classroom is **Padlet**, an online bulletin board of sorts. Students and teachers post virtual notes that can contain text, images, Web hyperlinks, and videos. Although not as quick as TodaysMeet, the addition of the multimedia appealed to the students in a big way.

Padlet is most effective as a classroom tool when the teacher poses a question and students answer that question by posting notes to the virtual board. Padlet can be used in both synchronous and asynchronous learning situations. As students post to the virtual board, their content is instantly available for all to view. They also have the option to post anonymously.

The **ShowMe** app is an iPad screen-casting app that allows the user to record videos with a simultaneous voiceover. Additionally, users have the ability to import pictures for annotation. The power of incorporating this application is in the development of both visual literacies and oral communication skills. Completed and rendered screencasts are published to a secure Web page where they can be viewed by the student, teacher, or parents. Students can use this app to explain concepts, reflect on reading, or record an instructional video.

Integration of the ShowMe app provides students the opportunity to engage each essential element of literacy. When using ShowMe, students organize their thoughts, write scripts, narrate, create visual representations, edit the visuals, and listen to themselves as they replay and share their screencasts with classmates. Consider this example:

> In a third-grade class, the teacher asked a group of students to engage in a readers' theater that was recorded through ShowMe. The students chose pictures and annotated the pictures as they recorded their voices reading the readers' theater excerpt. The power came when the students would watch the video and analyze their own fluency and ability to convey the message of the story verbally.

Aurasma is an augmented reality application that uses visual references or trigger images to activate a database of video overlays (known as *Auras*). Using a mobile device with a camera and the Aurasma application, a user can frame a trigger image and a preset video or picture Aura will appear on the screen. The Aurasma application can be downloaded on most mobile computing devices, including tablet computers and smartphones.

The Aurasma application offers the potential to evoke meaningful literary responses. The teacher can begin by creating auras for specific pages in a book assigned for students to read independently. Before assigning the text, the teacher should read the novel and develop specific questioning that supports deep literary reflection in relation to literary elements of the novel. For each book the students would use for this activity, the teacher should draw an original mark on the pages on which questioning auras would be created. Consider this example when using the app:

> One teacher drew a star in the top right corner of each page that would serve as the trigger image. Then with the app, the teacher would use the literary response questions to create text pictures to be used as the Auras that correspond directly to the literature. Equipped with their phone and the Aurasma app near them, students would read the book independently and as they see the star in the top right corner of the pages they would use their device to hover over the page to view the questions.
>
> Upon reading each augmented reality question, they would respond by answering the question in their journal before continuing to read. The participating students loved the challenge to think in different ways about the text and they enjoyed using technology in collaboration with traditional text. The Aurasma tool allows the teacher to be creative and guide students toward meaningful response without direct verbal contact. As an extension, students can create their own auras as a way of communicating with their peers as they read the same literature.

FINAL THOUGHTS

Technology can be used for many purposes in urban literacy settings. It not only increases motivation, but it has the potential to connect students to real-world skills. Using social media applications in the classroom provides students the opportunity to develop twenty-first-century skills in a socially responsible way. Additionally, social media can be used as a tool for expression of understanding as well as a repository of experiences for students. It is imperative that the K–6 teacher be deeply engaged and open while using social media as a tool for learning.

Students are learning through technology that is infused in every part of their lives. Incorporating innovative uses of social media and mobile learning applications enhances student understanding of content and contributes to the learning of twenty-first-century literacies. As urban elementary students engage in learning through technology, they find connections to their lives outside of the school walls. This sets the foundation for literacy, learning, and living in our digital world.

REFERENCES

Avi, & Mordan, C. B. (2013). *Iron thunder: The battle between the Monitor & the Merrimac: A Civil War novel*. New York: Hyperion.

Bradbury, R. (1991). *The pedestrian/838*. New York: Samuel French Trade.

Clayton, R. B., Leshner, G., & Almond, A. (2015). The extended iSelf: The impact of iPhone separation on cognition, emotion, and physiology. *Journal of Computer-Mediated Communication, 20*(1), 119–35.

Gebhard, M., Shin, D. S., & Seger, W. (2013). Blogging and emergent L2 literacy development in an urban elementary school: A functional perspective. *CALICO Journal, 28*(2), 278–307.

Holloway, D., Green, L., & Livingstone, S. (2013). Zero to eight: Young children and their internet use. Retrieved from https://www.commonsensemedia.org/research/zero-to-eight-childrens-media-use-in-america-2013.

Lenhart, A. (2015). *Teens, social media & technology overview 2015: Smart phones facilitate shifts in communication landscape for teens*. Washington, DC: Pew Research Center. Retrieved from http://www.pewinternet.org/files/2015/04/PI_TeensandTech_Update2015_0409151.pdf.

Mayer, R. E. (2005). Principles for managing essential processing multimedia learning: Segmenting, pretraining, and modality principles. In R. E. Mayer (Ed.), *Cambridge handbook of multimedia learning* (pp. 169–82). New York: Cambridge University Press.

National Association for Media Literacy Education. (2010). Media literacy defined. Retrieved November 30, 2015, from http://namle.net/publications/media-literacy-definitions/.

Navalpakkam, V., Rao, J., & Slaney, M. (2011). *Using gaze patterns to study and predict reading struggles due to distraction*. Proceedings from CHI '11: Extended Abstracts on Human Factors in Computing Systems, New York (pp. 1705–10). doi: 10.1145/1979742.1979832.

New London Group. (1996). Pedagogy of multiliteracies: Designing social futures. *Harvard Educational Review, 66*(1), 66–92.

Roe, B., & Ross, E. (2006). *Integrating language arts through literature and thematic units*. Boston: Pearson Education.

Soto, G. (2006). *A fire in my hands*. Orlando, FL: Harcourt, Inc.

Talbert, T. L., & Trumble, J. (2014). *An education prof. goes back to high school, finds that technology is no longer a tool but a context*. Retrieved from http://hechingerreport.org/education-prof-goes-back-high-school-finds-technology-longer-tool-context/.

Turkle, S. (2012). *Alone together: Why we expect more from technology and less from each other*. New York: Basic Books.

Vygotsky, L. (1978). Interaction between learning and development. *Readings on the development of children, 23*(3), 34–41.

Chapter Thirteen

Preparing Pre-Service Teachers for Differentiation via Instructional Technology

Leanne Howell and Brent Merritt

No two students are alike, regardless of their age or grade level. In fact, national demographics indicate that the PK–12 student population is less alike than ever before (Strauss, 2014). With variations in student differences, avenues of learning and methods of teaching should reflect the use of varied and differentiated instruction if all students are to maximize their full academic potential.

One recent national report card (National Center for Education Statistics, 2011) highlights that 53 percent of Native American, 51 percent of African American, and 49 percent of Hispanic American fourth-grade students are reading below basic reading and fluency levels in literacy performance. Students from different ethnic backgrounds, low socioeconomic status, and those who speak languages other than English are consistently identified to be "at risk" for literacy success in school.

Because of the challenges and circumstances presented by these data, traditional approaches to teaching no longer seem the best avenue for ensuring the academic success for diverse student populations. As such, the need to differentiate instruction in classroom settings has never been more important (Howell, 2011).

Differentiated instruction is a concept centered on the belief that students learn in many different ways. When considering the best approaches for instruction, successful educators must take into account the aforementioned myriad students' needs in the instructional process: their economic status, culture, language, and background experiences (Ladson-Billings, 2006), as well as their readiness, preferences, and interests (Tomlinson & Imbeau,

2010). Putting students' varied needs into focus, it is essential that teachers be trained and skilled to use strategies that ensure the learning experiences offered in classrooms are differentiated and appropriate.

DIFFERENTIATED INSTRUCTION

Differentiation is far more than a toolbox of teaching strategies. It encompasses a philosophy about teaching and learning that recognizes all students are different, and therefore, all instruction should be tailored to reflect those differences. Differentiated instruction is non-negotiable in diverse classrooms. It is not a matter of *if* but rather a matter of *how*.

Tomlinson (1999) challenges educators to look at differentiation in two broad components—an *instructional* component and a *student* component. The first, considered an instructional component, encompasses three areas of instruction—*Content*, *Process*, and *Product*. One, two, or all three of these components can be modified either in isolation or simultaneously as assessment occurs and impacts instruction.

The second, considered the student component, can also be divided into three areas: *Interest*, *Student Profile*, and *Readiness*. These three areas should help inform instruction, and like the first component, should be driven by assessment.

Regardless of which component is being addressed (instructional or student), several important tenets should be considered in planning for differentiated instruction. The following section elaborates on authentic and continual assessment, the presence of constructive learning, and students as the drivers of instructional processes.

Assessment Is Authentic and Continual

Authentic assessment is a critical component of differentiated classrooms. This type of assessment begins with standards that are aligned with curriculum. In turn, this curriculum is filled with strategies to best suit students' needs and ultimately result in academic growth. Assessments are continual and flexible and used throughout the learning process to appropriately gauge what skills have been learned and which ones need revisiting (Tomlinson, 2014). Pre-assessments are essential to determine what students do and do not know before planning for instruction. Additionally, post-assessments are also important components of the instructional process so that student progress can be used as an indicator of growth.

Constructivist Learning Is Present

Constructivism, or student-centered learning, centers on the idea that students construct meaningful learning by building on previous knowledge and experience. Constructivism involves students being active, rather than passive, participants in their own learning. Teachers who teach with this tenet in mind often assume the role of a facilitator, guiding students to experience their own "ah has" in the learning process (Smith & Throne, 2007).

Students' Needs Guide the Instructional Process

Driven by continuous assessment, students' needs are at the forefront of all instructional planning and teaching. Although standards steer and guide instruction, the focus in student-centered classrooms is not on a one-size-fits-all model, but rather on considering student choices as pathways for learning. Students are considered key players in their own learning process.

One student's road map for learning is seldom the same as anyone else's in the classroom. Tomlinson (2014) insists that teachers who aim to differentiate instruction must consider the content, process, and product of the learning experience, based on student need.

In sum, the basic foundation of differentiated instruction is to purposefully plan curriculum and instruction that adheres to each student's learning needs while maximizing the capacity to learn (Roberts & Inman, 2008; Van Garderen & Whittaker, 2006). Differentiated instruction provides students multiple opportunities to take in new information, organize this information to scaffold new knowledge, and then rely on this scaffolding to help them actually process new knowledge (Heacox, 2012).

When differentiation is the framework for instructional decisions, teachers select instructional avenues and materials that ultimately maximize academic success for every student in every classroom during every day of the school year.

TECHNOLOGY AS AN INSTRUCTIONAL TOOL

One tool for successfully differentiating instruction that is gaining momentum in classrooms is the use of instructional technology (Adams, 2011). Specifically, instructional technology facilitates the discovery of authentic knowledge and offers many avenues for students to research and share new knowledge with their peers.

New instructional technologies are consistently being introduced to offer teachers vast opportunities for differentiating instruction. Additional evidence supports the idea that classrooms rich with technology encourage students to be creative and think critically, while constructing their own knowledge rather than regurgitating simple facts, dates, and numbers (Matzen & Edmunds, 2007).

Not surprisingly, endless studies support the effectiveness of technology in K–12 education (Adams, 2011; Hite, 2005; Hughes, 2008; Lee, Linn, Varma, & Liu, 2010; Watson, 2007). In fact, some research even points to larger percentages of students experiencing academic success when technology is used as a tool in their classroom (Watson, 2007). This academic success may be a result, in part, because of increased student engagement when one-to-one technology is used (Manugurerra & Petocz, 2011).

More specific to urban learners, instructional technology has been found to be a useful tool with low-income children, primarily because of the embedded motivational properties (Laffey, Espinosa, Moore, & Lodree, 2003). Information presented within the realm of an interactive medium with added components of sound, video, and animation can also increase student engagement of reluctant learners (Couse & Chen, 2010).

In consideration of culturally and linguistically diverse students, the use of early and swift academic interventions to differentiate instruction is paramount because these urban learners often enter their early school experiences academically behind their nonminority or affluent peers (Tough, 2008).

THE USE OF INSTRUCTIONAL TECHNOLOGY TO DIFFERENTIATE INSTRUCTION

The following case study offers as a glimpse into how one Professional Development School (PDS) in a Central Texas school district collaborated with district personnel and university faculty to engage and prepare pre-service teacher candidates to use instructional technology to differentiate literacy instruction with small groups of students. Within the context of the case study, an outline of the weekly professional development series offered to these candidates is described.

Then, examples of how pre-service candidates actually used instructional technology to engage, assess, and differentiate for their diverse K–4 student population are presented. Next, feedback from pre-service candidates about their experiences is examined. The chapter concludes with recommendations for practice to others in the field who aspired to impact literacy instruction through the use of instructional technology.

If teachers are to maximize the benefits of instructional technology to impact literacy achievement, they must possess the knowledge to select devices and then use appropriate software applications. As such, they must also possess the self-efficacy to believe they can do this successfully, with integrity and purpose.

More specific to this case study, it was important to provide pre-service teacher candidates not only with content and pedagogy surrounding instructional technology, but also to ensure they had the skills and self-efficacy to use this instructional technology on a regular basis in the contexts of real classrooms. To do one without the other would not yield lasting results or fully prepare them as future educators to teach in our technology-abundant society with fidelity.

Self-Efficacy and Constructivism in Using Technology

Bandura's self-efficacy theory (1997) provides a basis for understanding the role of pre-service teachers' beliefs about their own ability to actually integrate technology into their future teaching practices. Specific to this case study, Bandura's theory suggests that teachers' pedagogical decisions are influenced by self-efficacy beliefs pertaining to their own capabilities of using technology in classrooms settings. Therefore, with this theory as guide, it seems that increasing pre-service teacher candidates' knowledge and application of instructional technology will, in turn, increase their self-efficacy beliefs. Hence, in this case, it is the connection between their specific knowledge and Bandura's theory that ultimately affects the degree to which pre-service teacher candidates actually incorporate technology into pedagogical practices to enhance literacy opportunities for children.

Another theory important to this case study is the use of instructional technology occuring from the epistemological standpoint of contructivism (Reiser, 2001). This theory places emphasis on the acquisition of knowledge and the notion that knowledge is acquired through an active process of learning between learners and their phsycial and social surroundings, rather than merely being accumulated or received. Through avenues offered within the realm of instructional technology, students are able to construct new knowledge to their prior schema and create different pathways to learning.

Context

At Sullivan Elementary (pseudonym) pre-service teacher candidates used instructional technology to differentiate instruction and create authentic learning experiences for their students. Located in a central Texas school district, a 1:1 technology initiative school district, Sullivan Elementary just completed its first year as a PDS, partnered with a local university. Reflective of this technology initiative, iPads were provided by the district for teacher candidates, as well as elementary students and teachers, to use as instructional supplements.

During the fall semester, one hour a day, four days a week, pre-service teacher candidates (who were in their junior year of their college experience) planned and taught small groups of kindergarten through fourth-grade students in the areas of English/language arts. Guided by curriculum standards, these candidates, along with their mentor in-service teachers and their university faculty, collaborated in weekly curriculum planning meetings to help the candidates prepare and implement academically appropriate literacy lessons for their students.

EMPOWERING AND PREPARING PRE-SERVICE TEACHER CANDIDATES

Learning

Beginning the third week of the fall semester, the pre-service teacher candidates at Sullivan participated in a weekly professional development series (table 13.1) to address appropriate ways to use instructional technology to assess, differentiate, and ultimately engage their diverse groups of students in learning processes and outcomes.

Sessions were approximately one hour in length and were conducted in a room designated for professional development on the Sullivan campus. Dur-

Teaching with Technology: A Professional Development Series Offered to Pre-Service Teacher Candidates

Session 1: iPad Classroom Management, Digital Citizenship
    Flipped PD via *Edmodo*
Session 2: SAMR, TPACK, ISTE, TEKS
    An interactive overview of technology standards using *NearPod*
Session 3: Work Flow
    Google Drive, Edmodo
Session 4: Creativity and Innovation Apps
    iPlayground Task Cards: Book Creator, Popplet, PicCollage,
    DoodleBuddy (or other drawing app)
Session 5: Assessment 1 (Exit Tickets)
    Socrative, NearPod, Padlet
Session 6: Assessment
    Infuse Learning, Blendspace, Kahoot, Google Forms, Rubric (RubiStar)
Session 7: Challenge Based Learning
Session 8: Research and Information Fluency
    iWorks: Pages and Keynote
Session 9: Critical Thinking and Problem Solving
    iWorks: iMovie
Session 10: Assessment and Task Card Activities
Session 11: Instructional Technology Showcase

ing each session, candidates explored software applications recommended and demonstrated by the instructional technology team. Candidates were challenged to discover ways the software applications could be used to deepen student learning. After candidates became familiar with these applications, they were required to actively use these elements of instructional technology on a regular basis in their planning and teaching of literacy.

Throughout the professional development series, led by the Sullivan instructional technology specialist, candidates participated in hands-on learning in various aspects of instructional technology use, primarily in the form of Apple iPads. With International Society for Teaching in Education (ISTE) standards (2015) as a guide, candidates explored elements of digital citizenship, workflow, and basic iPad applications.

Further in the series, candidates explored applications as platforms for students to collaborate, communicate, create, and engage in critical thinking. Additionally, applications pertaining to assessment, challenge-based learning, and research were also introduced, explored, and used on a regular basis.

Using

Soon after the technology series began, candidates were required by the PDS faculty to use instructional technology in small-group teaching. With each student having access to an iPad in the classroom, all students in each small group were able to personalize instruction. The instructional process was initially driven by pre-assessment, resulting in differentiation for each student in the small group.

Over the course of the semester, candidates used a wide variety of applications to engage students in active literacy learning. Kindergarten students snapped photos of peers with their iPads as they reenacted parts of an unfamiliar story. Then using *Book Creator*, students were asked to put events of the story in order to make their own books.

Although some students were able to sequence many events, others were only able to sequence a few. The use of this application allowed candidates to meet their kindergarten students at the appropriate instructional level, ensuring that all students experienced some level of academic success.

Book Creator was also used regularly in second through fourth grades. Third-grade students created a book to inform peers of the steps in "how-to" do a task, and students across the hall in another classroom used *Book Creator* to collect information about a "buddy" and then create a brief "Buddy Biography."

Across all grades, from kindergarten to fourth grade, students also used *Book Creator* to create colorful and detailed books to inform others of their new knowledge gained through inquiry-based learning experiences connected to content standards in English/language arts and social studies. After weeks of researching their own questions pertaining to topics like animals, heroes, and celebrations, students created their own books to share their new information with peers.

Before presenting, students worked with partners to plan, draft, edit, and publish final copies of their books to ensure their products accurately displayed their newly acquired knowledge. Then, students reviewed each other's products, using rubrics to peer assess. In the end, all products were retrieved electronically by the pre-service teacher candidate and assessed, using the same components of the rubrics. Students' electronic books were used throughout the year for students to read to others and share with parents.

QR Reader was another application that pre-service teacher candidates used on a regular basis. Used across all grade levels, this application proved to be an excellent tool for differentiating the learning experiences of the students. In one fourth-grade classroom, candidates used QR codes to help students master skills of making inferences and drawing conclusions.

Based on pre-assessments, one candidate designed different QR codes, based on ability, for each student in her small group. Although each student was asked to complete the same tasks, each had his or her own QR code that, when scanned, went straight to academically appropriate research material tailored to the student. This proved to be a great way for teacher candidates to differentiate the learning experience while maintaining students' self-esteem.

QR Reader was used more widely as an avenue for students to actively research topics of interest or topics within the curriculum. Across all grade levels, candidates took the time to find ability-appropriate information about topics their students were researching.

Using the personalized QR codes, students actively collected information and researched aforementioned topics such as heroes, cultures, and celebrations; they felt confident in the process as they accessed reading materials from a collection gathered by the teacher candidates based on abilities, interests, and reading levels.

Additionally, teacher candidates used apps like *Kahoot* and *Socrative* to differentiate assessments for the students. Using these resources, candidates were able to create quizzes and exit tickets to formatively assess students' understanding of standards pertaining to comprehension, sequencing, and summarizing. The assessment for each student matched the learning processes and outcomes pertaining to each standard.

FEEDBACK FROM CANDIDATES

Pre-service teacher candidates overwhelming confirmed that their self-efficacy toward the use of instructional technology increased as a result of the professional development experiences. Further, many expressed a strong relationship between the use of instructional technology and the ability to differentiate for their students.

Two components appeared to be essential to their growth: actively *learning about* instructional technology and then having opportunities to *use* these newly discovered applications and approaches on a regular basis to differentiate instruction for their students. According to one candidate, "I loved learning about the different ways to use instructional technology, but I loved just as much being asked to use what I had learned to experiment with it myself in a real-world setting."

Another candidate noted that it was nice to get to practice using instructional technology with so much support from the PDS faculty. This candidate shared that she knew where to go to find help, answers, or needed instructional support. Still further, one candidate pointed out that all too often ideas from professional development are only presented, with no opportunities to put those ideas to real-world use.

Several candidates were overwhelmed at the potential of the technology tools to differentiate instruction. One reported, "Differentiation is so much easier when I use instructional technology. It allows me to plan different things for my students and none of them ever seem to care that they are all doing different things. They are all so engaged and mesmerized with their own learning."

Candidates also reflected on the importance of having access to iPads for troubleshooting and extensive learning themselves. Although most of the candidates were considered to be tech savvy, many were unfamiliar with the educational uses and potential for inciting new learning. Most had not previously used the applications learned about in the professional development series, so they felt it essential to have ongoing access to iPads to ensure they fully understood the uses and applications of specific tools before they presented them to their students.

ESSENTIAL INGREDIENTS OF PROFESSIONAL DEVELOPMENT

This two-pronged process of professional development provided pre-service teacher candidates the opportunity to become more proficient in their use of instructional technology and increased their related self-efficacy to ultimately differentiate learning experiences for their students in the content area of literacy. This unique opportunity helped many candidates alleviate the fear of how to tailor curricula to meet the needs of their students, especially in the content area of English/language arts.

Just as affirmed, these candidates benefited from not only learning about the use instructional technology to differentiate, but also practicing using it as part of their own educational preparedness in becoming future teachers. In turn, the students with whom they worked with benefitted from differentiated literacy instruction as a result of instructional technology.

RECOMMENDATIONS FOR PRACTICE

Instructional technology has the potential to be a useful tool to successfully differentiate literacy instruction for diverse student populations. For technology integration to be effective, several key factors must be considered. First, professional development is essential for in-service and pre-service teachers to effectively be stewards of instructional technology to benefit students. Professional development must occur as part of a two-part process: learning about and then using the applications designated for differentiation in literacy instruction.

Second, educators should be encouraged to develop grade-level or campus communities of support. Systems of communication should be fostered to help not only empower them to use instructional technology but to also support each other in questions, inquiries, and troubleshooting. On campuses where there is an instructional technology specialist, this professional should be the key person to coordinate and organize support.

Next, adequate time must be taken by in-service and pre-service teachers to explore the applications and programs intended for use in the classroom. Troubleshooting is an essential step in reducing valuable instructional time. Additionally, students must be taught how to use instructional literacy applications. It cannot be assumed that students know how to use apps planned for instruction. Deliberate attention and time should be taken to ensure each student has the app downloaded and is familiar with using it.

Finally, there is a critical need to involve parents. It is vitally important to inform them of how instructional technology is being used in best practices to differentiate instruction in literacy. Share the list of applications used in the classroom and encourage parents to engage in the learning process with their children at home as extensions to learning that occurs in the classroom.

FINAL THOUGHTS

Differentiated instruction encompasses the use of teaching tools and strategies to give diverse students every opportunity to experience literacy success. The use of instructional technology can help support and scaffold instruction and offer extended learning opportunities for diverse students; however, in-service and pre-service teachers must have the self-efficacy and training to feel confident using it in the classroom.

The case study presented the successful iteration of training and support for pre-service teachers in their use of instructional technology to assess, engage, and empower their students in literacy instruction. New possibilities inspired by the presence of technology provide an exciting opportunity for educators to rethink the design of diverse classrooms in ways to best suit the needs of every student. Differentiated instruction is no longer an option in K–12 classrooms, but an opportunity to inspire hope of academic success for every student.

REFERENCES

Adams, L. G. (2011). Engaging middle school students with technology: Using real-time data to test predictions in aquatic ecosystems. *Science Scope, 34*(9), 32–38.

Bandura, A. (1997). *Self-efficacy: The exercise of control.* New York: W. H. Freeman and Company.

Couse, L., & Chen, D. W. (2010). A tablet computer for young children? Exploring its viability for early childhood education. *Early Childhood Education, 43*(1), 75–98.

Heacox, D. (2012). *Differentiating instruction in the regular classroom: How to reach and teach all learners.* Minneapolis, MN: Free Spirit Publishing, Inc.

Hite, A. S. (2005). *Are we there yet? A study of K–12 teachers' efforts at technology integration.* (PhD Diss.). Retrieved from Dissertation and Thesis: Full Text (Publication No. AAI3168028).

Howell, L., & Lewis, C. (2011). Hope is alive! Envisioning the future possibilities of urban schools. In L. Howell, C. Lewis, & N. Carter (Eds.), *Yes we can! Improving urban schools through innovative educational reform* (p. ix). Charlotte, NC: Information Age.

Hughes, K. E. (2008). *A mixed methods case study of the influence of teacher professional development for technology integration on subsequent student achievement.* (PhD Diss.). Retrieved from Dissertations & Theses: Full Text (Publication No. AAT 3304229).

International Society for Teaching in Education (ISTE). (2015). *ISTE Standards.* Retrieved October 30, 2015, from http://www.iste.org.

Ladson-Billings, G. (2006). From the achievement gap to the education debt: Understanding achievement in US schools. *Educational Researcher, 35*(7), 3–12.

Laffey, J. J., Espinosa, L., Moore, J., & Lodree, A. (2003). Supporting learning and behavior of at-risk children: Computers in urban education. *Journal of Research on Technology in Education, 35,* 423–40.

Lee, H., Linn, M. C., Varma, K., & Liu, O. L. (2010). How do technology-enhanced inquiry science units impact classroom learning? *Journal of Research in Science Teaching, 47*(1), 71–90.

Manuguerra, M., & Petocz, P. (2011) Promoting student engagement by integrating new technology into tertiary education: The role of the iPad. *Asian Social Science, 7*(11), 61–65.

Matzen, N. J., & Edmunds, J. A. (2007). Technology as a catalyst for change: The role of professional development. *Journal of Research on Technology in Education, 39*(4), 417–30.

National Center for Education Statistics. (2011). *The nation's report card: Reading 2011* (NCES2012-457). Retrieved from http://nces.ed.gov/nationsreportcard/pubs/main2011/2012457.asp.

Reiser, R. A. (2001). A history of instructional design and technology: Part I: A history of instructional media. *Educational Technology Research and Development, 49*(1), 53–64.

Roberts, J., & Inman, T. (2008). *Strategies for differentiating instruction: Best practices for the classroom.* Waco, TX: Prufrock Press, Inc.

Smith, G. E., & Throne, S. (2007). *Differentiating instruction with technology for K–5 classrooms.* International Society for Teaching in Education. Retrieved from www.iste.org.

Strauss, V. (2014, August). For first time, minority students expected to be majority in U.S. public schools this fall. *The Washington Post.* Retrieved from http://www.washingtonpost.com/blogs/answer-sheet/wp/2014/08/21/for-first-time-minority-students-expected-to-be-majority-in-u-s-public-schools-this-fall/.

Tomlinson, C. (1999). *The differentiated classroom: Responding to the needs of all learners.* Alexandria, VA: ASCD Publishing.

Tomlinson, C. (2014). *The differentiated classroom: Responding to the needs of all learners* (2nd ed.). Alexandria, VA: ASCD Publishing.

Tomlinson, C., & Imbeau, M. (2010). *Leading and managing differentiated classrooms.* Alexandria, VA: ASCD Publishing.

Tough, P. (2008). *Whatever it takes: Geoffrey Canada's quest to change Harlem and America.* New York: Houghton Mifflin.

Van Garderen, D., & Whittaker, C. (2006). Planning differentiated, multicultural instruction for secondary inclusive classrooms. *Teaching Exceptional Children, 38*(3), 12–21.

Watson, S. J. (2007). *A national primer on K–12 online learning.* Retrieved January 1, 2012, from http://ww.nacol.org/docs/national_report.pdf.

Chapter Fourteen

Professional Development and Classroom Resources for the Urban Elementary Literacy Educator

Sherry McElhannon and Jessica Rogers

To successfully meet the needs of a diverse classroom and drive students toward success in literacy, teachers must first have a strong foundational knowledge of literacy instruction (International Reading Association [IRA], 2010). Teachers strengthen this foundation as they engage in professional development designed to increase their knowledge of their subject area.

However, professional development programs must also build on this strengthened foundation by exposing teachers to the latest research in the field, working to establish a depth of understanding based on theories and student behaviors (Joyce & Showers, 2002). As teachers "learn more about the subjects they teach, and how students learn these subjects," they can create successful frameworks for teaching literacy (Garet, Porter, Desimone, Birman, & Suk Yoon, 2001, p. 916).

Not all professional development programs are created equally. Just as students in a particular classroom have different educational needs, the learning needs of educators are unique as well. The traditional "six-hour update," "set and get" style of professional development is becoming obsolete and is being replaced with a number of flexible, collaborative, and often sustained or ongoing programs of professional development that have been proven to be more effective in producing long-term change in the classroom (Guskey, 2000).

Culturally affirming literacy instruction and professional development can be a powerful tool that can help begin and guide the conversations that need to take place among educators. As teachers are exposed to unbiased research regarding different literacy strategies and different cultures, they can gain new understanding of their students and the unique challenges faced in each ethnic group (Banks, 1993b).

It is vital that professional development provide time for teachers to really understand new research and then allow for collaboration as they seek to apply it, along with best-practice instructional techniques in their diverse classrooms.

To create a professional development program that will result in literacy instruction that is more relevant to students of color, both structure and content must be considered. Those responsible for scheduling professional development must learn to recognize the important elements that must be present to make any professional development program effective, the general characteristics of strong professional development, and the various manifestations of those characteristics in alternative models of professional development.

COMPONENTS OF SUCCESSFUL PROFESSIONAL DEVELOPMENT

Professional development can be defined as "those processes and activities designed to enhance the professional knowledge, skills, and attitudes of educators so that they might, in turn, improve the learning of students" (Guskey, 2000, p. 16). During professional development sessions, the focus must not only be on building the teachers' repertoire of strong, research-based literacy strategies, but also on developing cultural understanding and awareness that will drive the selection of high-impact strategies for their diverse learners.

Within a professional development setting, teachers are students, and they need the same elements in their professional learning that they are expected to provide for their students in their classroom (Lieberman, 1995). All learners need a positive environment, rich in collaboration and encouragement (Scheeler, Ruhl, & McAfee, 2004). They need time to interact with new information and make it their own and to "see the new methods from the pupils' perspectives," so they can help students have the same kinds of experiences (Darling-Hammond & McLaughlin, 1995, p. 598).

Great care should be taken to avoid superficial implementation of knowledge, and learners need both time and ongoing support from administration to develop authentic or deep understanding of new information (Darling-Hammond & McLaughlin, 1995, p. 597; Joyce & Showers, 2002, p. 81). Additionally, one method of instruction will not meet the needs of every student and teachers must also be provided with a variety of opportunities to meet their students' learning needs (Guskey, 2000).

As leaders of professional development work to create an ideal learning environment that encourages culturally responsive attitudes, develops a positive community of learning, incorporates a variety of instructional strategies and structures, and models characteristics of effective professional development, teachers will be able to experience firsthand how learning can be transformed for diverse students in their own classrooms.

Research-Based

An essential component for success in any profession is "the continual deepening of knowledge and skills" that is firmly grounded in "major theories, research, and best practices" (Garet et al., 2001, p. 916; IRA, 2010). Understanding of the theories must take place on such a level that teachers can implement that theory in the classroom and see improvement in student learning. Teachers must move past superficial understanding and seek mastery of new theories and ideas because they are then "more likely to replicate results obtained in research settings with their own students" (Joyce & Showers, 2002).

Research generally has significant implications that will require teachers to make major changes in thought or practice. Change is difficult, regardless of years of experience, and teachers should be guided through shifts in thought about new information received before they leave the professional development session (Sparks & Simmons, 1989).

Cultural Understanding and Affirmation

By definition, the act of affirmation is positive, encouraging, and supporting, and so developing an attitude of cultural affirmation is a prerequisite to setting a positive focus. As a whole, school systems are predominantly pessimistic, and phrases like "you don't know our kids" and "they're just lazy" are common during professional development sessions.

These types of phrases are poison for school culture and must be addressed at the beginning of any professional development. It seems like educators are always analyzing test results and applying Band-Aids to issues that arise without ever truly determining the root of the problem with struggling students. The media, politicians, and sometimes even administrators also seem to be constantly highlighting problems in schools. This negativity results in the creation of a deficit view or thinking process among educators "where students of poverty [or color are] thought of and taught as substandard" and teachers come to believe that students in a particular group do not "have the ability to learn and succeed like their wealthy peers" (Banks, 1993a, p. 33).

The deficit-thinking mind-set is often supported by the campus routines that were designed to close achievement gaps, namely the segregation of student data into categories by race, gender, socioeconomic status, and so on.

By highlighting groups of students that are performing below the acceptable level, teachers begin to think that certain students are not able to learn as much or as well as others, and they lower their standards accordingly.

Professional development must be designed to encourage teachers to think positively (Guskey, 2002). Research consistently supports the idea of a self-fulfilling prophecy, where "if teachers *expect* students to be high or low achievers, they will act in ways that cause this to happen" (Gay, 2000, p. 64). Once a teacher adopts a negative stereotypical belief about a certain group of students, those students are eventually excluded from "participation in substantive academic interactions" and "education has failed" (Gay, 2000, pp. 59–60).

As teachers analyze their expectations and current beliefs, they must realize the power they hold over students' ultimate success or failure in the classroom through the delivery of instruction. Becoming aware of their own "cultural blinders" and how they can "obstruct educational opportunities for students of color" is the first step in being able to change their perception and actions (Gay, 2000, p. 70).

The next step in the process is to engage in positive discussion with other professionals that does not focus on segregated data but on what students can do. These conversations should be "informative and analytical, and they should involve individuals who are in positions of authority or expertise to help teachers make better sense of their behaviors and improve them" (Gay, 2000, p. 72). Teachers should take the opportunity to reflect on the strengths of their students, the qualities and skills that each student is bringing to the classroom, and learn how to capitalize on those strengths.

Positive Focus

When administrators require teachers to attend a specific training and implement specific strategies because of poor student performance, professional development can be viewed as a form of punishment and teachers quickly turn against learning and growth. In such sessions, teachers often feel blamed for their students' performance and in turn blame the school environment or even their students (Jones et al., 1999). When professional development begins with negative connotations, it cannot have a positive impact on student performance.

Instead, leaders must maintain a positive environment that encourages growth, support, and meeting students' needs. Though the acquisition of new information is important, professional development should focus primarily on guiding teachers to think about how they can add to their professional knowledge, discover new interests, and ultimately grow as a professional.

Professional development sessions should help teachers feel safe to explore new ideas and theories, share their own thinking, and listen to the thoughts of others without feeling rushed or pressured for immediate results (Glazer & Hannafin, 2006). When teachers are learning in a positive, safe environment, they are more inclined to make a positive difference in their students' lives (Marzano, 2003).

Collaboration

Research consistently shows that "cooperation, collaboration, and community are prominent themes, techniques, and goals in educating marginalized Latino, Native, African, and Asian American students" (Gay, 2000, p. 187). Because of the value these cultures place on connectedness and collaborative problem solving, along with the central role played by cooperation in these groups' learning style, it is clear that working in groups allows students from these cultures to be more successful (Gay, 2000). Teachers need to experience this type of learning within a professional development setting.

Teaching tends to be a fairly isolated profession, however Darling-Hammond (2008) suggests that "[t]eachers learn best by studying, doing, and reflecting; by collaborating with other teachers; by looking closely at students and their work; and by sharing what they see" (p. 8). Consequently, time for collaboration must be included in the structure of the professional development environment.

Through collaboration, teachers can learn not only about instructional practices, but also about each other. Beginning conversations about differences in cultures and experiences will not only strengthen their ability to collaborate with other professionals, but it will help teachers better understand and meet the needs of the students in their classrooms.

Practical, Hands-On Experiences

In the classroom, after students are exposed to new material, effective teachers provide multiple and varied opportunities for students to explore and interact with the material, with the ultimate goal being mastery of that concept. The same should be true for teachers encountering new research or instructional strategies. Research shows that, to impact student learning, professional development should not only focus on content and methods of teaching, but it must also be "linked to daily classroom practice" (Guskey, 2000, p. 17).

Within the context of collaborative groups, teachers need to be able to process, practice, and apply what they have learned. They need to try a new strategy, ask questions if it does not seem to be working, and try it again. New strategies seldom work "out of the box" and often require adjustments based on a particular classroom and set of students. Professional development should be the time where teachers can work on those adjustments while they have access to expert support and input from colleagues (Reeves, 2012).

SUSTAINING PROFESSIONAL DEVELOPMENT

Students in a classroom also receive ongoing support from their teachers after exposure to new material. The teacher is there every day to correct misconceptions, encourage and support understanding, and even provide yet another explanation when necessary. Professional development support needs to be ongoing, a term which should be "measured in years" (Hiebert, 1999, p. 15) and sustained if it is to be effective (Guskey, 2000).

Professional development sustained over a long period of time gives teachers the support and encouragement they need to overcome inevitable roadblocks and challenges encountered while implementing a new strategy or learning a new culture or perspective.

Too often, a teacher will learn about a new instructional strategy or framework in a six-hour workshop and return to the classroom with enthusiasm and the best intentions for implementation, only to be met with resistance and challenges from students, parents, or even other teachers. Although the teacher knows the new strategy to be best practice, with no support, it is easier to go back to old, familiar, and perhaps less effective methods of teaching.

Instructional Coaching

To help teachers add "new practices to existing repertoires . . . technical assistance of some form at the classroom level [is] essential" (Joyce & Showers, 2002, p. 85). Instructional coaching is a highly flexible and personal method of professional development in which an individual skilled in an area "provide[s] intensive, differentiated support to teachers so that they are able to implement proven practices" (Knight, 2006, p. 29).

The coach can have a number of titles, such as literacy coach, curriculum coach, instructional coach, and play a number of roles such as gathering resources for teachers, assisting with lesson planning, leading professional learning communities (PLCs), or even coteaching a lesson.

Instructional coaches can be district employees or outside consultants hired to work alongside teachers in the classroom. An on-site coach takes advantage of existing relationships and increases teacher access to personalized assistance; however, district employees that serve as coaches risk becoming overextended as they perform coaching duties as well as their "other duties as assigned."

An outside consultant hired as a coach is free to work with teachers without distractions like testing or hall duty. However, involvement of the consultant is usually limited to the contract outlined by the district and they are more likely to be viewed as "spies" from administration, which could undermine trust.

When establishing coaching relationships, cultural background should be considered, along with personality and experience. The combination of cultural experiences would impact both teacher and coach and better enable the teacher to meet the students' needs.

Personal Learning Networks

Personal learning networks (PLNs) are another effective method of ongoing support and professional development for teachers. PLNs are established through the teacher's social media platform of choice—Twitter being the most popular—and allow the teacher to connect with experts in their field and educators around the world. Once established, the flow of information from a PLN is constant, it is always "on," allowing teachers to join the conversation on their own time. Because teachers are typically isolated in their classroom all day, the asynchronous nature of a PLN, available anytime, anywhere, is quite appealing (Trust, 2012).

As the name suggests, PLNs are the ultimate in personal professional development. Though it can take time to build, a PLN can be constructed to specifically support each individual teacher's individual and unique interests. It is also flexible, so as teachers acquire new interests or move on to new goals, the PLN can quickly change and grow as well. Some teachers might just be seeking answers to questions, but others might find the "real-time interaction tools are useful for building relationships and seeking one-on-one support" (Trust, 2012, p. 134).

Developing a PLN as a teacher can also serve as a model of life-long learning for students developing and using their own age-appropriate PLNs (Flanigan, 2012). Even the youngest children can participate as a whole class in building a shared PLN, and responsibility can gradually be released as they become more confident digital citizens until they are able to build their own PLN. Connecting with teachers or classrooms around the world can provide a global perspective to students whose exposure to other cultures is often limited.

Professional Learning Communities

Although PLCs are often spoken of interchangeably with PLNs, they are actually quite different in focus and structure. PLCs are a type of action research, a collaborative and systematic process of self-directed professional development where teachers work to analyze and address a specific problem. While a PLN typically has the goal of self-improvement for teacher, increasing their knowledge or craft in a certain area, a PLC is focused on finding ways to increase student achievement.

For a PLC to be effective, all teachers involved must share a "common vision to improve teaching and learning" and be "willing to put aside personal agendas for the good of the group" (Venables, 2011, p. 24).

The members of a PLC are "in constant pursuit of data" because they realize the data can share valuable information about student learning (Venables, 2011, p. 93). As each teacher looks at his or her own data or student work, he or she engages "in an ongoing cycle of questions that promote deep team learning" (DuFour, 2004, p. 8).

As a group, they discuss their findings with openness and honesty, digging beyond surface-level comments and analysis to really determine the root of the problem (Venables, 2011). As a group, teachers can create a plan to address the issue and to improve the results in a specific area. Then, they repeat the process, either revisiting a previous issue to check progress or tackling a new issue.

Student Data Focus

Implementing too many new things at one time can only lead to disaster. Professional development must be highly focused, and that focus should be established clearly and consistently. To determine a focal point, administrators must identify a weakness or area of need by looking objectively at a comprehensive body of data collected by the school through observation of learning and instruction, benchmarks, and diagnostic tests, not just the results from state standardized tests (Joyce & Showers, 2002).

Once the weakness has been identified, research can begin to determine what constitutes best practice for that area. Through research, administrators should be able to refine the area of weakness to establish small, manageable goals. For example, if the data reveals that African American students are not reading at the same level as the other students, professional development simply aimed at trying to "close the gaps" is too broad.

Research reveals that there are several best practices that have been proven to be effective in improving student success as a whole, such as establishing high standards for all students, detecting and discussing bias in literature, or providing relevant topics for students to study. Any of those individual best practices would be an effective focus for a professional development program (Garet et. al., 2001).

Once a focus has been established, a majority of professional development should be centered on that focus. A lesson study, a highly focused model of professional development, involves teachers on a campus working collaboratively to plan, teach, observe, and critique individual lessons, and repeating the process until the lesson is perfect (Dudley, 2011).

Adequate Time

Genuine acquisition of new information is a gradual process that cannot be rushed. Professional development must allow time for teachers to move comfortably through the stages of appropriation to put a new instructional theory into practice. Initially, teachers need to actually read the research and theory to support a new instructional practice and understand the origins of the practice. After reading, there must be time for discussion and for teachers to process how the new practice will look with their teaching style in their classroom before they can implement the practice.

During the implementation phase, teachers will need time to tweak and refine the practice until they are "masters" (Garet, Birman, Porter, Desimone, & Herman, 1999). The success of this process will depend greatly on the teacher's values, knowledge, and ongoing support.

It is ambitious at best to expect teachers to fully understand their own beliefs and subconscious thoughts about culture, learn about other cultures, change their mind-set, learn a new strategy, and then apply that strategy to meet all students' needs within the space of a traditional six-hour professional development session. Teachers need time to learn, think, discuss, and apply new information. This process can only effectively happen within the context of sustained professional development (Glazer & Hannafin, 2006).

Administrator Support

By taking the time to objectively identify an area of weakness, refine the problem into an achievable goal, and establish a professional development plan that will address this weakness, administrators communicate their support to their teachers (Lindstrom & Speck, 2004). Change is slow, however, and once an administrator chooses a focus for improvement and establishes a professional development plan, they must continue to support their teachers as they strive to reach the established goals.

Ample support through resources and finances is essential, but the gift of time might be the loudest way an administrator can support classroom teachers (Bredeson, 2002). Many times in education, if results are not immediate, educators move on to the next thing in search of a quick fix. These trendy programs and "one-shot workshops based on the most current educational fad" (Guskey, 2000) simply widen the achievement gaps between struggling and high-performing students.

No matter how focused the series of professional development sessions may be, administrators should also be careful not to inundate teachers with professional development sessions or to take time away during professional development sessions with administrative or organizational activities (Bredeson, 2002). Teachers are typically overwhelmed with the daily activities in their classrooms, and rarely do they have time to read the research, much less make it practical and applicable in their classrooms.

Administrators can also support their teachers as they identify and deal with personal stereotypes by being a part of that process (Bredeson, 2002). Dropping into a professional development session, sitting next to and having conversations with teachers, and being transparent about working through their own stereotypes can help administrators demonstrate a tremendous level of support as they seek to change the culture of thinking in their school.

Administrators can also lead by example as they consciously set a positive tone in staff meetings and communication with teachers, and make a point to identify and highlight strengths within their teaching staff.

Choice

Ultimately, the success of a professional development plan or initiative comes down to the teachers. Teachers must be on board, and the best way to get them on board is to allow voice and choice in the process. Just like students, when teachers have a voice in something, they are more likely to see its importance (Kirk & MacDonald, 2001). After the administrator selects a focus area, the teachers should meet together as a team to identify non-negotiables, things that need to be in place for success.

The ultimate way for teachers to have a voice in their professional development is through an Edcamp, or "unconference." Edcamps typically follow the basic structure of a traditional conference such as being held on a specific date and developing specific break out session time slots, but the topics for the breakout sessions are not decided ahead of time (The Edcamp Foundation, n.d.). Instead, they are generated and selected by participants on the day of the event. "Edcamp strives to bring teachers together to talk about the things that matter most to them: their interests, passions, and questions."

Teachers who attend Edcamp can choose to lead sessions on those things that matter, with an expectation that the people in the room will work together to build understanding by sharing their own knowledge and questions" (The Edcamp Foundation, n.d., para. 3). This type of professional development appeals to teachers who are motivated by curiosity to research and learn new information in their field and are willing to share that information with others as well.

CLASSROOM RESOURCES

The age of information has put untold resources at our fingertips, but as a classroom teacher, do not overlook the amazing resource you have in your school librarian. It has been said that librarians are the "original search engine" and that is absolutely true. Librarians are in the business of connecting people and information, so ask for what you need. If they don't have it, they can probably find it for you or send you to someone who does.

The following list of online resources is certainly not exhaustive, but will provide a starting point for further research. Many of these resources provide reading lists that will help highlight a variety of texts and authors and will help teachers begin immersing themselves and their students in multicultural literature of the highest quality. Some resources will provide lesson plans and ideas that teachers can adjust for their own students, and some provide ideas and resources for hosting events or activities that can help promote cultural awareness in your community.

Organizations

Center for the Study of Children's Multicultural Literature (CSMCL)

The CSMCL is an educational research center composed of librarians and academic experts in the field of multicultural literature. Their goal is to "preserve the richness of many cultures" and to provide "access to multicultural children's books with high literary and artistic standards." Their website includes information about grants to fund multicultural literacy initiatives and activities, and their "Best Books" list, which includes titles for children and young adults.

Cooperative Children's Book Center (CCBC)

This research library supports the teaching, learning, and research related to children's and young adult literature at the School of Education at the University of Wisconsin–Madison. They have compiled a list of recommended reading in the area of multicultural literature for children and young adults, as well as several bibliographies and book lists, which include books by or about people from a variety of races and cultures.

El día de los niños/El día de los libros (Children's Day/Book Day)

Also known as *Día*, Children's Day/Book Day is celebrated annually on April 30 and emphasizes the importance of literacy for children of all linguistic and cultural backgrounds. Día is funded by a partnerships between the Association for Library Services to Children (ALSC) and the CSMCL and is celebrated with library programs around the country. A variety of resources are available on the Día website, including free webinars, articles, research, and practical ideas for educators who want to impact literacy. Book lists, logos, and planning kits for planning your own Día event are also available.

We Need Diverse Books

This organization advocates for "essential changes in the publishing industry to produce and promote literature that reflects and honors the lives of all young people." Their website provides an extensive and well-organized list of places to find diverse books, including authors to look for and book awards that highlight diverse literature. Research substantiating the need for diverse literature is also included, as well as information about how to get involved in the movement.

General Resources

Authors of Diverse Literature from the International Literacy Association

This list of authors and illustrators represents many cultures and races and is an excellent resource for building a collection of quality literature for children.

Diversity in YA

This website was founded by two authors who celebrate all kinds of diversity. Their goal is to "bring attention to books and authors that might fall outside the mainstream." In addition to lists of diverse books for young adults, this site provides analysis of data regarding diversity in young adult literature, guest blogs from authors about their books, and community discussion about diversity in literature.

Exploring Diversity through Children's and Young Adult Books by Author Cynthia Leitich Smith

This collection of information provides background information on multicultural reading that will assist in curriculum building, collection diversification, and planning group reading. Linked within the page are bibliographies of children's and young adult books, with brief descriptions, organized by grade level. Smith has also provided extensive resources in the areas of Asian heritage themes, multiracial themes, and Native American themes in literature.

Hear Diversity (Books on Tape)

This initiative from Books on Tape extends the call for diverse literature to include audiobooks and highlights "the critical role audiobooks play in connecting diverse books to their young adult audiences." Audiobooks can bridge the gap created by a lack of decoding and fluency skills to allow young people struggling with literacy to see and hear themselves in books.

This website provides categorized lists of audiobooks, as well as samples of the story which can be played from the website.

"How to Choose the Best Multicultural Books" from Scholastic.com

This lengthy article covers the selection of literature dealing with a variety of cultures and races, and includes a short list of key criteria to use when selecting books, reviews of ten children's books for grades K–8, author lists, and advice from children's authors and illustrators.

How to Tell the Difference: Guide to Evaluating Books for Anti-Indian Bias

Published by Oyate, a Native organization that works to ensure the honest portrayal of Native American lives and history, *How to Tell the Difference* is a resource to help authors, educators, and parents evaluate books about native peoples. Although the book is available for purchase, an excerpt of the criteria from the book is included on the website.

Selection of Awards and Book Lists

Amelia Bloomer Book List, from the American Library Association

A book list, compiled annually, of well-written and well-illustrated books with significant feminist content, intended for young readers (ages birth through eighteen).

Coretta Scott King Book Award from the American Library Association

Designed to commemorate the life and works of Dr. Martin Luther King Jr., and to honor Mrs. Coretta Scott King for her courage and determination to continue the work for peace, the Coretta Scott King Book Awards annually recognize outstanding books for young adults and children by African American authors and illustrators that reflect the African American experience. Further, the award encourages the artistic expression of the black experience via literature and the graphic arts in biographical, social, and historical treatments by African American authors and illustrators.

Pura Belpré Award from the American Library Association

The Pura Belpré Award, established in 1996, is presented to a Latino/Latina writer and illustrator whose work best portrays, affirms, and celebrates the Latino cultural experience in an outstanding work of literature for children and youth.

Notable Books for a Global Society from the International Literacy Association

Selected by the Children's Literature and Reading Special Interest Group (CL/R SIG), an organization chartered by the International Reading Association ([IRA] now known as the International Literacy Association), these twenty-five books represent the best in diverse children's literature. The books come from a variety of genres, and are vetted for accuracy, authentic depictions, and displays of leadership and cooperation.

FINAL THOUGHTS

Unfortunately there is not one "silver bullet" best practice that will reach all students of color in a classroom at once. The mere suggestion that there might be such a strategy perpetuates the types of blanket stereotypes and assumptions that the culturally responsive teacher seeks to negate. The only way to improve literacy instruction is for teachers themselves to be immersed in culturally affirming literacy instruction.

To be successful, best practices for culturally affirmed literacy instruction that are learned in a professional development session must be supported by administrators, through time and resources, and the entire campus must work together to develop a positive environment that sets and holds all students to high academic standards.

REFERENCES

Banks, J. A. (1993a). *Multicultural education: Issues and perspectives* (2nd ed.). Boston: Allyn and Bacon.

Banks, J. A. (1993b). The canon debate, knowledge construction, and multicultural education. *Educational Researcher, 22*(5), 4–14.

Bredeson, P. V. (2002). *Designs for learning: A new architecture for professional development in schools*. Thousand Oaks, CA: Corwin Press.

Darling-Hammond, L. (2008). Teacher learning that supports student learning. *Teaching for Intelligence, 2,* 91–100.

Darling-Hammond, L., & McLaughlin, M. W. (1995). Policies that support professional development in an era of reform. *Phi Delta Kappan, 76*(8), 597–604.

Dudley, P. (2011). *Lesson study: A handbook*. Retrieved from http://lessonstudy.co.uk/wp-content/uploads/2012/03/new-handbook-revisedMay14.pdf.

DuFour, R. (2004). What is a "professional learning community"? *Educational Leadership, 61*(8), 6–11.

The Edcamp Foundation. (n.d.) *What is an Edcamp?* Retrieved from http://edcamp.org.

Flanigan, R. L. (2012). Professional learning networks taking off. *Education Digest: Essential Readings Condensed for Quick Review, 77*(7), 42–45.

Garet, M. S., Birman, B. F., Porter, A. C., Desimone, L., & Herman, R. (1999). *Designing effective professional development: Lessons from the Eisenhower Program [and] Technical Appendices*. Washington, DC: U.S. Department of Education.

Garet, M. S., Porter, A. C., Desimone, L., Birman, B. F., & Suk Yoon, K. (2001). What makes professional development effective? Results from a national sample of teachers. *American Educational Research Journal, 38*(4), 915–45.

Gay, G. (2000). *Culturally responsive teaching theory, research, and practice.* New York: Teachers College Press.

Glazer, E. M., & Hannafin, M. J. (2006). The collaborative apprenticeship model: Situated professional development within school settings. *Teaching and Teacher Education, 22*(2), 179–93.

Guskey, T. R. (2000). *Evaluating professional development.* Thousand Oaks, CA: Corwin Press.

Guskey, T. R. (2002). Professional development and teacher change. *Teachers and Teaching: Theory and Practice, 8*(3), 381–91.

Hiebert, J. (1999). Relationships between research and the NCTM standards. *Journal for Research in Mathematics Education, 30*(1), 3–19.

International Reading Association. (2010). *Standards for reading professionals: A reference for the preparation of educators in the United States.* Newark, DE: International Reading Association. Retrieved from http://www.reading.org/general/currentresearch/standards/professionalstandards2010.aspx.

Jones, M. G., Jones, B. D., Hardin, B., Chapman, L., Yarbrough, T., & Davis, M. (1999). The impact of high-stakes testing on teachers and students in North Carolina. *Phi Delta Kappan, 81*(3), 199–203.

Joyce, B. R., & Showers, B. (2002). *Student achievement through staff development.* Alexandria, VA: Association for Supervision and Curriculum Development.

Kirk, D., & MacDonald, D. (2001). Teacher voice and ownership of curriculum change. *Journal of Curriculum Studies, 33*(5), 551–67.

Knight, J. (2006). Instructional coaching. *School Administrator, 63*(4), 36–40.

Lieberman, A. (1995). Practices that support teacher development: Transforming conceptions of professional learning. *Innovating and Evaluating Science Education: NSF Evaluation Forums, 1992–94*, 67.

Lindstrom, P. H., & Speck, M. (2004). *The principal as professional development leader.* Thousand Oaks, CA: Corwin Press.

Marzano, R. J. (2003). *What works in schools: Translating research into action.* Alexandria, VA: Association for Supervision and Curriculum Development.

Reeves, D. B. (2012). *Transforming professional development into student results.* Alexandria, VA: Association for Supervision and Curriculum Development.

Scheeler, M. C., Ruhl, K. L., & McAfee, J. K. (2004). Providing performance feedback to teachers: A review. *Teacher Education and Special Education: The Journal of the Teacher Education Division of the Council for Exceptional Children, 27*(4), 396–407.

Sparks, G. M., & Simmons, J. (1989). Inquiry-oriented staff development: Using research as a source of tools, not rules. In S. DeJarnette (Ed.), *Staff development: A handbook of effective practices* (pp. 126–39). Washington, DC: National Staff Development Council.

Trust, T. (2012). Professional learning networks designed for teacher learning. *Journal of Digital Learning in Teacher Education, 28*(4), 133–38.

Venables, D. R. (2011). *The practice of authentic PLCs: A guide to effective teacher teams.* Thousand Oaks, CA: Corwin Press.

Index

About the Editors

Dr. Lakia M. Scott is assistant professor in the School of Education at Baylor University. She currently teaches elementary reading methods and courses in diversity and multiculturalism. Scott has more than a decade of combined teaching experiences at all levels of education. Her current research interests include: creating urban literacy initiatives to advance student academic outcomes, increasing multicultural awareness and perspectives in teacher education programs, and extending the discussion on the academic and cultural relevance of historically black colleges and universities. She has publications that align with best practices for teaching African American and Hispanic/Latino(a) students. Some of these works include: *English as a Gatekeeper: A Conversation of Linguistic Capital and American Schools* (2014), *Micro-aggressions and African American and Hispanic Students in Urban Schools: A Call for Culturally Affirming Education* (2013), *Understanding the Urban Dialect: Code-Switching and Technology Integration Models to Enhance Literacy Practices for Twenty-First Century African American Learners* (2013), and *Appropriating the Language in Urban Classes via Rap Parties* (2013). Scott is also the coauthor of two book publications: *Last of the Black Titans: The Role of Historically Black Colleges and Universities in the 21st Century* (2015) and *Unshackled: Education for Freedom, Student Achievement and Personal Emancipation* (2014). She is currently conducting research on national reading and language intervention programs for urban students with specific focus on the urban dialect.

Dr. Barbara Purdum-Cassidy is a clinical assistant professor in the Department of Curriculum and Instruction at Baylor University. She currently teaches elementary language arts methods to pre-service teachers and advanced methods of teaching writing in the Department of Curriculum and

Instruction. Cassidy has more than twenty-five years of combined experiences at the elementary, middle, undergraduate, and graduate teaching levels. She has published research articles that examine best practices for teaching urban students. Some of these works include: *An Analysis of the Ways in Which Preservice Teachers Integrate Children's Literature in Mathematics* (2015) and *What are They Asking? An Analysis of the Questions Planned by Prospective Teachers When Integrating Literature in Mathematics* (2015). She is currently conducting a multiyear study that examines the effects of project-based instruction on urban students' reading and writing achievement. Her current research interests include creating urban literacy initiatives to advance student academic outcomes, project-based instruction, and preservice teachers' beliefs and efficacy for teaching writing.